EXPERIENCING DESIGN

EXPERIENCING DESIGN

THE
INNOVATOR'S
JOURNEY

**JEANNE LIEDTKA, KAREN HOLD,
and JESSICA ELDRIDGE**

Columbia Business School
Publishing

Columbia University Press
Publishers since 1893
New York   Chichester, West Sussex

Library of Congress Cataloging-in-Publication Data

Names: Liedtka, Jeanne, author. | Hold, Karen, author. | Eldridge, Jessica, author.
Title: Experiencing design : the innovator's journey / Jeanne Liedtka, Karen Hold,
    Jessica Eldridge.
Description: New York : Columbia University Press, 2021. | Includes index.
Identifiers: LCCN 2020058119 (print) | LCCN 2020058120 (ebook) |
    ISBN 9780231194266 (hardback) | ISBN 9780231550734 (ebook)
Subjects: LCSH: Technological innovations. | Design.
Classification: LCC HD45 .L476 2021 (print) | LCC HD45 (ebook) |
    DDC 658.4/063—dc23
LC record available at https://lccn.loc.gov/2020058119
LC ebook record available at https://lccn.loc.gov/2020058120

Columbia University Press books are printed on permanent and durable acid-free paper.
This book is printed on paper with recycled content.
Printed in the United States of America

c   1 0   9   8   7   6   5   4   3   2   1

Book design by Leigh Ayers

To all of our students
who inspire us as they work to make the world a better place

CONTENTS

PART ONE
INTRODUCTION

HOW DESIGN SHAPES US AS WE SHAPE DESIGNS

"Real isn't how you are made," said the Skin Horse. "It's a thing that happens to you. . . . It doesn't happen all at once. You become. It takes a long time. That's why it doesn't happen often to people who break easily, or have sharp edges, or who have to be carefully kept. Generally, by the time you are Real, most of your hair has been loved off, and your eyes drop out and you get loose in the joints and very shabby. But these things don't matter at all, because once you are Real you can't be ugly, except to people who don't understand."[1]

— MARGERY WILLIAMS BIANCO, *THE VELVETEEN RABBIT*

We want to start this book with a radical premise: that the transformational power of design thinking (DT, as we lovingly refer to it) lies not in what it encourages us to *do*, but in who it encourages us to *become*. Like our childhood friend, the Velveteen Rabbit, DT gives us a chance to become more *real*—to get in touch with our authentic human selves, to restore some of the wonder and creativity that we had as children, but have lost. Being a design thinker doesn't rely on whether you went to design school or not, or have innovation in your job title. The path is there for all of us, if we are willing to make the journey. We become design thinkers by *experiencing* design.

But like any journey to becoming anything that really matters, you need to prepare to get some hair rubbed off. It is a journey of jubilant highs and frustrating lows. People who break easily—who lack the confidence and courage to be vulnerable and to dream about what is possible; who have sharp edges and think they already know everything they need to know; who have to be carefully kept because they want to be in charge and in control—they may not make it. We wrote this book for those who want to *try*. We wrote this book because, after 10 years of dedicated research on the subject, we know that the payoffs to DT done well—to ourselves, our families, our communities and our organizations—are also very real. DT makes us better innovators and better human beings, in a world that desperately needs more of both of those.

But the path there is not nearly as obvious as it might seem.

In daylong hackathons and workshops, DT can seem easy. But our research demonstrates that doing it well is *not* easy. Practiced at a superficial level, even great design tools like ethnography and prototyping don't go deep enough to create the shifts in mindset and skillset that achieving DT's most significant impacts requires. Novice design thinkers may *do* DT activities, but do not experience the shifts that reveal new and deeper levels of who they themselves *are*. It is the *becoming*, not the *doing*, that is key to achieving transformational results. *Becoming* involves changing how we see the world and the rules we use to navigate it. It requires challenging beliefs about ourselves (and others) and letting go of some deep-seated fears. Fully leveraging DT's possibilities requires moving beyond performing the activities it prescribes; it demands that we experience it fully. More so than any other approach to innovation, DT experiences create the space for us to get in touch with our more authentic selves.

You are probably wondering what authenticity has to do with innovation. A lot, it turns out. Many of the barriers to creating powerful new futures are *personal*. Sure—the cultures and processes of organizations can foster them or get in the way. But organizations only change when the people within them change.

In explaining the challenges to building learning organizations, Fred Kofman and Peter Senge explain: "Creating organizations skilled at learning requires fundamental shifts in how we think and act as individuals, as well as organizations."[2] All change relies on personal transformation, Edward Deming, the central figure in the Quality movement, observed. We need to *be* someone new to create something new.

Maybe we've been looking for innovation in all the wrong places. Or we have just been overlooking some of the right ones. We have looked outside of ourselves to external forces—technology, customers, other industries—all valid and important, but what have we missed by largely ignoring the creator and focusing on only what they create? How might we tap into the wellspring of innovation within the innovator and unlock the creative potential in each of us? Accomplishing this involves helping them find their higher, better self—the self who has the courage to ask "What if anything were possible?", who doesn't run from any prospect of failure, who can detach their ego from their idea, and who can listen to others through the perspective of what others want to say rather than what they want to hear.

How can DT help us do that? By first shaping the experience of those who use it, before it shapes what they design for others. But success on this journey relies on much more than helping innovators to better understand their customer's journey—it requires an awareness of what is going on behind the scenes in their personal journeys.

We live, we are told, in the "age of experience." Experience is not just about *how we think*, it is immersive in a way that centers on what *we perceive* and *feel*. It is intensely personal and subjective. But *whose* experience matters? Most discussions of DT focus on

---

AUTHENTICITY

The idea of authenticity has preoccupied philosophers and psychologists for many years. For German philosopher Martin Heidegger, it involves accessing what he called the "withheld"—our higher and better self that lies awaiting emergence. There are preconditions for summoning our withheld. One is *voice*—the ability to express ourselves in ways consistent with our inner thoughts and feelings. *Active engagement* is another. The recognition of the *power of emotions* to our sense of self is a third. Heidegger stresses that the withheld cannot be summoned—it can only be *invited* into a space prepared to welcome it. Finding our authentic self is a developmental process—one of continually *becoming*. Influential developmental psychologists like Erich Fromm, Erik Erickson and Carl Rogers have all stressed the power of authenticity and the enhanced psychological benefits of acting in ways that are true to oneself, with Abraham Maslow's hierarchy of needs, and its apex of self-actualization, perhaps the best known. These theories provide useful insights into what the process of becoming entails and what it takes to encourage its exploration. When Heidegger's invitation to bring what we normally withhold into a conversation is accepted, the results are transformational—for us, for our customers, for our organizations and, quite possibly, for our world.

the experience of the customers we are designing for. But where does the inspiration and facility for creating those new customer experiences come from? It comes from changes in the innovator as a person. Their experiences—of empathy, of meaning, of collaborative co-creation, of transitioning from *knower* to *learner*—set the stage for DT to work its magic.

Decades of research on adult learning are very clear on one point—we learn about what *matters* to us. We learn because we care. DT's human-centered focus engages us by giving us experiences that matter, that impact us at a deep personal level. By connecting us with a more authentic version of ourselves, it motivates us to change. Change happens when we combine new knowledge with *will*. Many innovation methodologies bring new knowledge—few engage body, mind and spirit to forge will like DT does.

Not to get too existential, but who is that self that we are connecting to? Who are we beyond a kind of Freudian sense of ego and id? Psychologist Jerome Bruner argued that "the self is not a *thing*, but a point of view that unifies the flow of experience into a coherent narrative." So we are a story we tell ourselves. That story, that point of view, creates a personal stance that innovators carry with them into the process. "It is the personal stance that travels with the researcher through the process of engaging with the problem, thinking it through, reaching confident conclusions and making these accessible to an audience," argues designer João Ferreira.[3] Of course, each of us is the lead actor in our story—we occupy its center.

Within this story of us, we are part of a broader collective experience; our story lies at the nexus of a web of relationships. "De-centering" us from our own story is perhaps DT's most significant first step in challenging us to become someone new. We are part of the world, not the center of it. "You're not stuck in traffic," designer Kevin Slavin argues. "You are traffic."[4]

Without providing these kinds of de-centering experiences for the innovator, DT projects are likely to generate mostly mundane ideas and lackluster results instead of powerful outcomes. DT might still *feel* good to use, but fail to produce the changes in

THE WORLD ORBITING US

Faculty gathered to hear one of our colleagues present his research strategy. In his presentation, he offered a summarizing image: he and his research topic were at its center in a large circle. A variety of other faculty and their research surrounded him in smaller circles. After a moment of stunned silence, the rest of the room erupted into laughter. It was affectionate laughter—he was a great guy and we all respected his work. But really? Talk about ego on display! The funniest part of the story was that he was totally baffled as to why we were laughing. Finally, a kindly colleague said, "Bill, the rest of us just never realized that we were orbiting around you." But our real problem (that remained unspoken) with Bill's image was not that his model was wrong—we were all carrying around the same model in our heads—it was just that we each thought that our name belonged in the center of the circle, not Bill's.

individual mindsets and group dynamics that lie at the heart of its transformational value. In our decade of teaching DT to thousands of managers, engineers, scientists and others not trained in design, and studying scores of organizational DT projects as well, we have learned that going deep with design—where the crucial payoffs are—requires more than changing the activities that innovators do; it involves creating the conditions that shape who they become, that create the space that invites their best selves to emerge. Understanding what the foundation of DT's success—its *social technology*—looks like and means for creating powerful developmental pathways for learners is essential for innovators and their leaders.

WHY A *SOCIAL* TECHNOLOGY?

Today we think of computers and smartphones when we hear the term "technology," so it may seem a strange term to describe the very human phenomena we are talking about here. In fact, the juxtaposition of the digital with the human is what makes DT so powerful! Think about the incredible advances in digital technology that we have witnessed over the past 20 years or so. Decades ago, capturing the computing capacity of the latest iPhone would have required a tall building covering multiple city blocks. But what about corresponding advances on the human side? Not so impressive. Some of the "advances" made possible by the digital revolution—tweeting, texting,

and email—seem to damage, rather than enhance, our ability as humans to collaborate, especially across difference. Social media seems to produce the opposite of the social technology we need: rather than helping us leverage our differences to find higher-order solutions, it inflames them in ways that make productive (or even just civil) conversation even more difficult to achieve; it divides and polarizes.

So we think the time has come to liberate the term "technology" from its modern meaning, bring back the missing human dimension, and create a different kind of technology—one that catalyzes collaboration and encourages conversations for change across difference; one that helps us locate our better (rather than worse) selves by creating a space for respectful and inclusive conversations that invite all of us to make what we withhold visible to each other. The more artificially intelligent our world becomes, the more important it is that we access what makes us human.

Acknowledging this human element doesn't mean rejecting technology: it means complementing it with a human dimension. Derived from the Greek, meaning "science of craft," a *technology* is a collection of techniques, skills, and processes for transforming knowledge into practical outcomes. Therefore, understanding innovation as an intensely personal and *social* process—with an accompanying need for a social technology—ties it to human emotions, to the complex interactions of people, and to the way the best solutions emerge from interactions with each

Social media quote

great session description

AI rebuttal

other. It highlights the need for a human-centered collection of tools and processes that foster enhanced inclusion, empathy, collaboration *and* productivity.

Such a human-focused technology needs to be teachable and scalable to achieve for innovation what Total Quality Management (TQM) did for quality in the 1980s and 1990s: invite people at all levels of an organization to become involved in making an abstract concept *real* in practice. DT is innovation's equivalent of TQM. Practiced by organizations as diverse as global corporations, start-ups, government agencies, hospitals, and high schools, it makes possible the kinds of changes in the innovation space that TQM did in quality. It is democratizing innovation and unlocking hidden opportunities—not just to tap into new sources of value that senior leaders simply cannot see, but also to explore new dimensions of ourselves. Creating transformational experiences for others on the *outside* first requires transformation on the *inside*.

ABOUT THE RESEARCH

This book reflects the cumulative learning from over a decade of work researching DT. In our first study, more than 10 years ago, we set out to explore the role that operating managers in large organizations played in innovation. We interviewed more than 70 successful growth leaders, focusing on identifying the specific practices leading to their success. We reported these results in our first book, *The Catalyst: How You Can Lead Extraordinary Growth*. Meanwhile, DT was on the ascent. As we examined the behaviors and mindsets we observed in our growth leaders, the parallels between these and the formal DT methodology became obvious. Could teaching the DT toolkit help less intuitively growth-oriented managers see new opportunities? We hoped so then and *know* so now. Over the next seven years, we created a database of in-depth studies of DT projects in action (reported in two books, *Problem Solving with Design Thinking* and *Design Thinking for the Greater Good*). For the past several years, we have been on a new mission to translate these cases and qualitative results into more quantitative ones that demonstrate and quantify the impact of DT in practice. We will share some of those results in Chapter 2.

Throughout this research journey, we have been interested in how nondesigners learn DT. We've developed a methodology (*Designing for Growth*) and project handbook (*Designing for Growth: A Field Guide*), and helped thousands of people learn and practice DT, both in person and online. Our big Aha! came when we looked seriously at competency building, rather than just teaching tools and process. The key to deep learning, we realized, was using tools and process to facilitate a series of *experiences* for our learners. These experiences, we saw, did more than skill building; they created personal transformations. As we dug deeper, we also saw that student personalities and preferences impacted their learning path in significant ways that we needed to recognize and support. (Stay tuned for more on this in Part 4.)

Lest we be accused of espousing a kind of new age narcissism in the name of innovation, we want to ground this discussion in the most pragmatic terms to demonstrate that design makes for good business. It's effective and productive and as much of a win for organizations as it is for individuals. So let's examine what drives DT's game-changing potential by exploring the kinds of outcomes that innovation needs to accomplish for organizations, along with the advice leaders get about how to achieve them, and the challenges that arise when they try. Then, we will look more closely at how DT's social technology not only unlocks an innovator's deeper sense of self, but addresses these organizational blocks to innovation in more productive ways in the process.

OUR INNOVATION WISH LIST

Consider a set of big-picture outcomes that organizations want innovation processes to deliver—an innovation wish list. We suggest four simple and straightforward starting points. We want innovation to:

1. Give us **choices that create better value** in the moment;
2. **Reduce the risk and cost** of innovation efforts;
3. **Increase the likelihood** that new ideas actually get implemented; and
4. Improve our long-term choices by making both **individuals and organizations more adaptable** in a changing world.

Sometimes we have to settle for only one or two of these, but ideally, we would like to achieve them all. Each one comes with an accompanying set of challenges. Let's look at these in more detail.

Start with the obvious: we expect our innovation processes *to give us better choices*—ones that enhance value both for those for whom we design and for the organization itself—that allow us to make their lives better by offering useful and differentiated products, services, and experiences. Our choice to emphasize "value creating" rather than "novel" is deliberate. Artists may pursue novelty for its own sake, but in our world, we care about *usefulness*. We know that outcomes that matter are often *not* novel—they result from recombining things that already exist or are borrowed from other places. Think of wheels on luggage: two parts—wheels and bags—present for thousands of years, but not combined until about 1970, by a tinkerer frustrated with his family's inability to pack light. Now imagine your next sprint through the airport without your roller bag. *That's* value creation, not novelty.

Generating more valuable choices for those we design for starts by asking better questions. So many innovation opportunities are lost at the starting gate, when we rush to solve the obvious problem. Not surprisingly, accepting conventional problem definitions generally leads to finding obvious, conventional solutions. Asking a more interesting question—or treating the obvious one as testable—is a solid beginning for cultivating better choices. But this creates a dilemma: *how do we hold action-oriented people, who are eager*

BROADWAY'S *HAMILTON*

One of our favorite examples of the power of recombining existing elements to produce something entirely new is the Broadway musical sensation *Hamilton*. On the surface, each and every element of *Hamilton* has been around a long time:

- Stories of U.S. founding fathers go back to George Washington and his cherry tree
- The Broadway musical dates back to 1857
- Hip-hop's official birthday is 1973, making even it just about 50 years old—other inspirations like jazz and R&B have been around even longer

Individually, there's nothing new here . . . but put them all together and magic happens. Lin-Manuel Miranda's musical, based on the life of Alexander Hamilton (one of the more obscure founding fathers), became the biggest Broadway phenomenon in decades, delighting entirely new audiences who had little previous interest in Broadway (or history). Why? Because of its creative recombination of existing elements.

to get to answers, *in the question?* We can also improve solution quality by better understanding those for whom we design, but this provides another dilemma: *people rarely know what they want until they see it.* A third route to improving solutions is through diversity: bringing new voices into idea generation loosens the grip of our personal mental blinders and helps us work collaboratively to identify better, higher-order

focus groups

solutions. But this comes with its own challenge: *conversations across difference can deteriorate into divisive debates about whose answer is best.*

Let's move on to the next item on our wish list—reducing **the risk and cost of innovation efforts.** Stepping into the innovation space inevitably changes the physics surrounding the work we do: uncertainty is as unavoidable a force during innovation as gravity is when we walk on Earth. Though denying and avoiding risk may be our natural inclination, such actions provide a quick trip to expensive failures. Accepting and actively *managing* risk is what matters. Generating better choices (see wish list item #1) is a good place to start, but how do we know what "better" looks like in a world of uncertainty? Achieving it means creating and managing a *portfolio* of options. But most of us have been taught that there is only one right answer, *so moving forward with multiple ideas looks "inefficient."* But we also know that stopping ideas is almost as hard as starting them. Our ideas are our babies—and being willing to "call our own baby ugly" (as a manager in one of our studies described it) does not come easily. *How do we know which ideas to keep and which ones to call ugly?* Experimentation, of course! We need to focus on conducting fast, cheap experiments to winnow out the ideas that don't work. But few of us have been taught how to be good testers, so we *allow unrecognized biases to taint experiments.* And even if our experiments are good, our culture trips us up: *backing an idea that fails, in most organizations, is more likely to be seen as incompetence than successful experimentation.*

AKA there are no bad ideas in the "what if" phase

GETTING OUR WISH LIST ACCOMPLISHED

Wish List	Advice	Conventional Solution	New Challenge
	Start with better problem definitions	Spend more time understanding the problem	Action-oriented people rush to answers
1. **Better Choices**	*Come up with better ideas*	Develop a deeper understanding of the needs of those you are designing for	People we design for don't know what they want
		Incorporate a more diverse set of perspectives	Team conflict ensues
	Generate multiple ideas	Be willing to create many ideas	Multiple ideas seem "inefficient"
2. **Reduced Risk/Cost**		Be willing to kill many ideas	Hard to let go of our egos and "call our own baby ugly"
	Keep the good ideas and kill the bad ones	Conduct experiments	Cognitive biases make us bad experimenters; Failures aren't seen as learning, but as incompetence
3. **Increased Likelihood of Implementation**	*Ensure implementers are aligned and committed*	Build emotional engagement	Emotion trumps reason in testing
4. **Increased Individual and Organizational Adaptability**	*Engage local intelligence*	Localized control of innovation	Chaos and incoherence with too many cooks in the kitchen

Next on our wish list is increasing the *likelihood of successfully implementing our new and improved ideas.* Research tells us that there is no shortage of advice on that: we need implementers who are aligned and committed. Change involves engaging emotion, not just reason. Desire, psychologists tell us, is a more powerful motivator of behavioral change than goals and objectives. But doesn't that conflict with the objectivity required to run the experiments we just talked about? When innovators fall in love with their ideas, and *emotion trumps reason during testing*, they are in trouble.

Finally, the last innovation outcome on our wish list is more ambitious than the previous three, but also more important to long-term survival: *making us and the organizations we inhabit more adaptable to ongoing change.* Of course, getting good at understanding customer needs (#1) and experimenting (#2) help accomplish this—but they are not all we need. Omnipotent leaders may be able to ensure success in a stable and predictable world; but in a chaotic and confusing one, it is local intelligence that carries the day. Local intelligence, however, only pays off with local autonomy. Together, they allow for multiple approaches and more variation across an organization— and those are good things. In a Darwinian race for survival of the fittest, more variation in the gene pool fosters successful adaptation. When stability dominates, *reducing* variation to get efficiencies works, but with high uncertainty, *increasing* variation maximizes adaptability. In this new world, a diverse set of locally tailored solutions, assessed through experimentation

and shared across local geographies so that they can learn from each other, improves success. Broadened network connections increase adaptability. But isn't that kind of *local control likely to lead to chaos* as everyone goes their own way?

So we have an obvious wish list and lots of advice on how to get there—but every bit of it is accompanied by a set of challenges we must first overcome. Who can blame leaders for trying harder to control by doubling down on efficiency and rationality, even though research tells us that trying to ratchet up control backfires?[5] Without new toolkits, how can we operationalize new ways of thinking and behaving? Achieving the seemingly simple innovation outcomes on our wish list—better choices, decreased risk, and increased implementability and adaptability—while managing the challenges involved in getting there requires acknowledging the human element. Notice that our challenges to successful innovation are all *human,* not technical, so we need new social technologies to address them. Cue design thinking.

DESIGN THINKING'S CORE PRACTICES

In Chapter 2, we will explore how DT addresses each of the challenges we've noted. But first, we need to back up a bit and look at the core practices that define DT—a feat not as simple as it sounds, as there seems to be a bewildering array of different models on offer. Some come from consulting firms, others from universities (including our own), some are homegrown, developed by organizations themselves. So many models, so little time! The good news is that despite the different terms and models in use, our research demonstrates that we are all talking about pretty much the same thing. At its heart, we see five core practices at work:

FIVE CORE PRACTICES

1. Develop a deep, **empathetic understanding** of the needs and context of those for whom (and with whom) we are designing

2. Form **diverse teams**

3. **Create multiple solutions** and make them tangible and testable

4. Foster **conversations that encourage dialogue** instead of debate

5. Offer a structured and **facilitated process**

PRACTICE #1:

Develop a deep, empathetic understanding of the needs and context of those for whom (and with whom) we are designing

Not surprisingly, the aim to develop a deeper understanding of stakeholders' contexts—particularly those we are designing for—lies at the heart of DT. This shows up as a focus on developing empathy for the stakeholders being served and using an array of ethnographic tools to identify deeper insights which allow us to reframe problem definitions and generate better solutions. Rather than relying solely on quantitative data such as surveys and market analyses, DT is deeply interested in the details of people's lives and their unmet needs. This pursuit of insights into unmet needs *precedes* the pursuit of solutions by shifting innovators' mindsets from egocentric to empathetic.

important shift

PRACTICE #2:

Form diverse teams

Another core practice is the use of diverse teams. Many positives come from bringing diverse perspectives into the conversation. Diversity brings new data and ways of looking at the problem that help us produce novel insights and solutions. It also requires new ways of working together so that teams can capture the richness of difference. But what kind of diversity? Our favorite advice on this comes from evolutionary biologists who advocate for what they call *requisite variety*—this happens when your repertoire of available responses (which is determined by who is on your team) matches the complexity your problem presents.

PRACTICE #3:

Create multiple solutions and make them tangible and testable

Creating and testing multiple solutions fosters learning in action, another hallmark of DT at work.

Three key components of this practice stand out: (1) generating a *portfolio* of possible solutions, rather than a single "true" one; (2) treating these potential solutions as hypotheses to be tested in action through iteration and feedback from stakeholders; and (3) creating low-fidelity prototypes to support this testing. Successful learning in action also requires adopting new mindsets that overcome basic human fears around failure.

PRACTICE #4:
Foster conversations that encourage dialogue instead of debate

Dialogue is central to innovation because knowledge is created through social interaction and conversation. Dialogue happens when people talk *with* us, not *at us*. Successful design-oriented conversations are most vividly illustrated by what they do *not* do: accept obvious and conventional problem definitions, utilize debate, or focus on options already visible at the start of the process. Instead, they treat the problem definition as a hypothesis and focus on understanding, rather than arguing, across different perspectives. They look for solutions to emerge *during* the process. Since most of us have been rewarded for forceful debating rather than peaceful inquiry (did your high school have a Dialogue Team as well as Debate Team? We think not . . .) we need new rules to keep these conversations collaborative and productive.

PRACTICE #5:
Offer a structured and facilitated process

Having a structured process, ideally with supportive mentoring, is key to helping those learning DT get comfortable trying out the new ways of thinking and behaving that it requires. This idea of tightly structuring creative processes may seem counterintuitive, but rather than stifling people's creativity, the right structure actually *frees* it. The previous four practices—understanding user needs, forming diverse teams, creating multiple solutions, and fostering dialogue—are much harder for learners to accomplish without defined tools and methods. Activities like face-to-face ethnographic research with customers, deep immersion in their perspectives, co-creation with stakeholders through dialogue, and the design and execution of experiments are foreign to most nondesigners. DT's structured processes make them feel safe. The presence of simple, seemingly innocent templates lures people into change conversations they might otherwise resist and enhances their creative confidence as well as the quality of their output. Trained designers may find structured processes inhibiting and off-putting, but the rest of us need them! The aim of this structure is to offer simple rules that guide the innovation conversation toward more productive outcomes. Most of us are driven primarily by a fear of making mistakes, so we prefer preventing error over seizing opportunity—we choose *inaction* rather than action when a choice risks failure. But there *is* no innovation without action. DT's structure gets people to *try*.

HOW DT'S SOCIAL TECHNOLOGY WORKS

How does DT make new ways of thinking and behaving feel safe, while helping innovators to find their more authentic selves on the way to improving organizational outcomes? It starts by giving innovators a specific and familiar set of activities to perform—gathering data, identifying insights, establishing design criteria, generating ideas, and prototyping and testing those ideas.

Behind the scenes, these seemingly simple DT activities set the stage for an innovator's personal transformation by initiating a sequence of personal experiences that they *feel*. These experiences, triggered by DT activities, ultimately change the innovators themselves—not just what they produce.

We do not necessarily learn from our experiences. We can wander through them in our habitual mindsets and stay exactly who we were at the start. Most assume that an innovator's journey through the DT activities is fairly straightforward and linear, a set of steps that they do to reach a set of outcomes that are driven by user needs and tested for market viability. But when innovators dig below the "doing" to fully experience DT, their journey is much more introspective and involved. To change us, to produce deep learning, our experiences must be what pioneering educator John Dewey called "educative": they must progress in a structured way that combines *action* and *reflection*. In DT, data gathering forces an educative experience of **Immersion** in users' lives that shifts innovators' frames of reference and engages their emotions, helping them see and care about new possibilities while paving the way for more effective teamwork. Developing insights offers a **Sensemaking** experience that transforms voluminous data points into new knowledge and builds enthusiasm and emotional commitment. Specifying

DESIGN THINKING LOOKS LIKE A SET OF ACTIVITIES THAT INNOVATORS DO

DISCOVERY

TESTING

Gathering Data   Identifying Insights   Establishing Design Criteria   Generating Ideas   Prototyping   Experimenting

design criteria drives an **Alignment** experience, with other stakeholders, around what really matters in future designs, whatever they turn out to be. Generating ideas collaboratively offers opportunities for an experience of **Emergence** in which higher-order solutions are jointly developed. Creating prototypes stimulates an experience of **Imagining** as innovators work to make ideas feel real to both teams and stakeholders. Designing and conducting experiments leads to an experience of **Learning in Action** that guides innovators through the tough journey from knower to learner.

DT's social technology pushes innovators to question their assumptions, shift their mindsets and discover new skillsets, taking them closer to becoming their most authentic selves—curious, aware of their biases, open to creativity and wonder. The experiences

wow

of each phase are connected, flowing into one another; as innovators venture to each next step of "doing," they journey further into their own potential. The experiences are powerful because they are educative—they are sequenced in such a way that their effects are _cumulative_ as the journey progresses. They insist on both action and reflection. As a result, they trigger fundamental shifts in mindsets as well as skillsets. Their human-centeredness creates a space for Heidegger's invitation to us to explore our better selves. In doing so, who innovators _are_ changes—they _become_ more empathetic, confident, collaborative, and comfortable with learning in action. This is the culmination of DT's social technology: an innovator's personal transformation through the process of doing-experiencing-becoming.

"DOING" DRIVES EXPERIENCES THAT DRIVE PERSONAL TRANSFORMATION

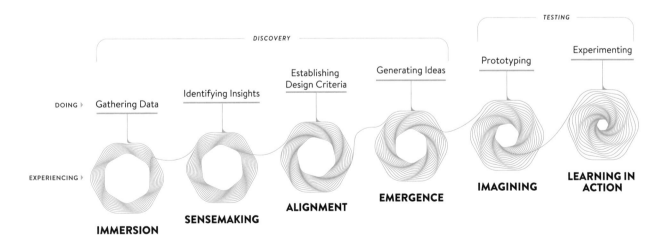

As we studied more deeply what this model of doing-experiencing-becoming looked like in practice, we stumbled across a guiding philosophy from the world of occupational therapy (OT): doing-being-becoming. As we investigated further with the help of a seasoned OT therapist (thank you, K!), the parallels to the progression in DT became evident. The focus of OT work, we learned, is not just addressing a patient's disability, it is also about restoring the loss of identity that can so often accompany it. Carefully planned activities (*doing*) help the patient regain a sense of self-efficacy and who they are (*being*), and this reconnects them with the larger world, helping them to find themselves in a new future (*becoming*). A multifunctional team of specialists—medical caregivers, psychologists, and therapists—work together to implement an assessment and treatment plan, taking into consideration the elements of task, environment, and person that shape and impact the patient. Activities must contain a "just right" challenge—not too hard and not too easy. Getting this wrong may cause the patient to disconnect from the process.

This got us thinking about the losses involved in the partial selves we bring to our professional lives in organizations: the loss of the creative, fearless children we once were and the multifaceted emotional humans that we still are (that we now show only to our families and friends). We realized that this process, from the world of OT, of restoring a lost self was right on target as we looked at an innovator's journey. What so many of us have lost—and what DT can help us to find—goes so much deeper than just creative confidence.

THE JOURNEY OF DOING-EXPERIENCING-BECOMING

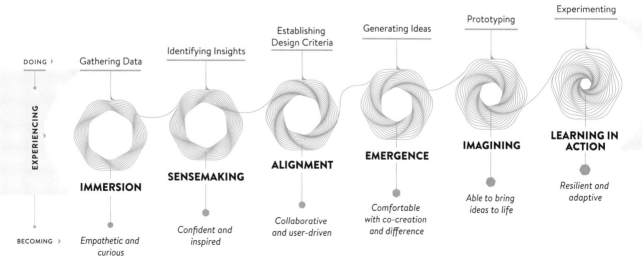

DOING-BEING-BECOMING *IN OT*

TIM'S STORY

Tim suffered from schizophrenia and lacked the basic life skills he needed to care for himself. Working with his occupational therapist, he decided to tackle cooking skills and selected the activity of preparing a "Sunday roast" as a good place to start—the activity was not too complicated, posed few safety hazards, and had symbolic value as a culturally cherished family ritual. Making the roast (doing) built Tim's sense of self-efficacy (being) and connected him to the traditions of a larger world (becoming). Succeeding at this prepared Tim to move on to his next set of challenges with heightened confidence.

Perhaps it can help to recapture even that sense of wonder, as one innovator we spoke with hoped for:

> As we grow older and supposedly "wiser" we tend to forget the childlike wonder and imagination that we all had when we were younger. We squash that with logic, analysis and all forms of "correctness." It pays to stop and ask myself, "What if anything were possible?" to rekindle that ability—and something incredible just might happen.

This book explores, for each phase of experience, how DT done well invites innovators to bring their more authentic self into the innovation conversation. In Chapter 2, we focus at the organizational level,

reviewing new research that looks at *why* DT works and helps us to accomplish our organizational innovation wish list. With that understanding of outcomes as a backdrop, we get personal. In Chapters 3 through 9, we turn to the innovator's own journey and unpack the kinds of changes in mindsets and skillsets that each phase unlocks, examining the new behaviors that the transition from novice to competency involves. Chapters 3 through 6 (Part 2) look at the Discovery phases occurring during DT's "fuzzy front end." Chapters 7 through 9 (Part 3) examine the challenging back-end processes involved in Testing.

Part 4 looks at the ways in which this personal journey to *becoming* is experienced by different personalities. All innovators do not share the same journey: people with different needs and preferences follow different paths. Doing design deeply rather than superficially is never easy, but navigating particular phases is easier for some people than for others. Many of our readers will already be familiar with the idea of the different innovation journeys as experienced by two characters we have called Geoff and George.

Geoff and George were archetypes that we created to illustrate differences in the mindsets and experiences of the managers with whom we worked. As our research has progressed, we have been able to identify more precisely how deeper differences in personality shape diverse DT learning journeys. In Part 4, you'll meet four different profiles that we've developed based on our experiences teaching DT to thousands of people. Understanding the different paths that these four take is critical for innovators working in diverse teams and for leaders and facilitators interested in better supporting individuals in their learning process.

Finally, in Part 5, we focus on helping you assess and accelerate progress in your own DT learning journey, as well as that of your organization.

GEOFF AND GEORGE

Geoff and George are old friends who have been with us since we published our first book on innovation over 10 years ago. Each is an archetype—a blend of multiple people we interviewed during our research. They capture for us two very different approaches to innovation and growth. George, a successful manager, finds himself struggling with the uncertainty inevitable in innovating. George is a perfectionist who worries a lot about making mistakes and lives his life trying to avoid them. Because moving into uncertainty leads logically to more mistakes, George avoids that too—and with this comes the avoidance of many new experiences. In contrast, Geoff expects to make mistakes. For him, success is all about learning. Because learning only occurs when we step away from the familiar, Geoff is accepting of the uncertainty that inevitably accompanies new experiences.

These differences in mindset drive alternative responses to moving innovation forward. Geoff has a deep and personal interest in his customers as people, rather than as demographic or marketing categories, and focuses on improving their lives, not just selling them products. This empathy, when combined with his broad repertoire of experiences, helps Geoff to see opportunities that others miss. As he moves an idea forward, Geoff never puts all his eggs in one basket; instead he adopts a portfolio-based, experimental approach. In contrast, though George also cares about his customers, his focus is more on selling them his products, rather than understanding their lives and the unmet needs. George bets on a much more traditional analytic approach, trying to find—and then "prove" conclusively with data—that he has found the one right answer.

George's approach, though successful in a stable world, is fatally flawed when the environment becomes uncertain and hard to predict, whereas Geoff intuitively has the mindset and skillset to succeed. But we need the Georges of the world—they bring valuable skills to contribute to any innovation conversation, especially in testing. The good news—Geoff's natural inclinations map directly onto design tools that we can teach to George.

CHAPTER 2

WHY DESIGN THINKING WORKS

n Chapter 1, we introduced our organizational innovation wish list and the challenges associated with accomplishing it. In this chapter, we want to go back to that list and look more systematically at both the challenges themselves and how DT helps organizations to surmount them.

WISH LIST ITEM #1:
Better choices

The advice on how to get to better choices in Chapter 1 had three parts, each of which came accompanied by its own dilemma to be resolved: (1) spend more time understanding the problem instead of rushing to solve it—but *action-oriented managers want to get moving*; (2) get to know the needs of the people you are designing for—but *people don't know what they want when you ask*; and (3) incorporate a more diverse set of voices—but that often leads to *team conflict and worsened decision quality*. All three of these challenges are addressed directly by DT's core practices.

First, DT's structure holds people in the problem to gather data on current issues and context *before* letting them move to idea generation. It taps into our natural curiosity about other human beings to get us excited about Discovery. During that data gathering, DT uses another core practice—focusing on user needs. This focuses on using ethnographic and projective tools that don't *ask* people what they want, but instead to go deeper to pay attention to what they *do* to discover what they need but can't articulate. This same focus on user needs reduces team conflict by giving members a common focus and agreed upon design criteria. Finally, DT's emphasis on dialogue provides a set of conversational rules—like turn taking, listening to understand, and possibility thinking—that allow diverse groups to leverage their differences to find better solutions than anyone brought into the room. DT deliberately slows down the process throughout to allow for individual learning and reflection and the collaborative emergence of better solutions.

WISH LIST ITEM #2:
Reduced risk and cost of innovation

Advice to achieve this in Chapter 1 focused on two critical activities: generating multiple ideas rather than a single "best" one and then winnowing these down through testing with users. But we acknowledged a double-edged sword here as well—on the multiple-idea side, *it seems "inefficient"* to keep generating lots of ideas when you have found a good one early on, and innovators also find it hard to let go of their ideas and are *loath to acknowledge their babies as ugly*. On the experiment side, *cognitive biases make most of us poor experimenters*—plus we live in organizational cultures (and often have individual mindsets) that punish what

we see as "failure"—so innovators *find it hard to see the failure of an idea as evidence of learning rather than having made a mistake.* There are multiple layers to how DT addresses these issues. Let's start by stepping back to look at the well-researched topic of human error and how it interferes with making good choices.

THE SOURCES OF BIAS

Cybernetics scholar Ranulph Glanville once advised: "Accept that error is endemic. There is always error. The question is not to eradicate error, but how do we manage error, how do we live with error?"[6] Digging deeper into the challenges of managing error takes us straight to the work of psychologists who have studied decision-making for a long time. They have identified upwards of 180 different kinds of biases that affect our ability to make good decisions. We want to call out 10 specific biases that cause especially serious problems for innovators, both during Discovery at the front end of DT and in Testing at the back end.

DT's ability to fight these common biases accounts for its ability to help us achieve our wish list along many dimensions. These biases sort into three categories:

CATEGORY I BIASES: **The source of error lies within us and how we see the world.**

This first category relates to our inability to escape our own worldview, including our past (bias #1—projection bias), our current emotional state (#2—hot/cold gap),

10 BIASES TO WATCH OUT FOR [7]

1. **Projection Bias:** This is a tendency to project the present into the future, resulting in predictions that tend to overestimate the extent to which the future will resemble the present. This projection of an innovator's past interferes with imagining a new future and impedes both seeing novel ideas and accurately assessing their likelihood of success.

2. **Hot/Cold Gap:** An innovator's emotional state, whether hot (highly emotional) or cold (unemotional), has been demonstrated to influence assessment of the potential value of an idea, leading them to either under- or overvalue it in the present, impeding the accuracy of their prediction of how others (even themselves) will react in the future, when their emotional state is different.

3. **Egocentric Empathy Gap:** This bias causes innovators to consistently overestimate the similarity between what they value and what others value, and to project their own thoughts and preferences onto others. This leads to the creation of new ideas that they value but those they are designing for do not.

4. **Selective Perception/Functional Fixedness:** Here, innovators overestimate the effect of one factor at the expense of others, overreacting to specific stimuli and ignoring others, resulting in a more narrow set of ideas.

5. **Say/Do Gap:** Innovators often try to minimize the impact of their own biases by *asking* users what they want. Unfortunately, users are often unable to accurately describe their own current behavior, much less provide reliable data on their deeper needs and wants, resulting in the "say/do" gap between what they say now and what they will do later. Research demonstrates that consumers are not reliable predictors of their own purchase behavior for any type of goods studied.

6. **Response Bias:** The "say/do" gap is made worse, in some situations, by users' tendency to tell us either what they think we want to hear (few want to hurt our feelings!) or things that make them look good and are socially acceptable (of course we floss twice a day!). This is particularly damaging to managing innovation efficiently because it often results in false positives—users tell us they will use (but they won't). This causes us to invest in ideas that will ultimately fail.

7. **Availability Bias:** This causes innovators to undervalue ideas that are harder for them to imagine. Since the familiarity of an idea is likely to be inversely related to its novelty, this leads to a preference for more incremental solutions.

8. **Planning Fallacy:** When innovators *do* create new ideas, they often see an overly rosy future, characterized by overly optimistic predictions about how well it will be received, resulting in the "planning fallacy." They only rarely include considerations of failures.

9. **Endowment Effect:** Innovators' attachment to early ideas makes giving up their current solution more painful than the pleasure of getting a new and improved one.

10. **Hypothesis Confirmation Bias:** In what is perhaps the most commonly discussed bias, innovators search for facts that support their favored solutions, and find it hard to even recognize data that disconfirms them. Interestingly, even when a decision-maker's bias is revealed to them, they often fail to correct it.

our personal preferences (#3—egocentric empathy gap), and our tendency to be overly influenced by specific factors (#4—selective perception/functional fixedness).

How DT helps:

- *We collect deeper data:* By immersing ourselves as vividly as possible in someone else's experience, we reduce reliance on our own experiences as the primary source of information.
- *We see different perspectives:* By using diverse teams, we expose ourselves to the way others think, helping us surface our own hidden biases.

CATEGORY II BIASES: **The source of error lies with those we are designing for.**

We try to get accurate information from those we are designing for by asking them—but they are unable to accurately describe their own needs or give good feedback on new ideas (#5—"say/do" gap). They also tend to offer what they consider socially acceptable answers (#6—response bias).

How DT helps:

- *We ask open-ended questions:* Ethnographic conversations uncover hidden needs unlocked through probing and focusing on experiences and journeys.
- *We focus on behaviors, not intentions:* DT teaches us to value observation, and to focus our

questions based on actions, not attitudes and opinions (which releases users from potentially feeling judged).

- *We leverage immersive tools:* Storyboards and journey maps make new ideas tangible and allow potential users to see real strengths and pitfalls in solutions.

CATEGORY III BIASES: **The sources of error relate to how we handle the information we collect.**

We are poor scientists. We tend to be unimaginative (#7—availability bias), overly optimistic (#8—planning fallacy), and wedded to initial solutions (#9—endowment effect), and we find it difficult to see disconfirming data (#10—hypothesis confirmation bias).

How DT helps:

- *We treat everything as a hypothesis to be tested:* We actively seek disconfirming data and try to surface our assumptions during prototyping.
- *We explore many options:* By testing multiple solutions simultaneously, DT helps us invest less in any given option, making it easier to let go of our "babies."
- *We co-create:* We delay accepting early compromises and use collaboration across diverse perspectives to build higher-order solutions.

But individuals are not the only ones to suffer biases that aggravate error. Organizations are also replete with them—particularly around challenges to be customer-centric rather than organization-centric and the way they view the failure of ideas during experimentation as incompetence (rather than learning). Research has now demonstrated quite conclusively how design done well shapes organizational cultures in significant ways that make them both more learning oriented and more user-centric.[8]

Now back to our wish list.

WISH LIST ITEM #3:
Increased likelihood of successful implementation

Successful implementation, advice tells us, comes from implementers who are aligned and engaged—so the emphasis here is on building emotional commitment. Research on engagement demonstrates many positive outcomes associated with engagement, such as improved productivity and creativity, as well as improved likelihood of implementation success. DT is clearly very good at building engagement—this is one of the most prevalent outcomes seen in our research. DT's ability to engage people in Discovery shifts mindsets while involvement in idea generation fosters ownership. Even experimentation, traditionally treated as a method aimed primarily at improving solution quality through iteration, turns out to have a valuable, unanticipated side benefit: inviting implementers into Testing creates ownership and enthusiasm for change. But positive emotional engagement

could become a negative if it allows *emotion to trump objectivity during Testing*. Here again, DT's ability to teach innovators how to design and execute good experiments is key to ensuring that the human-centered empathy and emotion so important to the success of DT's Discovery phase does not interfere with objectivity and the data-driven nature of Testing.

WISH LIST ITEM #4:
Increased individual and organizational adaptability

We see a lot of evidence for the way in which DT accomplishes our final wish list item of increased adaptability. At the individual level, DT increases adaptability through a set of powerful psychological benefits to innovators' individual mindsets. It enhances their willingness to collaborate as well as their confidence to navigate changing and increasingly complex environments. It also fosters ownership of change. Use of DT bolsters innovators' creative confidence, creates psychological safety, and encourages open-mindedness and risk-taking—all essential to successful adaptation. At team and organizational levels, DT changes the interactions both within the team and with its stakeholders. It strengthens network relationships and enhances partners' willingness to collaborate, which is critical to increasing responsiveness to changing conditions. In turn, enhanced collaboration produces new resources for problem solving and allows the pooling of existing ones (contributing to wish list item #2—reducing the cost and risk of innovation efforts). DT's ability to successfully foster system-level conversations across difference drives more effective resource allocation.

One particularly powerful driver of adaptation, as we discussed in Chapter 1, is the ability to tap into local intelligence. Doing so requires giving localized control of innovation, but this presents a dilemma: how to avoid *chaos and incoherence* when control from the top is relaxed. Researchers who study complex adaptive systems argue for the power of localization through identifying what they call "simple rules" that allow freedom at the local level, but coordination centrally.[9] Using DT as such a set of simple rules offers clear, centralized guidelines for process but affords people in different parts of a system the freedom to identify and solve their own problems while maintaining a centralized discipline and capability for sharing what each locality learns. It offers the best of both worlds.

Finally, DT's ability to foster trust-building across stakeholders critically enables reducing risk and increasing adaptability. One of our colleagues, an expert in change management, calls trust "the currency of change." We live in a world where organizations' and individuals' abilities to adapt and change quickly is critical. They do that most efficiently and most effectively in an environment where trust exists.

These positive effects of DT are corroborated by a growing body of research that quantifies DT's payoff and impact on performance in the business world. Consulting firms like McKinsey and research organizations like Forrester have devoted extensive effort

to measuring ROI.[10] Preliminary reports from these sources show impressive outcomes: Forrester assessed the ROI of IBM's investment in DT competencies, in a small sample of client-facing teams, at over 300%. Similarly, McKinsey, with data gathered from 300 firms over a five-year period, reported additional revenue growth of 32% and return to shareholders of 56% for firms with top design capability scores.

But how does DT produce these impressive returns? Many of the positive impacts of its social technology role lie beneath the surface in how the human-centered effects that we have talked about play out in how people think, converse and act. We have argued that DT's outcomes resemble an iceberg with multiple layers of impact, most of them lying hidden below the surface.[11]

Like an iceberg, only DT's most obvious impacts show above the waterline. These are the most easily counted—like cost savings and sales increases—and usually relate to standard organizational measures.

ASSESSING THE ROI OF DESIGN THINKING

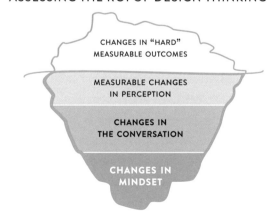

But the most powerful work, and the hardest to count, happens beneath the surface.

Some impacts, just below the waterline, remain measurable (if not countable)—often through surveys that measure people's perceptions around how satisfied they are with a product's performance, like Net Promoter Score (NPS). These perceptual measures clearly relate to the countable things like sales increases. Though that link is more challenging to quantify precisely, these benefits are just as real.

Deeper still, we find DT impacts innovators' *inner conversations* with themselves. These are changes that are less about what people say or do in their interaction with each other and more about shifts in individual mindsets—how innovators think and what they believe. This is where *becoming* shows up.

We have focused our latest research on the question of how we identify and measure these deeper impacts.

We now understand *why* the ROI in previous empirical studies done by Forrester and McKinsey is so high, and *why* DT plays such a prominent role in fostering the achievement of our innovation wish list. It offers a rich and diverse array of positive outcomes for individuals and their organizations—many below the surface and difficult to detect using our usual financial and activity-based measures. But all are just as real.

THE SWEET SPOT—THE MOST POWERFUL ACCELERATOR OF IMPROVED OUTCOMES— IS RIGHT IN THE MIDDLE. WE CALL THIS THE **MINIMUM VIABLE COMPETENCY**.

THE IMPACT OF EXPERTISE

Clearly, DT done well delivers significant benefits. But what does it mean to do it well? What role does an individual's level of expertise play? How much training is enough? These questions surface a longstanding debate in the DT field about whether we can—or should—teach DT to nondesigners. Critics (often design experts) argue that teaching DT to nondesigners is akin to "allowing people to practice medicine without a license" and that "DT needs to be left to the experts" (yes—that is a direct quote from one of our interviewees). On the other side, proponents of "democratizing" design (like us) have argued that even a little design is better than none.

Findings from our latest research on the value of expertise suggest that both parties are right *and* wrong.[12] Expertise definitely matters in our data, but not in the linear way you might expect. Instead, expertise operates through a series of *thresholds* (think novice, intermediate and expert) and only certain thresholds matter. This may come as a shock to some, but neither *novice* expertise nor *expert* status seem significant to improving outcomes. The sweet spot—the most powerful accelerator of improved outcomes—is right in the middle. We call this the *minimum viable competency* (MVC) that innovators need to reach in order to

OUR NEW RESEARCH

In our latest research, done with our colleague Kristina Jaskyte Bahr at the University of Georgia, our goal has been to explore the entire iceberg, above and below the water. Based on what we had learned over a decade spent studying DT in action, we developed a simple online diagnostic survey (contained here in the appendix) that looks across multiple levels of analysis—individual, team, organizational, and even system level—at DT impacts. To date, we have gathered data from over 1,000 DT users (from business, nonprofit and government organizations globally) in successive waves of surveying.[13]

Our research findings illustrate the wide array of diverse outcomes that DT is capable of producing. Our factor analysis groups them into five categories.

What we've learned:

DT produces increased solution quality and implementability. Our research into why DT improves quality and implementability suggests that the reason relates to the human element. It is not only the result of reducing Category 1 biases by introducing data from users, it also comes from holding innovators in the problem space long enough to reframe the problem. Quality is also impacted by the enhanced engagement of employees and by creating conditions for higher-order ideas to emerge *during* stakeholder conversations. Not only does DT help us come up with better ideas, it also assures a higher likelihood of actually implementing those ideas as well. DT acts like a form of change management, engaging implementers in activities like prototyping and testing that build enthusiasm and ownership of new solutions, and keeping them motivated during the hard work of iteration.

We also observe important relationship-building impacts from the use of DT related to network capability and resource use. This has to do with creating shared purpose and a greater commitment to collaboration, but also comes from pooling resources across partners. Tapping into the power of local capability-building by allowing autonomy, while assuring quality by offering tools instead of standardized solutions, allows adaptation to local conditions and takes advantage of local intelligence. This, in turn, feeds into better solutions. DT fosters the ability to work collaboratively with a broader network of stakeholders, adding their capabilities and resources to ours. Our research also demonstrates that DT builds trust, which produces many positive outcomes as diverse as increased efficiency and enhanced collaboration.

Finally, our research suggests a set of powerful impacts at a personal level. Practicing DT shifts innovators' mindsets and beliefs, as well as their skillsets. It builds their creative confidence and a sense of psychological safety that, in turn, fosters a willingness to try new things. These individual shifts are critical to engaging a broad group of people in the task of adapting to an increasingly turbulent world.

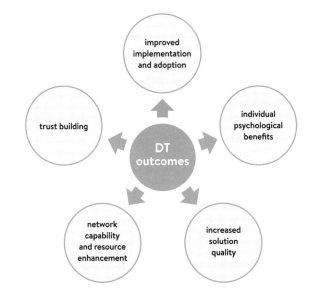

optimize the use of DT. (Apologies to Lean Startup for brazenly riffing off the minimum viable product [MVP] concept they have made famous.)

What does this actually mean for innovators and their organizations? It means that, in our research, achieving impact at every level of the iceberg requires getting innovators' skills beyond the threshold of novice: they need to be fully literate in DT tools and methods. And they need to cross over into the intermediate threshold of expertise. So one-day hackathons or an occasional sprint are not enough to get there. On the other hand, four years of design school aren't necessary for literacy either: innovators need not reach the level of expert. The intermediate threshold is what we need to clear to maximize benefits across all five impact factors.

This finding really got us thinking: What does that intermediate threshold, that middle ground between novice and expert where the real payoff to DT lies, look like? What are the MVCs that characterize it? How will I know when I have reached them? These questions set us on a path to thinking about DT as a progression through a series of experiences that, in turn, produce identifiable new mindsets and skillsets that show up in an accompanying set of behaviors. When we see these *behaviors*, we know that MVC—that intermediate threshold where DT's power lies—has been reached. We will review a detailed checklist of what these behaviors look like at each phase of the DT process in the coming chapters. Here are some quick examples of what we see, by experience phase:

MINIMUM VIABLE COMPETENCIES
(some examples)

IMMERSION

- Listens to understand needs rather than test solutions
- Aware of own biases and blinders
- Able to probe deeply for any unarticulated needs/beliefs

SENSEMAKING

- Distinguishes between an observation and an interpretation
- Remains patient with iteration and search
- Develops informed inferences that are actionable

ALIGNMENT

- Listens heedfully and respectfully to teammates' views
- Attentive to the rules of dialogue, like turn taking
- Willing to let go of own perspective and be open to others

EMERGENCE

- Pursues multiple possibilities
- Actively engages in co-creation, looks for opportunities to build on the ideas of others
- Stays in the possibility space despite time pressure

IMAGINING

Able to capture, in the mind's eye, a vivid image of the experience a concept will create for users

Develops immersive prototypes that facilitate feedback conversations

LEARNING IN ACTION

Focuses on testing critical assumptions

Explores disconfirming data with curiosity rather than rejecting it

These behaviors that indicate that an innovator has reached the MVCs are visible above the water line—we can measure and track them (at least using perceptual measures—more on this in Part 5). But they only happen when those experiences at the different phases of DT produce fundamental shifts in how innovators see the world. This takes us back full circle to where we started—to the *doing-experiencing-becoming* cycle. This is the foundation for the next two parts of this book: examining the way in which innovators' experience of DT's different phases triggers different aspects of personal transformation, of *becoming*, that allows them and their organizations to reap the full benefits of DT.

So—let's get started!

PART TWO
THE DISCOVERY PROCESS

INTRODUCTION TO THE DISCOVERY PROCESS

In Part 1 of this book, we shared evidence, from our own research as well as that of others, that demonstrated the diverse positive impacts that DT's transformative potential offers, and looked at how these can help organizations achieve their innovation wish lists. In doing so, we hoped to make a case for why every individual and organization interested in improving their innovation capabilities needs to pay attention to the journeys of their innovators, as well as those of their customers.

We highlighted DT's role as a crucial social technology and laid out our case for the importance of recognizing the difference between *doing* design activities and *experiencing* the shifts in mindsets and skillsets that accompany *becoming* a design thinker. Recognizing and cultivating this depth of experience is key to maximizing DT's impact.

In the remainder of this book, we want to turn our attention to examining, for each experience phase, what the journey to minimum viable competency (MVC) looks like. In each chapter, we begin by describing the mindset shift DT aspires to achieve. We look at the science behind such shifts, what makes them hard to accomplish, and the payoff when we succeed. For each stage, we provide a checklist of the specific behavioral milestones that *becoming* requires so that you can assess where you and your team are today. Finally, we share ideas for how you, as both an individual innovator and a leader of others, can achieve a deeper experience. Along the way, we pay particular attention to how activities translate to experience—how *doing* shapes *becoming*.

Part 2 looks at the Discovery process and the first four phases of the innovator's journey: Immersion, Sensemaking, Alignment, and Emergence. In Part 3, we will examine the Testing process and the experiences of Imagining and Learning in Action. Part 4 explores how the journey differs across different personalities. We bring our discussion back to you and your organization in Part 5.

So, on to Immersion!

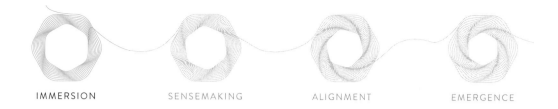

IMMERSION   SENSEMAKING   ALIGNMENT   EMERGENCE

CHAPTER 3
IMMERSION

SANJAY

As the design team began data gathering on the needs of recently arrived refugees, Sanjay struggled with the process. His teammates seemed obsessed with the "plight" of the refugees, focusing on how hard they had it. But Sanjay wasn't so sure, for reasons he explained: "My father was a refugee as a child. His family lost everything and he had to rebuild his life from scratch." His dad had built a great life for his family. Seeing the structured support local refugees were already getting, Sanjay was skeptical that their needs were not already being met as he talked with social service workers. Then he met Kwame, a boy from the Congo. "Meeting Kwame," he explained, "was pivotal. Until that point I was convinced that the lives refugees were leading in the United States are somewhat comfortable (in comparison to what was standard for me back home). Kwame helped us understand the journeys refugees undertake to get here. His clothes were frayed. His shoes had holes in them. He failed his first English test because he didn't know the meaning of the word 'celery.' He applied for jobs for his parents and accompanied them to interviews. We went on to have similar eye-opening experiences with other refugees. My skepticism disappeared." ■

The experience of Immersion changes Sanjay. Though his team feels otherwise, his early "expert" interviews with local social workers and refugee agencies seem to confirm his suspicions that things are not all that bad for local refugees. This data, interpreted through Sanjay's own personal experiences, sets up a comparison between the local refugees' experience and the objectively worse ones his own father once faced, leaving him unsure that a serious problem exists. Then he spends time with a boy with holes in his shoes, forging an emotional connection. He develops empathy for Kwame, and for the other refugees he later meets, shifting his perspective dramatically from egocentric and detached to empathetic and engaged. This is the Immersion experience at work. It is more than a set of activities that Sanjay performs. In the process of *doing* ethnographic data gathering, he has an *experience* that is personal and human centered. This experience changes *him*—not just what he knows, but also what he feels and believes. It puts him in touch with his more authentic self and connects him to others around him, not just Kwame.

Though ethnography might be viewed as just an alternative approach to data gathering that focuses on obtaining qualitative rather than quantitative data, its impact, when done well, goes much deeper than that: it triggers a level of personal engagement, both cognitive and emotional, that is entirely different than conducting a survey or even doing an "expert" interview. When design is done well, data gathering initiates more than a deepened understanding of the problem and the needs of the people being designed for; it also creates an experience of Immersion that shifts how the innovator sees and interacts with the world.

In this chapter, we will examine the profound personal impact that results from innovators' willingness to immerse themselves in the experience of others, and the power of awakening to the realization that others are unique individuals with unique (and valid) needs and behaviors that may differ from one's own. Immersion sets the stage for the entire sequence of DT experiences that come later. Nowhere is the difference between *doing* and *becoming* more visible than in Immersion. A few ethnographic interviews conducted for detached data-gathering purposes do not empathy make!

IMMERSION ACTIVITIES[14]

- Conducting research using design tools like ethnographic observation and interviewing
- Preparing conversation guides
- Exploring the job to be done of those you are designing for
- Creating journey maps
- Using projective tools (like collage) to explore unarticulated needs
- Mirroring or shadowing users
- Asking users to prepare diaries or photo journals
- Capturing key takeaways to share

WHAT DOES AN INNOVATOR'S MINDSET SHIFT LOOK LIKE DURING IMMERSION?

As innovators experience Immersion, they move from *unconsciously* seeing only through the lens of their own perspective to *consciously* seeking to better understand, value, and adopt the perspective of others. Let's explore what we mean.

IMMERSION MOVES INNOVATORS...

FROM A MINDSET THAT IS...	TO A MINDSET THAT IS...
Egocentric	Empathetic
Certain about the accuracy of one's own perspective	Aware of personal biases
Detached and distant	Curious and personally engaged
Impatient and anxious to problem solve and generate solutions	Willing to invest time to understand current reality before developing solutions
Accepting of the obvious and conventional definition of the problem; treating it as a given	Critical of the obvious definition; treating it as a hypothesis

THE SCIENCE BEHIND IT

The development of empathy is a primary driver of these shifts in mindset during Immersion. Psychiatrist Dr. Mark Goulston[15] argues that immersion in others' problems, from the perspectives of those having them, changes people. He describes how his own listening changed as he worked with suicidal patients: "Now I always try to hear them from their *inside out* rather than from my intellectual *understanding in*. I think this enables my patients to feel better understood and, consequently, less alone."

Empathy is a complex phenomenon. Researchers who study it distinguish between *affective* empathy, an emotional connection that carries with it the ability to feel *with* another, and *cognitive* empathy, the mental processing associated with perspective taking and understanding another's thoughts, beliefs, or intentions. Both have a critical role to play in DT processes. We need a balance between affective and cognitive empathy. Too much or too little of either can be problematic: cognitive empathy without an affective component can merely make us better manipulators; affective empathy without perspective taking leads us to gravitate to others like us rather than to those who are different.

MIRROR NEURONS AT WORK. Some scientists believe that empathy is innate, and is explained in part by the presence of mirror neurons. Mirror neurons are responsible for activating the same neural pathways in our brain when we observe or mentally "see" an activity as when we actually perform that activity (we will come back to this later as one of the reasons why visualization is so powerful). Extending this logic, we can feel *with* others experiencing pain, for instance, without us having to actually experience it ourselves. According to scholars Pier Francesco Ferrari and Giacomo Rizzolatti, mirror neurons make it possible for us to understand the actions and intentions of others.[16] They are the biological root of empathy. Because all humans are born with mirror neurons, we all have the capacity to understand others' actions and intentions, they argue. Other scientists ascribe less import to mirror neurons, arguing that the development of empathy is much more a function of nurture (culture, socialization, and learning experiences) than of nature.

THE BIOLOGICAL CIRCUITRY OF FEAR CAN DECREASE OUR WILLINGNESS TO ENGAGE WITH OTHERS. Even if we believe we *are* wired to engage and intuit others' thoughts and feelings, this is not enough to spur action. Our biological circuitry of fear can interfere with Immersion's ability to develop empathy. Fear resides in a deep brain lobe—the amygdala. Part of the limbic system that controls our emotional responses, the amygdala has played a crucial role in human survival since time immemorial. It holds our fight-or-flight instinct, which has protected us from dangerous animals and predators. But the limbic system can also short-circuit the rational executive-functioning portion of our brain, the neocortex, responsible for higher-order brain function and cognition. So what once saved us may be diminishing our ability to engage with others. We have to help the neocortex combat the strong biological circuitry of the amygdala so that we reject the fear that accompanies engagement.

CULTIVATING CURIOSITY IS KEY TO LEARNING. Research by psychologist Paul Silvia shows how curiosity plays a critical role in triggering engagement instead of avoidance, by helping us overcome feelings of uncertainty and anxiety.[17] Indulging our curiosity creates a virtuous cycle, motivating learning that, in turn, motivates interest. His research suggests that the sweet spot to maximize motivation and learning is simultaneously complex *and* understandable. By counterbalancing the instinctive anxiety and uncertainty that rule our choice to engage, the sweet spot provides the motivation to immerse ourselves in new things, places, or experiences.

OUR BIASES BLIND US. It is not only our brain's wiring and evolutionary impulses that inhibit our capacity to understand the needs of others—flaws in human decision-making processes also play a major role. In Chapter 2, we discussed the various types of biases that hinder our ability to make good decisions. During data-gathering activities, Category 1 biases are especially problematic. The egocentric empathy bias, in which we consistently overestimate the similarity between what we value and what others value, is a particularly powerful proclivity that works against impactful immersion. Researchers Van Boven, Dunning, and Loewenstein[18] note that "a venerable tradition in social psychology has documented people's tendency to project their own thoughts, preferences, and behaviors onto other people." Similarly, Nickerson[19] describes the power of selective perception and the "pervasive human tendency to selectively perceive, encode and retain information that is congruent with one's own desires."

WHAT MAKES IMMERSION SO HARD?

At a personal level, even beyond our brain circuitry and biases, innovators find the Immersion experience difficult for many reasons:

STEPPING INTO THE UNKNOWN IS INTIMIDATING. People who prefer structure, clarity, and specificity find the ambiguity of this early stage of the DT process unnerving. They like to start with a well-defined problem that has visible solutions *before* they try to solve it. As one innovator told us:

> *To me, seeking for the unknowns while not knowing what you're looking for is one of the most challenging things in DT.*

Stepping into open-ended exploration can be unsettling. A colleague who works with MBA students noted that his students generally displayed a lot of

THE PROMISE AND PERIL OF MAPS

It had been a long day on the hiking trails of Yosemite National Park, but the Mariposa Grove of giant sequoias still waited. So I (Jeanne) retrieved a map of the Grove at the visitor center and set off to find the trees it indicated: the "Grizzly Giant" (thought to be, at 1,700 years old, the oldest in the grove), the "Loving Couple" (two trees joined in an interesting way at the base), and so on. These were named by Galen Clark, the original protector of the grove in the mid-1800s, as a way to make visitors care about the trees and protect them from timbering interests. I was disappointed when the famed grove turned out to be no more impressive than these few individual trees. Giving my map to another tourist who didn't have one, I headed back, deciding to take an alternative route to the parking lot. Though the path was well marked at the trailhead, 20 yards in, I was all alone and lost. I slowed my pace and began to look around at the forest surrounding me. It was amazing! There were giant sequoias everywhere, their majesty undeniable. I was awed. It really *was* a grove, I realized. How had I missed it before? My devotion to the map had not served me well. Had I not given it up, I would have found every tree it indicated, but missed seeing the grove itself. The map had given me confidence and a mission, but also created a myopia that kept me from being fully present and blinded me to what I was really looking for. Focused on it, I almost literally "missed the forest for the trees."

confidence, yet they found exploring strangers' decision processes intimidating: "Often students seem to feel that they could run any major corporation the day after graduation, but find talking to a shopper in a supermarket terrifying." People crave maps to help them navigate the unknown. But a map can also create a detachment and goal orientation that can actively impede actually *seeing* what is going on around us.

Mapmaking is a tricky business—we need maps that guide rather than blind us. We need the structure of DT's methodology and tools paired with the freedom to explore without constraint.

WE LISTEN TO JUDGE RATHER THAN TO UNDERSTAND. Many people treat their beliefs as truths; when faced with something that looks contrary, they reject it immediately. Creativity breakthroughs often require keeping alive sets of tensions: between what we believe and what others believe, between possibilities and constraints, between allowing our conversations to diverge or forcing convergence. Innovators have to be willing to listen to the unfamiliar and treat what they believe to be true as a hypothesis. As one innovator explained:

> I experienced the paradox of the path to becoming creative. . . . Different frames of reference can drive creativity. . . . Moving forward, I will not be too fast to reject things that look contrary but will spend time to look at them and try them out.

IT IS CHALLENGING TO BE FULLY PRESENT AND NOT LISTEN THROUGH THE SOLUTIONS WE ALREADY HAVE IN MIND. Human beings are natural problem solvers. We are anxious to solve, so we immediately begin hypothesizing answers and then listen to our interviewees through the lens of the solutions we are already imagining. One innovator offered:

> I automatically start thinking of solutions based off my experience. It's hard for my brain to imagine seeing something from someone else's perspective. I used to be a UX designer in my past life and was so surprised to see people confused by our designs—they were so obvious to me.

Immersion requires listening openly and being fully present to the experience of another, not listening selectively through our own preconceptions. When innovators experience this, it can be truly inspiring. As one told us:

> Ethnographic research has been my favorite part of the design thinking process. At that point, the world is your oyster, and there's a genuine sense of wonder about where the conversation is going to go. . . . There's magic in probing and asking open-ended questions without a clear agenda. It is so much more freeing to not have a predetermined solution in mind and to be able to genuinely and curiously learn more.

So we need to put our theories aside. As Sherlock Holmes famously noted, "It is a capital mistake to theorize before one has data. Insensibly one begins to twist facts to suit theories, instead of theories to suit facts."[20]

WE'VE BEEN TAUGHT THAT "REAL" DATA HAS NUMBERS AND THAT THE PURPOSE OF DATA GATHERING IS PROOF. For many of us, quantitative data inspires confidence that our findings are "accurate." We have been trained to value "hard data" as the best (and often only) input into decision-making. Qualitative ethnographic research makes no such promise of accuracy, so we are reluctant to take that path. But this perspective fails to appreciate that data has many uses—and also limitations. In the front end of DT, we gather data to *inspire* better ideas, not to test or "prove" they are worth pursuing. How do you "prove" a future that does not yet exist? We can't expect to use data from the past to successfully predict the future if we are trying to change it. In such an endeavor, sample sizes and statistical significance are irrelevant. Our quest is to figure out what the future *should* look like. This is why some designers look for "extreme" users to help them figure out where the future may already be happening and learn from it. To paraphrase a quote attributed to William Gibson, the noted science fiction author, "The future is already here—it is just not very evenly distributed."

OUR BACKGROUND AND EXPERTISE INTERFERE WITH SEEING SOMETHING FROM SOMEONE ELSE'S PERSPECTIVE. It is often difficult to understand another person's thinking, feelings, and motivations. "Experts" (engineers, professors, physicians, lawyers, and the like) are trained to view problems through the lens of their profession's worldview, which makes it challenging to understand the perspective of nonexperts like students, patients, and clients. The more different from us people are, the harder it is to see the world through their eyes. As explained by a leader of a team dedicated to rethinking strategy at a large children's hospital serving low-income families:

> *The people that I work with are often very physically uncomfortable with our customers. I've taken some people from hospitals along for interviews (in homes) where they're made physically uncomfortable by the socioeconomic conditions, by this new environment.*

British psychologist John Bowlby, working in the 1940s, showed that infants' strong attachments to their mothers protected them from strangers, but also limited their comfort in interactions with people they did not know. We are wired to attach to our own groups.

Then, there are the people we dislike. The bad news about Immersion is that you don't just get to develop a deep understanding for the people you like. You have to extend to all the benefit of accepting them as rational human beings making a set of choices that make sense to them. In order to influence them toward a different set of choices tomorrow, you have to understand why they are making their choices today. The reluctance to do this can show up as excluding them from research conversations or discrediting their point of view. One innovator we talked to refused to engage with contract employees who potentially held an important outside perspective because of his own deeply held knowledge bias. He said: "Contract people just don't know. They don't have the knowledge, the background, the history, they just don't know. That introduces mistakes."

Given all of the challenges to achieving Immersion, you may question if it is really worth all this trouble. Not surprising, the answer is an unqualified *absolutely!*

WHY DOES IMMERSION MATTER SO MUCH?

IMMERSION SETS THE STAGE. Immersion is the foundation for every one of the significant outcomes we talked about in Chapter 2. Empathy is essential— the mindset it triggers kick-starts the entire experience journey of an innovator. Using ethnographic tools to immerse practitioners in the day-to-day lives of those for whom they are designing provides a direct *sensory* experience. Walking a patient to the lab is a very different experience than examining a process map. Not only does it unearth human-centered data and deeper insights, the emotional connection provides the cornerstone for DT done well. At one of our research sites, the team leader explained why involvement with the personal stories of those they served was so critical to helping staff move from a profession-centered "place of judgment" to a "place of possibilities":

> Rather than "this is how the system works and how they should be using it," we want to help staff shift their lens—get them out of their expert hat and into a beginner's mindset that is willing to look at the problem differently.

At one university medical center, a doctor described the critical impact of clinicians realizing, after journey mapping patients' experiences, that the care they were currently providing was not what they thought:

> We can think all kinds of things about how we believe the system is working, but then seeing the reality of how it was really working, it was shocking to see how far from our intentions reality had come. Patients needed someone to be present for them. Despite a flurry of activity, nothing was changing for them. We needed to feel their blockages and struggles.

Behind every problem definition lies a set of unarticulated assumptions, beliefs, and experiences that lead each person to define the problem a certain way. Unless these are surfaced early in the process and challenged, mindsets do not shift and opportunities to ask a more powerful question are lost. Immersion softens our boundaries and challenges our way of thinking to create space for alternative perspectives. This drives the problem reframing that is critical to better solutions. One innovator shared her insights:

> I found that I unintentionally limited my perception to find solutions only for the activity itself and blinded myself to other parts of the experience. This awakening moment let me see the unseen parts of myself and see the unseen parts of the user's experience. I feel like I now see the other part of the iceberg under the water.

IMMERSION ENCOURAGES US TO LISTEN MORE OPENLY TO ALTERNATIVE VIEWS. The ability to see new and more creative opportunities often rests on this kind of reframing of the problem in ways that tap into the diversity of perspectives available. The boundaries of a solution space are a function of the cumulative repertoires of team members—but only if they can tap into the richness of each member's contribution. Tapping into the power of the collective is core to why DT works. It relaxes our conviction about the "rightness" of our own view, and the "wrongness" of those who think differently, as it did with Sanjay. In this difference lies great potential. Getting people with different perspectives into the conversation expands the problem space. Immersion invites us all to confront our perspectives and biases, as well as those of others.

THE POWER OF MIRRORING

One especially memorable story from our research takes place in an institute serving adults with Asperger's Syndrome. A young designer visited one of the residents, Pete, at home. She observed him doing destructive things—picking at a leather sofa, ripping a magazine, and creating indents in a wall by rubbing against it. She wondered how she could design solutions that would prevent such behavior in the future. On her second visit to Pete's house, she took a more empathetic approach, and decided to mirror Pete's behavior. She discovered, to her surprise, the sensory enjoyment that came from ripping paper, flipping a magazine, picking at the leather on a couch, or holding an ear against a wall. Unable to ask Pete directly what he liked about doing these things, she experienced them for herself. On her first visit to his home, she had used her own frame of reference and labeled Pete's acts as negative and destructive. On her second visit, she began to truly empathize with Pete—the paper, sofa, and wall revealed vital clues that helped her understand the things Pete liked to do. She explained: "I thought empathy was innate, but now realize that it can grow and evolve. For this to happen it requires a perceptual shift in thinking that is open to different ways of being in the world."[21]

IMMERSION SETS UP THE SHIFT TO A HYPOTHESIS-DRIVEN MENTALITY. For most innovators, DT provides their first introduction to being hypothesis driven, and Immersion brings home the complexity of meeting the needs of human beings who do not see the world as we do. Few of us are raised with a hypothesis-driven mentality. Instead, we have been taught that there is a single "right" answer and that we can find it and prove it analytically, in advance of action. In contrast, hypothesis-driven thinkers believe that there are many possible answers, and that finding out which ones are superior is only possible through experimentation in action. Both ways of thinking have merit—both perform well, but under different circumstances. When the ability to predict based on existing data is good and the problem is clear and agreed upon, analytic methods are usually quicker and more efficient. This is the world of "tame" problems. In a complex and uncertain world, however, where extrapolating from the past is problematic, where elements interact in hard-to-predict ways, or when there is no clear agreement even on what the problem actually is, hypothesis-driven models carry the day. Persistent problems are often complex or "wicked" (in designer speak). This is the land where innovation lives. Hypothesis-driven approaches marry generative and analytical research. Many of us have been taught that we can be creative (entirely intuitive) *or* data driven (guided by numbers on a spreadsheet). Hypothesis-driven approaches demonstrate that, in a complex world, we need to be both—success in any innovative endeavor relies upon it.

IMMERSION CULTIVATES OUR CURIOSITY AND TEACHES US TO ASK GOOD QUESTIONS. This helps us discover needs that people can't tell us they have. Immersion creates the conditions for innovators to observe new perspectives, new relationships, and new needs that stakeholders cannot articulate clearly.

As Paul Silvia observed, this combination of being complex (the human being part) and understandable (through the structure of DT tools) hits the sweet spot for motivating curiosity and learning. As observers, we are able to empathize with the needs of our stakeholders but still retain a critical distance that helps us to intuit latent needs, even ones that our stakeholders cannot access on their own. This can drive new questions that lead to the identification of profoundly new insights that may even flip the problem on its head.

IMMERSION HOLDS US IN TODAY'S REALITIES.
As we talked about in Chapter 1, action-oriented people want to see results. They want to jump to the future and talk about *solutions*. This is a big problem if we are trying to innovate. We need to slow innovators down from jumping too early into envisioning a new future. The only clues we have about the optimal desired futures live in the present and the data we collect today. So that's where we have to start, because we cannot get to a new future without understanding the truth about the current reality of stakeholders' lives. Design's role is to help people envision new possibilities within the context of the current reality and identify what the gap looks like between the present and a desired future, so that we can think creatively about how to close it. As one innovator told us:

Based on the problems we were hearing it was easy for me to jump to solutions. Many of those problems held throughout the project and we

WHAT MAKES A GOOD QUESTION

Questions really matter in DT—they matter when we gather data, they matter when we brainstorm and they matter when we test. The questions we ask determine the boundaries of what we will see. If you get the questions wrong, the answers don't matter much. Formulating great questions is an art—but early on our advice is to keep them open-ended and exploratory. Despite the ambiguity all around, the right questions will guide anxious explorers to the answer. As Rainer Maria Rilke beautifully put it: "Try and try to love the questions themselves . . . Live the questions . . . you will gradually, without even noticing it, live your way into the answer."[22]

ended up addressing them with our solutions, but the reasons some of those things were problems were different from what I would have thought, and the solutions we came up with were wildly different from what I could ever have developed in those early weeks.

WHAT DO THE MVCs COMING OUT OF IMMERSION LOOK LIKE?

Individual innovators may start in different places as they enter the Immersion journey (more on this in Part 4), but we want them to arrive at the same destination, with a design mindset. But how do we detect this mindset in practice? As innovators experience Immersion, specific competencies develop that are reflected in their behavior. How do we know when we, or our team, have reached what we called MVCs in Chapter 2—the level at which DT's full impacts are maximized? In Immersion, we are looking for signals that the design thinker has moved beyond the activity of *doing* ethnographic research (while still listening through their usual egocentric and solution-focused mindset) to a DT mindset that listens openly and empathetically.

Here are some of the questions we suggest that you ask yourself:

AM I . . .

- ☑ Listening to understand rather than to test?

- ☑ Aware of my own biases and blinders?

- ☑ Asking good questions?

- ☑ Developing an emotional engagement and empathetic bond with those for whom I am designing?

- ☑ Fully present in the moment to the lived experience of my colleagues and those for whom I am designing?

- ☑ Searching for areas of opportunity rather than solutions?

- ☑ Probing deeply for unarticulated needs and beliefs?

HOW DO WE BETTER GUIDE AND SUPPORT OUR OWN SHIFT AND THAT OF OTHERS?

STAY DIRECTLY INVOLVED IN THE PROBLEM. Einstein suggested that spending 95% of the time thinking about the problem and only 5% thinking about its solution produces smarter innovation. But with today's "can-do" emphasis on speed coupled with our general impatience, innovators often feel pressured to run with the most obvious early solution and devote their energy to "selling" that. Instead, immerse yourself in the problem/opportunity as seen from the perspective of your key stakeholders. Don't delegate away all of your Discovery work. Though there is an important role for experts and mentors, insist that you and your staff be part of the team that does the work—otherwise others have the experience of Immersion, not you. Listening to someone else tell stories about your stakeholders, regardless of how compelling they are, is a weak substitute for the kind of direct involvement that forces your team to make eye contact with people stuck in the problem you're attempting to solve. *Becoming* is fueled by direct engagement.

FOCUS ON BEING FULLY PRESENT. This sounds a bit "new age" and abstract, but the truth is that we are rarely fully present to another. Instead, we are in our own heads, listening half-heartedly through our own filters. Ethnography offers the opportunity to step out of our own heads and into someone else's. Don't squander that chance and fritter it away by being only partly attentive.

LET GO OF "GETTING IT RIGHT." We can never know whether the observations we are making are "accurate." That is an uncomfortable position—but worries and self-doubt are usually unproductive. One innovator, looking back on the experience, told us:

> It's been a hell of a journey. I find some disappointment in how much self-doubt I have. I know that a lot of it is about hesitation around the process, but I know that the question "Am I doing this right?" is as much about the process as it is about my own competency. I should stop doing that, it's stupid.

An important part of letting go also relates to the need to control—controlling the interview, controlling the choice of solutions, and wanting to get our own way. Letting go of all of these is particularly important. One innovator described it this way:

> Maybe the reason I struggle with this mode of thinking in particular is that as a designer, we lack control. From beginning to end, we are required to listen and not speak. We can interpret observations and slowly shape them into criteria and potential solutions, but there aren't really any "end" decisions made until someone else makes

> them for us. For all the swift decision-making skills I have been taught, this is one space where we have to delay the gratification of knowing whether we've made a good decision or not.

Anxiety blocks fully experiencing. So we like to give our students a tongue-in-cheek list of what they *should* and *should not* worry about. In the early phases of their DT work, it looks like this:

USEFUL THINGS TO WORRY ABOUT

- Do we have the right interviewees?
- Are we getting the depth we need to uncover fresh insights? Are we probing enough?
- Is our debrief approach capturing the richness of what we learn?
- Is our team working well together?

USELESS THINGS TO WORRY ABOUT

- Will we be able to find a great solution?
- Will our ideas be too boring? Not original enough?
- Are we exploring too broadly?
- Are we doing the process right?
- Does our data make sense? Can we make sense of it?

BRING STRUCTURE AND FORETHOUGHT TO DATA GATHERING AND PROJECT MANAGEMENT. As you and your team begin to dig into *who* you need to talk to, *what* questions to ask, *which* tools to use, and *how* the team will divide responsibilities, the questions of who team members will study and where to find them require specific answers. Forethought and input here can make a significant difference in setting ourselves up for success and reducing the anxiety that can be a barrier to accepting Immersion. We advocate thinking through available tools: for understanding the user experience, we always recommend job-to-be-done and journey mapping. For complex value chain situations, we recommend utilizing a value chain mapping tool. Sometimes we find a "power alignment map" helpful. Set novices up for success by assigning the right research roles to the right team members. For instance, a faculty member would be a poor choice for interviewing students. It is difficult for authority figures to solicit honest responses from interviewees, despite how hard they try. Interviews work best when conducted by peers or outsiders who are not threatening or representative of the chain of command. We also find that methods for structuring aspects of the research, like debriefing key takeaways from each interview to share with other team members, lend themselves to the creation and use of templates—things we have been taught to decry as bureaucratic but that actually free learners to explore with less anxiety.

KEEP PUSHING DEEPER. Asking leading questions or accepting superficial answers will stall development of the deep understanding that Immersion seeks and stymie innovation success right out of the gate. Again, many of us are uncomfortable with classic ethnographic techniques like allowing lengthy silences after asking a probing question or repeating the same question to encourage an interviewee to share deeper thoughts with us. There is a steep experience curve to this work. Have patience with yourself and your teammates as you work on improving. Keep probing! To support this, we suggest having novices interview in pairs to allow one of them to concentrate solely on listening and probing while the other monitors the interview guide and takes notes.

DIVE INTO ACTION! In the past, we have eased cautious and timid team members into Immersion with seemingly easier research tools like secondary desk research in order not to overwhelm them with new experiences. This approach has had the opposite of our intended outcome. That kind of research doesn't produce the exhilaration and eye-opening depth of observations that interviews produce and can actually demotivate and accelerate novices' desire to move on. Instead, ease yourself and cautious team members into interviewing by practicing interviews with colleagues or watching videos on how to conduct empathy interviews—then push yourself out the door!

SLOW DOWN TO MOVE FASTER. In many organizations—and even personally—we have been programmed to worship at the altar of "efficiency." Much of DT can look highly inefficient to an outside observer. We must, however, understand that real efficiency happens when we speedily *implement* a scalable, risk-tested new concept, not how fast we generate the idea itself. The additional investment we make in the Immersion experience pays huge dividends later in the process. As one innovator commented:

> *Immersing myself in the user experience and allowing myself to wallow in a problem was really helpful. I have a hard time with things I deem inefficient, and I've written off wallowing as ineffective in the past. Now, I have an appreciation for slowing down to go fast.*

MAINTAIN POSITIVE MOMENTUM (OR PIVOT TO REGAIN MOMENTUM). There is a fine line between too much time for the Immersion phase and not enough. If you don't give yourself enough time, your research will feel superficial and clumsy and so will your Immersion experience. If you allow too much time, the process will slow down, learnings will be lost, and momentum will stall. The key is in the balance.

WHAT'S NEXT?

In our experience, those new to the Immersion experience rarely think that they have done "enough" data gathering and feel ready to move on. This is the nature of any creative process. When asked how he knew when his designing was "done," iconic architect Frank Gehry answered, "When I run out of money or time." A real strength of the DT process is to move us along to the next phase, even when we don't feel ready to go.

So on we go—knowing that we will never be done and that we will be circling back to do more research (next time with prototyped solutions) later in the process. A successful experience of Immersion sets the stage for an innovator to move on to Sensemaking, the phase to which we now turn.

CHAPTER 4
SENSEMAKING

MELANIE

When Melanie's design team set out to explore how to improve the financial health of survivors of domestic violence, the work was very personal. As a child in a home with abuse, she had always felt guilty that she had not been more able to help her own mother. This had led her to avoid topics related to domestic violence for most of her life. Doing the ethnographic research for the project was both hard and cathartic. She felt that she had a clear understanding of the women the team sought to help, as she listened to survivors discuss the impacts of the complex ecosystem and the challenges of trying to get help, and worked with her team to synthesize and make sense of their experiences. Though this was a subject she was confident that she knew all too well, she was surprised to find additional insights as she explored this new data. She realized that bouncing from person to person, as survivors attempted to get help, required them to tell their stories over and over again. Each retelling added further pain and insult. She also had never thought of even the existence of financial abuse before—only physical. She was shocked to realize that she herself had been a victim of financial abuse at the hands of her ex-husband, but had never recognized it as such. ∎

mmersion provides the raw material for doing design well. But our challenge now is to find the meaning in what we've observed. That meaning must reflect the perspectives of those we are designing for, not our own. Powerful insights that accelerate our ability to create better solutions appear when innovators successfully "make sense" of their mass of data in ways that uncover patterns, common themes, and unique differences, and point them in the direction of unfulfilled needs. Succeeding at Sensemaking can be a pivot point for novice innovators, triggering an epiphany in which they move from fear of failure and a lack of clarity about what they have learned during Immersion to experiencing an energizing confidence that they *can* meet the needs of those for whom they are designing, along with inspiration about how to do so.

Sensemaking happens at both individual and group levels. Like Melanie (and Sanjay from the last chapter), we all fall prey to interpreting data through our own background experiences, values, and expertise, despite the heightened awareness of these biases built during Immersion. Melanie cannot escape the influence of her past, no matter how hard she tries. Yet, as she stays with her data, she uncovers new insights that she had not seen earlier, about a subject that she believed she knew well. Reflecting on the experience of others gives her the opportunity to dig deeper and find meanings that she had missed in her own personal journey. These new insights are also facilitated by her interaction with her team. As they engage in collaborative Sensemaking, team members help each other to see new things. Each member of the team arrives at a place they would likely not have reached without the provocation of their conversations with each other.

The Sensemaking experience remains, for many, a "black box," a puzzle, resistant to "rules" for organizing it. Think about the mystery shrouding "Aha!" moments—we can't anticipate how and when they will come, we just know that when they do, it feels great! Whereas gathering data was active, making sense of it requires putting a pause on the action and *reflecting*. This movement between action and reflection is a hallmark of DT and an important driver of learning. This is almost invariably one of the most challenging phases in the entire DT process—but also among the most important. If Sensemaking fails to produce deeper insights, innovators lose confidence and are unlikely to produce creative solutions. Time and again, we witness the initial enthusiasm produced by DT's much-loved ethnographic tools dissipate as innovators struggle with Sensemaking, drowning in an ocean of information and floundering in the messiness of their search for deeper insights.

The activities that innovators do as part of the Sensemaking experience are aimed at making meaning of their observations, taming the messiness, and structuring their data so that they can learn from their observations in the field and translate this learning into the discovery of valuable insights. Together, these activities set the stage for another critical shift, not only in how innovators think, but in who they are.

WHAT DOES AN INNOVATOR'S MINDSET SHIFT LOOK LIKE DURING SENSEMAKING?

Successful Sensemaking drives a new kind of becoming, as innovators transition from being overwhelmed by the chaos of the process and unsure of what they have learned to being inspired, energized, and more confident in their ability to create value for those they design for.

As innovators move through the Sensemaking experience, they learn to mine their data to uncover what really matters to those for whom they are designing. In the process, emotional commitment to meeting those needs also grows. Let's look in more detail at what that means.

SENSEMAKING MOVES INNOVATORS . . .

FROM A MINDSET THAT IS . . .	TO A MINDSET THAT IS . . .
Uncomfortable with ambiguity	Willing to step into ambiguity to achieve greater understanding
Convinced problems are intractable	Inspired that problems are solvable
Struggling to understand the "why"	Clear around what is important to those they are designing for
Superficial in understanding the problem	Able to reframe the problem in ways that open up new possibilities
Looking for the "right" interpretation and fearful of getting it "wrong"	Persistent, willing to stay with their search and dig deeper
Conflict avoidant	Cognizant of the value of differing perspectives
Treating the problem definition as set in stone	Treating the problem definition as a hypothesis

THE SCIENCE BEHIND IT

Few mental processes are as surrounded by myth and misinformation as the generation of new insights. The fabled "Aha!" moment has been a source of fascination to researchers in different fields for many years. A diverse set of thinkers—philosophers, psychologists, neurologists, and more—have gotten into the act. It turns out that the instantaneous and dazzling "creative leap" across the chasm we have been taught to believe in actually looks more like the careful and slow work of building a bridge.

OUR BRAIN ON INSIGHTS. Experiments using neuroimaging indicate that the brain is predictable in how it behaves when developing an insight. Rather than a single neural event, "Aha!" moments are the culmination of a series of events that prepare the brain for an insight.[23] The brain's surge of energy that brings new insights into consciousness "occurs gradually rather than instantaneously and purposefully rather than serendipitously," Andy Dong and Erin MacDonald argue.[24] Our mind is really at work behind the scenes, sometimes unconsciously, to ready us for what looks like a flash of insight. Microbiologist Louis Pasteur traced the progress of breakthroughs in science to this preparation: "In the fields of observation, chance favors only the prepared mind." Sensemaking prepares the minds of innovators—gradually and cumulatively—to see insights and opportunities. The process underlying this is one that designers refer to as "abduction."

SENSEMAKING ACTIVITIES [25]

- Summarizing interview takeaways and insights
- Sharing observations with teammates
- Triangulating data from multiple sources
- Journaling to stimulate reflection
- Clustering observations to find meaning
- Capturing what we see in visualizations like posters
- Crafting personas that catalog difference in our data
- Creating maps of our user's journey
- Asking the Five Whys [26]
- Building Empathy Maps/360 Empathy Tool

ABDUCTION, ANYONE? More than 100 years ago, philosopher C. S. Peirce defined abduction as "speculative conjecture" that emerges from reflecting on the meaning of data. We can contrast abduction with deduction or induction. As professor Nick Dew explains:

> With deduction, your conclusions follow from your premises. For example, all roses have thorns; this is a rose, therefore it has thorns. Induction works in the opposite direction, from cases to general principles. For example, these plants are all roses; they all have thorns, therefore all roses probably have thorns. Abduction is less like these logics and more like inspired guesswork. It describes the

> *operation of making a leap to a hypothesis by connecting known patterns to specific hypotheses. For example, all roses have thorns; this plant has thorns; therefore it might be a rose.*[27]

So instead of assessing what *is* or what *must be*, abduction hypothesizes what *might* be. It looks at a set of observations and makes an educated guess at the larger pattern or theme that they represent. But what does that leap look like, and where does it come from? Answering these questions takes us to the topics of reflection and repertoire.

REFLECTION AND THE ART OF THINKING SLOW.

Reflection is a key element in Sensemaking. It happens when we take a step back and consciously examine our observations (and often our own thoughts, feelings, and actions) and then try to learn from them. It happens when we *pause.* Cognitive psychologist Daniel Kahneman calls this "slow thinking," or System 2 thinking.[28] Remember the biases we talked about Immersion helping us overcome in Chapter 3—projection, egocentric, hot/cold, and selective perception? They not only hijack us when we *gather* data, they are perhaps even more insidious when we try to *interpret* what that data means. Reflective thinking is what holds these at bay and allows us to see new things. It interrupts our habitual ways of thinking and prevents us from jumping to conclusions, from making inferences that live in our head instead of coming from the data.

In a related way, psychologist Chris Argyris talks about two kinds of learning.[29] Single-loop learning limits our solutions because we make corrections incrementally, without questioning the initial goal. Double-loop learning—when we critically question the question itself—allows us to break through to a fresh understanding. It is a kind of "metacognition" that happens as we reexamine our thinking process itself. For instance, departments in an organization may shift their processes to achieve the productivity goals set by leadership, in a single-loop process. If they instead ask *why* such parameters of success are important and evaluate whether they are the best metrics, that is double-loop. Argyris argues that double-loop learning is necessary for good decision-making in rapidly changing or uncertain contexts. The longer a decision-maker is stuck in single-loop learning, however, the harder it is to transition to double-loop learning. Again, impatience and a lack of awareness of their own blinders locks thinkers in both System 1 and single-loop ways of seeing the world.

INTUITION AND INSIGHT.

The leaps we make are often a product of our *intuition.* But where does intuition come from? Psychologists differentiate between ordinary and expert intuition. Ordinary intuition is just a feeling, a gut instinct. Expert intuition shows up as quick judgments, made based on the expert's repertoire. In the same way a tennis pro knows where the ball will go from the arc and speed of the opponent's racket, professionals develop a repertoire based on their past experiences. They define problems, create meaning, and make abductive leaps into what *might be* by relying on their repertoire. Contrary to popular belief, most of us don't suddenly "see" things we have not already seen. Our past makes us who we are and shapes what we see. Sometimes this is good and we want an expert's perspective, but other times, we want to step away from our habitual ways of seeing and adopt a "beginner's mind"—especially when we are trying to invent a new future.

So we need *provocations* to disrupt the habitual ways of seeing that characterize System 1 and single-loop learning. The experience of Immersion provides one set of provocations by confronting us with the needs of those for whom we design—that disrupts our ego-centric imposition of our own thoughts onto others. As a result, we enter Sensemaking more open to new ways of seeing the world. Another source of provocation, often especially important during Sensemaking, is working with a diverse team like Melanie's, wherein members constructively challenge each other, causing us to surface often unexamined beliefs and assumptions that get in the way of new ways of seeing (more on this next up in Chapter 5).

A PICTURE IS WORTH A THOUSAND WORDS.
Another critical source of provocation in DT is *visualizing* the data we are trying to process. Tools like flip charts, sticky notes, and postings on walls help innovators tame the mass of messy data, taking what is in the heads of individuals and making it visible. As designer Jon Kolko asserts:[30]

> One of the most basic principles of making meaning out of data is to externalize the entire meaning-making process. By taking data out of the cognitive realm (the head), removing it from the digital realm (the computer), and making it tangible in the physical realm in one cohesive visual structure (the wall), the designer is freed of the natural memory limitations of the brain and the artificial organizational limitations of technology. . . . Implicit and hidden meanings are uncovered.

Visualization becomes critical as we move from individual to collective Sensemaking.

To summarize, science tell us some interesting things about the experience of Sensemaking:

- It is cumulative over time and usually not a sudden flash of inspiration that comes from nowhere
- It involves making unavoidable leaps of judgment that are hard to prove "right" or "wrong" in the moment
- It requires slowing down to reflect and asking different questions
- It is both aided and impeded by our repertoire of experiences
- Making our inner thoughts visible helps, especially in collective Sensemaking

WHAT MAKES SENSEMAKING SO HARD?

Innovators find Sensemaking difficult for many reasons, many related to the science we've talked about:

INNOVATORS ARE OVERWHELMED BY THE AMOUNT OF QUALITATIVE DATA. Mentally processing large amounts of qualitative data is much more challenging than asking a computer to run regressions for us on quantitative data. It does not organize easily into Excel spreadsheets, so we have to find meaning the old-fashioned way—by ourselves. Not surprisingly, our cognitive circuitry often overloads; attempts at Sensemaking that lack structure can quickly get overwhelming. Enduring the ambiguity and messiness that getting to a deep insight involves can be mentally painful: it is uncomfortable for people who like to know where they are going (back to the need for maps). One innovator likened it to working on a giant jigsaw puzzle, but with a few twists:

> In a normal jigsaw puzzle you will usually get jigsaw pieces of a picture mixed up in one box with the completed outcome for reference on the outside of the box. . . . In design thinking, you have a much harder puzzle. First, pieces of data you get from the interviews do not come from one box—they come from various boxes. Second, those pieces of data from numerous boxes have been mixed up in one pile. Third, you don't have the completed picture. It is a mess!

Success requires what one of our favorite professors, many years ago, described as "wallowing in the data." "Wallowing" can be defined as "rolling about or relaxing in mud"—apt, but not something for which most creatures other than pigs have much patience. We are used to *analyzing* data, not wallowing in it. Sure—some innovators can just dive into the Sensemaking experience and feel comfortable taking the initiative to figure things out, but most of us need help to stay afloat.

DOING INTERVIEWS IS ONLY THE BEGINNING. Setting up successful Sensemaking requires significant work *after* the data gathering of Immersion is over. Prepping the data collected and organizing it into a format that captures the learning is essential and provides the foundation for deep insight identification, but can be time consuming and tedious. If innovators fail to do this homework or spend too much time debating how to do it, they may have little energy in reserve to do the hard work of mining it for deeper meanings. Since the search for insights also has no clear stopping point, this adds to the exhaustion and confusion. As one innovator shared with us: "It's hard to know when to keep discussion going in hopes of solidifying deeper insights or when it's better to move on and work on the next cluster." The outcome? They run out of steam.

INNOVATORS FIND IT DIFFICULT TO SEPARATE OBSERVATIONS FROM INTERPRETATIONS. The ability to sort factual observations/data points from interpretations is harder than you think. We are continually surprised at how bad intelligent people can be at recognizing what is a fact versus an interpretation they have made based on a fact. One of the approaches to making this work less challenging and exhausting is to layer the cognitive complexity. We do this by dividing the process into three parts: first, we process *observations* about current reality; next, we look for themes and turn these into *insights* about current reality; and then finally, we translate insights into *criteria* for future designs. Comingling the first two steps creates a confusing jumble of facts and inferences, and makes it hard to successfully layer.

WAITING FOR THE BIG "AHA!" Innovators and their teams slow Sensemaking down and imperil its success by resisting moving forward with data that is "not interesting enough." It is tempting to think that every individual data point should be interesting in and of itself to be an important contribution, but this is simply not true. People often need to lower their standard of what they think is "interesting" because how the individual data points *connect* in meaningful ways is what makes something interesting. Raw, individual data points are merely the building blocks of a great insight. Innovators that try to find utility in every piece of data risk losing sight of the bigger goal of connecting individual data points in meaningful ways and crafting insights that are informative, inspiring, and memorable. It's not about using every data point.

WE FORGET THAT INSPIRATION, NOT ACCURATE DESCRIPTION, IS OUR GOAL. Often, the hardest part of finding meaning in data is letting go of our traditional view that we are supposed to "prove" something is right. In DT, we do not pretend to describe an entire population with our small sample size. We cannot know how representative our interviewees are of the general population. But this doesn't matter—because our goal is to use data to *inspire*, not prove. As Tim Brown, IDEO's CEO, once observed:

> *The biggest barrier to innovation is needing to know the answer before you get started. This often manifests itself as a desire to have proof that your idea is worthwhile before you actually start the project—wanting to know whether you've got the right idea—or the assumption that you've got to have a business case—before beginning to explore something kills a lot of innovation.*[31]

Setting aside principles from quantitative research (like appropriate sample size) is critical if the true value of design research is to be realized. We frequently find this to be a sore point with learners, who struggle to let go of a view of data as descriptive of a generalizable reality. As one told us:

I'm sure this issue will work itself out as we progress through interviews, but it is an interesting question about design thinking and sample size—at what point are you okay making generalizations and how do you draw the line?

The true value of design research is *not* in proving an idea is good for everyone, but in inspiring better ideas that are right for specific people. If one unique person triggers an insight that is relevant, inspiring, and action-oriented, it is valuable. "Proving" in DT comes later during Testing.

TEAM MEMBERS ARE UNCOMFORTABLE WITH CHALLENGING EACH OTHER'S INTERPRETA-TIONS. One of the key takeaways from cognitive science is the need for an outside provocation to interrupt our habitual ways of thinking. This is one of the reasons why DT is much harder to practice alone, without a team. It is very difficult to see our own biases and blinders and surface our unarticulated beliefs and assumptions. We need others to help us. But many of us avoid conflict and confrontation—even of the gentle variety. Without a willingness to push each other, sometimes to the point of discomfort, finding deeper insights is hard to do well. We will talk more about this in our next chapter.

WHY DOES SENSEMAKING MATTER SO MUCH?

Sensemaking, in our experience, is the point in the process where we, as teachers, are most likely to "lose" our students. But defeat is not an option. Here's why:

SENSEMAKING SETS UP EVIDENCE-BASED IDEA GENERATION. The idea that DT is not data driven is a myth. Developing evidence-based insights is what qualitative data gathering is fundamentally about. Sensemaking promotes diligence in establishing solid evidence about a particular group of people's needs. That group may or may not be "generalizable," as we said before. For our purposes at this point in the process, we don't care. What we do care about is that the insights being developed emanate from the data we've gathered and not from our own heads.

Sensemaking uncovers implicit and hidden meanings, which come in layers. We have to access them layer by layer, like peeling an onion. We may "know" little about how the discrete elements of a problem or opportunity come together until we dive into the search for meaning and patterns. Much of the problem lies at the center of the onion, below the surface of what we *think* the problem is. The hidden meanings and true depth of the problem are only uncovered through Discovery. One innovator we talked to said:

There is a need to explore the unknowns—things that are not given or said. To me, seeking for the unknowns while not knowing what you're looking for exactly is one of the most important and challenging things in design thinking.

SENSEMAKING IS PERSONALLY PROFOUND. In Sensemaking, our goal is to uncover nuggets of knowledge that are relevant, valuable and important for developing new solutions. But in order to uncover what's important, we must give up old beliefs. Some innovators describe it as almost like walking through a door—there was an awakening where they crossed over a threshold of fear and discomfort into a more enlightened and deeper understanding of themselves, as well as those they designed for and with. This awakening often allowed them to see for the first time that their personal points of view, attitudes, actions, and behaviors had the potential to lead to resistance to change or criticism, blame and judgment of others' behaviors. It helped them develop an awareness of where they held personal biases that detracted from their ability to develop clarity around what was really important. In the struggle to understand the *why* behind their interpretation of observations, they developed an acceptance of contrarian points of view as opportunities for change.

AMUNDSEN EXPEDITION

Norwegian explorer Roald Amundsen's expedition reached the South Pole on December 14, 1911, triumphing in the race over a British party led by Robert Scott. Why they succeeded highlights the value of broadening the voices brought into the conversation. Scott and his peers thought their research team included all the necessary knowledge before embarking. Unfortunately, none of the so-called experts had any specific expertise in a polar expedition. It never dawned on Scott that the best way to survive or navigate the South Pole and its difficult terrain might be to learn from the people who had lived in similar conditions for generations. Meanwhile, Amundsen spent two years living among the native Inuits in preparation for his expedition and studied Inuit lives in great detail. He was intrigued by how the Inuits cared for their dogs, hunted for food, and used furs and skins as clothing. This openness to learning from strangers informed all of his planning, completely reframed his understanding of the problem and ultimately proved vital to his success.[32]

IT ENCOURAGES BROADER INCLUSION IN THE SEARCH FOR MEANING. For reasons we will explore more deeply in Chapter 5, bringing people with different perspectives into the conversation is a powerful force for deepening the insights that come out of it. Doing Sensemaking alone is difficult—we need to be exposed to the differing interpretations of others to stimulate our own. One of the challenges we have talked about is the very human rush to fix problems.

Because of that, we often don't pause to invite other people in who can help us surface the unarticulated assumptions about why a problem has been defined in a particular way. In the name of "efficiency," we talk to people who already think like we do. This false sense of efficiency sacrifices effectiveness for an illusory speed. If invited, others may identify parts of the problem or see patterns that we have overlooked. This takes us back, again, to the importance of problem framing and the way in which diverse perspectives motivate it.

SENSEMAKING LOCATES US IN THE PARTICULAR RATHER THAN THE GENERAL. One of the real opportunities in design is to design for difference and not just for similarity. Getting to solutions that are right for people means seeking to understand the needs of not only the average person in the middle of the bell curve, but also the needs of outliers at the extreme ends of the curve whose needs may be radically different from the norm. When teams actively look for themes and patterns, they see similarities and systematic differences in the attitudes, values, and behaviors of the different people they are trying to understand. The use of tools like personas helps innovators pay attention to these particulars and design for specific types of stakeholders—ones that are often ignored or underserved when we generalize across people and focus on the mean.

WHAT DO MVCs COMING OUT OF SENSEMAKING LOOK LIKE?

As with Immersion, as innovators become more comfortable and competent in Sensemaking, their level of capabilities increases. Here are the MVC behaviors we look for and the questions that we suggest that you ask yourself.

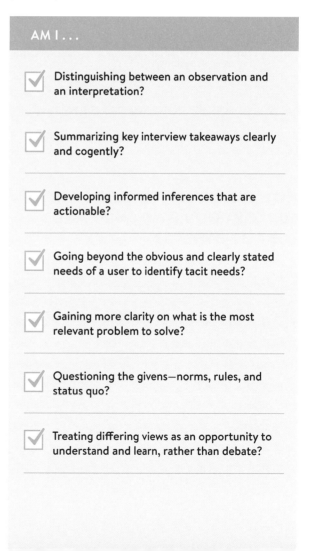

AM I . . .

- ☑ Distinguishing between an observation and an interpretation?

- ☑ Summarizing key interview takeaways clearly and cogently?

- ☑ Developing informed inferences that are actionable?

- ☑ Going beyond the obvious and clearly stated needs of a user to identify tacit needs?

- ☑ Gaining more clarity on what is the most relevant problem to solve?

- ☑ Questioning the givens—norms, rules, and status quo?

- ☑ Treating differing views as an opportunity to understand and learn, rather than debate?

- [x] **Willing to articulate the "why" behind my own perspective to teammates?**

- [x] **Controlling my need for closure?**

- [x] **Remaining patient with iteration and search?**

- [x] **Listening openly to those who disagree with my interpretations?**

- [x] **Productively challenging the perspective of others?**

HOW DO WE BETTER GUIDE AND SUPPORT OUR OWN SHIFT AND THAT OF OTHERS?

STRUCTURE = SAFETY = SUCCESS. More so than in any part of the DT process, creating a successful experience of Sensemaking benefits from carefully structuring the process. Getting to insights is a messy process for even the most seasoned designers. Guiding innovators through the cognitive complexity with structured approaches to finding meaning helps them to feel safe. Psychological safety is critical to keeping learners present and engaged despite the ambiguity around them. One innovator we talked to said:

To exercise early creativity under huge uncertainty is very uncomfortable and difficult for me. However, thanks to the safe learning environment, I now feel delighted to get this chance to try this out—to use design thinking and my creativity—to go out and collect clues, and to take this adventure.

As we mentioned earlier, we use a phased process. We begin by gathering together the most significant bits of data from the larger mass of qualitative data. We cluster these into a set of related bins. We then mine the bins for insights, looking first for the emerging insights that seem to be held in common, and then for differences across interviewees. Finally, we translate those insights into design criteria. We also find the use of tools like journey maps and personas very helpful here.

Having said that, it is important not to strong-arm data into frameworks that don't fit and that may obscure rather than reveal meanings. Remember Melanie's realization that despite her own childhood experiences of domestic abuse, there was more to learn? A related story that has long stayed with us was recounted by an Australian design team also trying to better understand and reduce domestic violence. The team saw a survivor's experience as a journey they were on and so employed journey mapping as a tool to structure the data and drive analysis. What the team eventually realized, however, was that the women who were victims of the abuse experienced themselves as caught in a *web*, not having a journey. The team's tools had shaped the search for insights in a way that was inconsistent with the actual experience of those they were designing for.

KEEP DIGGING. If Sensemaking has a mantra, it is undoubtedly "dig deeper." As we have said before, we uncover meaning in layers. Rarely are we able to cut immediately to the deeper layers. Instead, we must wade through more superficial ones on the way there. The persistence to keep reviewing and revisiting—to keep going back into the data—is essential. Giving up prematurely and settling for the superficial is always a great temptation, but its consequences are profound. As one innovator we talked with offered:

> I remember the phrase "deep insights lead to deep ideas," as especially powerful to me. I think we are wasting a lot of time and resources by not going the extra mile and getting to the meat of it. It's hard, but it's not impossible and the rewards are worth it.

Helping innovators to value surprises and seeming contradictions—to see them as good rather than bad— is important. When data tells us something confusing or unexpected, our initial tendency is to disregard it and quickly move on. But contradictions and surprises are the portal into new ways of seeing (Remember, Sherlock's insight about the dog who *didn't* bark in the night?). They show us where our current understanding is flawed and which of our assumptions need to be re-examined. They are a call to push harder towards more complex thinking—the kind necessary to resolve what seem like contradictions but are actually just artifacts of too superficial an interpretation of the data.

USE VISUALIZATION. As Jon Kolko advised us earlier in this chapter, get the data out your head and onto a space where you—and others—can all see and interact with it. Tools like flip charts, sticky notes, and posting on walls help to tame the mass of messy data—both for us as individuals and for the teams we work with. Working virtually, we have found software tools like Mural and Balsamiq to be great facilitators of this work. Much of this work is about making connections, and it is hard to connect the pieces if you can't see them all clearly laid out.

SLOW THE PROCESS DOWN. This is a phase of the DT process that is particularly important not to rush people through. We especially appreciate the ability to work an overnight into Sensemaking activities. Sleep can be a tremendous way to boost insights, playing a key role in memory consolidation. Sleep brings out hidden details that you might never have discovered otherwise. It provides incubation time that both insights and people need. The popularity of the "overnight test" exists for a reason. Innovators often return the next morning with renewed energy, clarity, and inspiration.

PROVIDE MORE PROVOCATION. The heart of Sensemaking relies on disruption, reflection, and learning to trigger new ways of seeing. Consider adding journals to encourage reflective thinking, or maybe fact/emotion boards (where we separate out facts and emotions). Push yourself and others to keep asking, *"Why do I care about this?"* to encourage problem *finding* rather than problem *solving* and to support double-loop learning.

DON'T LET PEOPLE GET STUCK. There are several places where we see innovators and their teams get stuck. One is at the transition point between a cluster of observations and the insight they suggest. Teams sit and stare glumly at a sea of Post-Its, circling around in a kind of analysis paralysis. To get them moving, we suggest picking the most obvious cluster, taking a first pass at an insight, and getting that up on the wall. When it is "good enough," we urge them to move on to a second cluster, and to circle back to the first cluster later to refine it. This usually transforms the free-floating anxiety about whether they are "getting it right" into energy to move forward. Another stall point relates to an inability to recognize the difference between the positive challenging of each other's perspectives and the negative of debates. Challenges to our way of thinking are one of the most effective provocations to disrupting our old views—but debates provoke defensiveness and anger, not additional insight. We define an activity as debating when team members begin to circle around an insight, each justifying and trying to sell their own "correct" interpretation of the data. Challenging perspectives, on the other hand, is about listening to understand and talking to build. Debating is about listening to argue against and talking to justify. We try to enforce a strict "no debating" rule.

COME ON, GET HAPPY. The relationship between positive affect and creativity is well recognized. Mood is one of the most widely studied and least disputed predictors of creativity. A negative mood, particularly anxiety, seriously impedes our ability to make new connections or think in new ways. It is especially damaging to the hard intellectual challenge posed by Sensemaking. Physical space profoundly shapes an innovator's mood and experience—big, open spaces broaden attention and thoughts. A positive mood facilitates insight identification. Those M&M's sitting in the center of the table are not just empty calories!

WHAT'S NEXT?

There is a magic moment when, out of the valley of darkness, innovators emerge with clarity around the deep needs of those they are designing for. They gain confidence that they will be able to create value for them. They are ready to move on to what we hope will be an experience of Alignment.

Or . . . maybe not. Perhaps instead they are still stuck in the valley and need to be airlifted out. Regardless, the time has come to move on, to move forward with what they've got, consoled by the promise that they can always circle back if it doesn't get them where they need to go in the next stage.

CHAPTER 5

ALIGNMENT

DALLAS, TEXAS

When a group of community organizations in Dallas, Texas, gathered to use DT to develop a prototype for what a community-centered care model for children might look like, they decided to begin with asthma, one of the most prevalent and utilization-intensive childhood diseases. Few of these leaders knew each other, and they started out much like the fabled blind men who each believed a whole elephant was like the single part of it they touched. Their journey to Alignment proved eye opening. One eaders of the effort described his experience of coming together and DT's role in facilitating it:

> *We had no clue how we related to each other. So we put together the asthma equation, a visual model for asthma, and the factors that were affecting these families and kids. When we put this together, people were stunned. We were all working on the same thing— but from different parts of the elephant. But none of us had ever looked at the whole elephant. . . . I had never pursued an ongoing collaboration before with such a range of uncommon partners, one with such a sense of purpose that was pulled together in that very structured and focused way—a group of people who had all been working hard to improve health for kids, but not working together. Doing God's work but with negligible*

impact and sustainability. Now we have a common agenda, shared measurements, and new funding opportunities. That is very different than anything I have ever experienced previously in the world of healthcare. ■

Welcome to the power of the experience of Alignment. In Immersion, our primary focus was the personal journey of each individual innovator, and the mindset shifts it encouraged. In Sensemaking, the individual was again primary, but the critical role played by the larger group or team was also highlighted, as members challenged each other's interpretations of the data in ways that broadened each individual's ability to find meaning. Now these individual journeys truly come together to create something greater than the sum of their parts: shared Immersion and Sensemaking experiences have laid the foundation for Alignment. As individuals' "prepared minds" work together, something powerful and profoundly personal happens to those involved. It happened in Dallas, where caregivers who had been struggling to do "God's work" in lonely isolation instead became a collective. The adrenaline surge accompanying this changes the innovator, as well as their group. They are not yet converging on *solutions*, but they take a critical first step toward them by aligning on the definition of the problem and the needs of those for whom they are designing.

Alignment bridges two crucial aspects of DT—content and process. The insights gathered on current reality are now translated into shared and specific criteria for future designs. That is the content piece, captured in the form of design criteria. Perhaps even more importantly, on the process side, individual innovators fuse into a collective with shared intentions and commitment to collaborative action. Together, these two elements create the conditions for success in the final phase of Discovery, fostering the emergence of truly transformational ideas. Without crossing both bridges, innovators' chances of achieving the kind of powerful outcomes DT is capable of (those we talked about in Chapter 2) are low.

Instead of parochial perspectives rooted in their own expertise or background, innovators' mindsets evolve and align around what truly matters to those they design for, and the criteria that any new design for them should aspire to. Design criteria play a pivotal but largely unheralded role in DT's social technology. Creating shared and specific attributes that an ideal design should meet set the stage for more productive idea generation, testing, and implementation. They encourage more productive idea generation by giving stakeholders the opportunity to develop a shared and user-centered frame of reference about what is important *before* they start generating ideas. They tell us what to pay attention to, reducing cognitive complexity, and challenge us to be more creative and user-centered in the solutions we generate. Later in Testing, relating the ideas back to these specific, already-agreed-upon principles sets up clear success markers that help teams avoid divisive debates. For implementers, having a hand in criteria creation fosters understanding and a sense of ownership that makes change more compelling. They are extraordinarily useful at every stage of the DT process. As one of our innovators pointed out:

> Design criteria's ability to use user insights to get multiple stakeholders to agree on goals and objectives, and then allow crazy creatives to go nuts with their weird brainstorming activities and games is a remarkable feat of social engineering.

As in Sensemaking and Immersion, Alignment too prepares innovators' minds, but this time communally—they become a collective that transcends their individual selves.

ALIGNMENT ACTIVITIES[33]

- Creating design criteria
- Dot voting
- Crafting POV (Point of View) insight statements
- Telling user stories
- Sharing journey maps
- Working with jobs-to-be-done
- Writing needs statements

BRIDGING CONTENT AND PROCESS

CONTENT
Insights on current needs

PROCESS
Individual thought

CONTENT
Criteria for future designs

PROCESS
Collective intention

WHAT DOES AN INNOVATOR'S MINDSET SHIFT LOOK LIKE DURING ALIGNMENT?

As individual innovators experience Alignment, they move from a reliance on their own personal perspective and beliefs to sharing a collective mindset committed to positive action. Let's look more deeply at what that transition looks like.

ALIGNMENT MOVES US . . .

FROM A MINDSET THAT . . .	TO A MINDSET THAT . . .
Prioritizes individual perspectives	Sees value in shared perspective making
Avoids different points of view	Welcomes different perspectives
Is reluctant to speak candidly	Is candid and comfortable with productive disagreement
Lacks trust in other stakeholders	Feels connected and trusting
Is driven to "win" alone	Is motivated to co-create and solve problems together
Believes in oneself	Believes in the power of the collective as well as the individual

THE SCIENCE BEHIND IT

In an uncertain world, the challenge of Alignment is not merely to get stakeholders to *agree* on what is already known—they must *learn* together about what remains unknown.

LEARNING TOGETHER. There are almost as many misconceptions about learning as there are about the "Aha!" moment. Most of us still carry around an outdated notion of learning as taking in new information, but learning theorists tell us instead that it is an active process of *constructing* knowledge, not *acquiring* it.[34] We construct knowledge from personal experiences, so our personal knowledge is drawn from our own perspectives. But learning is also a *social* process. Professor Betsy Campbell argues against the misnomer of learning as an individual cognitive activity, believing instead that it should be seen as a "conversational accomplishment" rather than a "cognitive epiphany."[35] Rather than "an invisible process inside the brain of an individual," she argues, it is the result of interactions among people. Heedfulness—paying respectful and open-minded attention to each other—is critical for accomplishing this. Such collective reflection builds the resilience of the group, her research suggests. Research on team reflexivity—the extent to which team members collectively reflect on, plan, act, and adapt—ties reflection to the essential ability to "unlearn" as necessary to give up old beliefs and take on new ones.

THE PARADOX OF DIFFERENCE. We know, from years of academic research, that more creative higher-order solutions are most likely to emerge when multiple perspectives are present in the conversation. In these circumstances, diversity is not a problem to be resolved—it is the path to new ideas. Yet research also shows that, while such diversity is essential to creative change *in theory*, it can produce negative results *in reality*.[36] This is the paradox: despite decades of study that offer a clear set of prescriptions for how to build and sustain collaboration, actually achieving it in the face of difference remains devilishly difficult. And diversity handled badly worsens decision quality rather than improving it. Therefore, dealing productively with difference is critical to learning our way to better decision-making.

TALKING ACROSS EACH OTHER. Working productively across difference is complicated by the unique ways of communication that specialized groups develop. Different groups literally do not speak the same language—they develop a unique vocabulary based on their expertise or ideologies. Miscommunication inevitably ensues when they try to bridge their differences. In order to communicate successfully across difference, researchers have demonstrated that the stakeholders involved need to develop a common lexicon. Avoiding chaos in these conversations also requires agreed-upon rules of engagement.[37]

Providing both of these accomplishes more than just agreement on terms and activities—it creates a safe space in which individuals can confront and explore different perspectives. Multiple researchers have examined the importance of creating safe spaces, not only to facilitate the exchange of information needed but also to build a sense of trust that encourages the informal interactions needed for successful collaboration.[38]

CROSSING BOUNDARIES. The boundaries that successful diverse groups must cross are complex, professors Boland and Tenkasi argue.[39] They are both interpretive (members give personal meaning to information and events) and political (as different interests clash). To create new knowledge collectively, groups must *transfer* information, *translate* across interpretive differences, and *transform* to rise above political differences. This takes time and requires both perspective *taking*—understanding and acknowledging the perspective of others while making one's own perspective visible and reconcilable to others—and perspective *making*—the creation of a coherent shared belief system. In DT, perspective taking is an individual effort initiated during Immersion, associated with the development of empathy. Perspective *making*, on the other hand, is a group activity that requires people coming together—not only to understand each other, but to forge something at a collective level that is new to all. The perspective-making discussion begins with the collective exploration of insights during Sensemaking and culminates with the creation of design criteria during Alignment. Research suggests that dialogue is a critical aid to perspective making.

HOW IS DIALOGUE DIFFERENT? William Isaacs, leader of the Dialogue Project at MIT, argues dialogue differs from ordinary conversation and has a well-defined set of qualities. He sees it as involving four key activities: voicing, listening, respecting, and suspending.[40] The International Institute for Sustained Dialogue defines dialogue as "a process of genuine interaction through which human beings listen to each other deeply enough to be changed by what they learn. . . . The intention is not to advocate but to inquire; not to argue but to explore; not to convince but to discover."[41] Dialogue uses language as a "device for connection, invention and coordination," as Fred Kofman and Peter Senge describe it.[42] Various approaches to dialogue have been prevalent for many years in fields like community development. *Future search* is a planning process that seeks to put the entire system in the room for a concentrated three-day retreat. *World Café* focuses instead on smaller, more intimate conversations with rotating groups discussing issues that matter to them. *Appreciative Inquiry* takes as its starting point the positive elements surrounding any issue, rather than the negative, and involves asking questions that improve a system's capacity to reach its positive potential. All of these approaches to dialogue share an emphasis on inclusivity, a willingness to share one's thoughts honestly and to listen with an open mind to those of others, an intention to act as a collective, and an openness to being individually changed by the conversation. Dialogue provides the path from **doing** to **becoming**.

CAN FLOW BE COLLECTIVE? We are all familiar with the idea of Flow, popularized by Professor Mikhail Csikszentmihalyi, in which individuals perform at their peak of capacity. Achieving Flow is the holy grail for Olympic-caliber athletes, for instance, who yearn to "enter the zone" where they are at their personal best. Recently, psychologists have begun to investigate the phenomena of *collective flow*. Like individual flow, collective flow is characterized by total absorption and enjoyment associated with the activity—but with additional benefits including a sense among members that they have surrendered self to the group. In fact, researchers have found that people prefer the experience of collective flow to solitary flow.[43] Collective flow is particularly powerful because of the well-recognized contagious effects of positive emotions that feed it. Social psychologists[44] find that collective flow is closely associated with a group's sense of self-efficacy—their belief in the power of the collective to accomplish their goals. They offer a formula, *shared challenge × collective competencies*, to assess the likelihood that a group will experience a sense of peak performance and collective flow. The more confidence a group has in its collective skills, they find, and belief in their shared challenge, the more likely they are to experience flow.

THE POWER OF MICROSTRUCTURES. Consultants Henri Lipmanowicz and Keith McCandless argue that the reasons organizations fail at engaging employees in deeper, more productive conversations tend to fall at two extremes: leaders either exert *too much* control at one extreme or *too little* at the other.[45] Finding the correct kind of microstructure—the way routine

DEMOCRATIC DIALOGUE AT THE UNITED NATIONS

Few institutions place more emphasis on dialogue than the United Nations (UN)—not surprising, given their peacekeeping mission. They have developed their own perspective on dialogue, "Democratic Dialogue," which they define as "the process of people coming together to build mutual understanding and trust across their differences, and to create positive outcomes through conversation." They emphasize the importance of developing a common language and note that only "coordinated meaning-making" provides a solid foundation for coordinated action. The principles that govern their approach include inclusiveness, joint ownership, and acceptance of mutual responsibility. In particular, they draw a clear differentiation between dialogue and negotiation, believing that the two can work in tandem, but must be recognized as distinct. Negotiation, for the UN, is a formal process with the hoped-for result of the end of a particular conflict. Their goal in negotiation is to reach a concrete agreement. With dialogue, however, they aim to change relationships. Negotiation, they believe, can stop wars—but only dialogue can create a sustainable peace.[46]

interactions are organized (things like the physical layout of the room, how participation is handled and groups are configured, the sequence of steps, and time allocation) is essential to good conversation. Conventional microstructures, they assert, are aimed at convincing, debating, and controlling. But merely loosening these, without adding new structures, is counterproductive. Instead, they advocate "liberating microstructures" that make it possible for groups of any size to significantly improve the quality of their discussions. Liberating microstructures are easy to accomplish (rearranging chairs, for instance, from auditorium style to circles) but can induce powerful changes in the way participants interact.

SO WHAT MAKES ALIGNMENT SO HARD?

Innovators find getting to Alignment difficult for many reasons:

THIS IS SOME DEEP STUFF. Genuine dialogue across difference touches us at our very core. Fully experiencing Alignment always necessitates surfacing differences rather than ignoring or suppressing them. Because these differences are often deeply rooted and value related, sharing them can induce fear. Entering a dialogue and voicing your views, rather than keeping them to yourself, makes us vulnerable. Creating candor requires changing mindsets and developing trust, as well as new behaviors. Crossing boundaries can feel

like dangerous work. Many people are conflict averse and reluctant to address difference head-on.

GETTING TO ALIGNMENT TAKES TIME. Similar to the blind men, each with their individual perspectives about what an elephant is like, conversations tend to start with everyone convinced that theirs is the only correct view. Getting to Alignment requires first exploring what each of us is actually looking at—and being open to the idea that our own view may be missing something. This is not a fast or efficient process. The patience and persistence needed to stay in the discomfort and work through it is often in short supply in a world where we are all in a hurry. For the UN, the presence of time pressure that they see as too great is one of the key warning indicators against attempts at dialogue.

THE KUMBAYA EFFECT. In our own work with organizations, we see the truth of Henri Lipmanowicz and Keith McCandless's observations on the need for microstructures in action. At one end of the spectrum, leaders view conversations about the future as the prerogative of executives and are doubtful that any good will come from inviting a broader group of voices into the conversation—so they over-control access and interaction. At the other extreme, leaders (often from the social sector) are committed to what we see as a naïve view of inclusiveness—that pretty much everyone deserves a voice in every conversation—and that just putting them all together in a room (without careful attention to how to organize the conversation) will produce a good outcome. We call the latter the "Kumbaya effect," where people with differences join hands and sing "Kumbaya" spontaneously. Both perspectives are exasperating—but one fails in private, while the other fails in public. Believers in Kumbaya, with their lack of attention to process and structure and naïveté about what it takes to successfully transcend difference, have done a great deal of damage to the reputation of inclusive conversations. Such conversations must be carefully designed and managed. They must have agreed-upon rules of engagement. Otherwise, they are likely to further polarize the parties involved, rather than bringing them together, and make things worse instead of better.

WHY DOES ALIGNMENT MATTER SO MUCH?

ALIGNMENT SETS THE CONDITIONS THAT ALLOW FOR THE EMERGENCE OF NEW IDEAS. If Alignment is not reached in advance of moving into idea generation, the likelihood of identifying solutions that all parties can support with commitment and enthusiasm is dramatically reduced. Based on evidence from almost a decade of research in the field, we believe that DT offers the kind of structure that diverse groups need to do the foundational work of finding shared perspective and purpose. It does this by holding diverse groups in the problem space to find shared meaning and build trust through a user-centered focus; by inviting new voices into a conversation with a

set of simple rules that encourage joint inquiry rather than debate; and by helping problem solvers iterate to improved solutions by making their ideas feel real, both to users and to implementers.

THE SEARCH FOR ALIGNMENT FORCES DIFFERENT KINDS OF CONVERSATIONS THAT MAY NOT HAVE HAPPENED OTHERWISE. All of the reasons that we have discussed thus far—the challenge of crossing boundaries, fear of the conflict that may result, and impatience with a seemingly fraught and inefficient process—create a strong urge to do what we have done in the past. That is generally to assemble the usual list of suspects who think like we do and with whom we are comfortable and confident that agreement can be reached in a relatively painless way. New kinds of conversations are unlikely to happen in such circumstances—and breakthrough thinking has a low probability of showing up. Strategist Saul Kaplan talks about why we need instead to explore "uncommon partnerships":

> Seeking collisions with uncommon partners who are wired to collaborate—and who are willing to do this without knowing the answer in advance—allows strategists to open up a space that Stuart Kauffman called "the adjacent possible."[47] New things happen because of the adjacent possible; when things collide randomly, new life forms are born.[48]

The challenge is to make these conversations candid. One of our longtime colleagues talks persuasively of the negative impact of what remains in the "unsaid." When things remain in the unsaid, they cannot be publicly acknowledged or addressed. So long as the truth as we know it remains unsaid, she argues, saying "yes" to collaboration doesn't mean much. Putting our differences on the table—*saying* them—is the first step in building a new world together. Issuing an invitation may get someone to show up, but it will not necessarily induce their active participation. Accomplishing this is one of the strengths of DT. As one innovator told us:

> *Human-centered design activities really allowed us to put lots of things on the table. Even if people didn't necessarily favor those ideas, they at least actually were put on the table. . . . I think if we had not used those activities, I don't even think they would have been brought to the floor.*

ACHIEVING ALIGNMENT FORCES A DEMOCRATIZATION OF VOICES. We have long known that hierarchy and authority are powerful inhibitors of new ways of thinking. One of our learners commented:

> *When you're tackling the problem, it's the sort of senior person, the more forceful person that dominates the conversation and moves things forward. And what I've seen is that people don't really support the idea—they're on the team,*

> *but they're not really engaged. But DT totally changed the dynamics such that people were all on equal footing and they felt like "I am learning because you have a different perspective and I want to learn your perspective and I want to learn how we can address the issue at hand."*

New thinking requires new voices, not dominance by the old ones. Real change requires commitment, not compliance. DT can create the conditions to give voice to those who otherwise would be unlikely to be invited—or, if invited, unlikely to speak.

THE ADMIRABLE ADMIN

Preparing to run a problem-solving exercise as part of a new initiative his agency was launching, a senior government official sent an email invitation to his expert staff. He was surprised to see the office receptionist, whom he had forgotten was on the distribution list, appear at the workshop. He considered explaining his mistake to her and suggesting that she need not stay, but decided against it and welcomed her instead. The workshop proceeded to generate many ideas, which were narrowed down through anonymous group process to the most attractive option to begin experimenting with. When the group disbanded, he asked the receptionist how she had enjoyed the workshop. Her answer: "It was great! And really cool to see that the idea I suggested was the one that got chosen."

ALIGNMENT HELPS PEOPLE STEP AWAY FROM THEIR ROLES AND STEP INTO COLLABORATION. One of the things we especially enjoy watching unfold in our workshops is the transition people make as they move from acting as representatives of their respective silos to thinking more broadly as a member of a collective. As one manager we interviewed told us:

> We had people that were experts in a lot of different things . . . an expert in venture capital, a CEO. We had somebody who had built an IT system, and physicians and regulators. You put all these people in the room and give them a problem and they might come up with very, very different ideas because they're looking at things from their perspective. What we found is the design thinking method helped us step away from our roles and focus on the issue and to get to know the other person's perspective and to get to know how they were thinking. And it was sort of the icebreaker that I think helped the teams then work together.

ALIGNMENT HELPS PROVIDE AN INCLUSIVE MECHANISM FOR INPUT. A framework for achieving Alignment that respects and elicits meaningful interaction and information from all members of a group, especially introverts, exponentially increases the amount of knowledge and ability that can be harnessed. It provides a mechanism to move from passive recipient to active contributor. One innovator told us:

> I have never considered myself to be much of an innovator. I have always been more of an incremental improver who finds ways to improve existing processes rather than taking exceptional new approaches to challenges. However, I really like how design thinking conceives roles for everyone in the innovation process, and how it broadens innovation to a wider set of people.

WHAT DO THE MVCs COMING OUT OF ALIGNMENT LOOK LIKE?

When we turn to the question of Alignment, our MVCs now belong to the collective rather than the individual. Instead of "Am I . . . ?" the question becomes "Are we . . . ?"

ARE WE . . .

☑ Giving careful thought to how we structure our conversations?

☑ Attentive to the rules of dialogue, like turn taking?

☑ Focusing on the issues that really matter, as expressed in the design criteria?

☑ Listening heedfully and respectfully to each other, ensuring that everyone feels heard?

☑ Able to make our different perspectives visible to each other?

☑ Willing to let go of our own perspectives to be open to those of others?

☑ Working to achieve a shared definition of the problem that we have agreed to solve?

☑ Aligned on a prioritized understanding of the qualities of the ideal solution, as expressed in design criteria?

☑ Contributing to the learning of others and learning together?

HOW DO WE BETTER GUIDE AND SUPPORT OUR OWN SHIFTS AND THAT OF OTHERS?

INVITE DIVERSE PERSPECTIVES INTO THE CONVERSATION DURING DISCOVERY. Many of the innovators we work with are surprised that engaging diverse stakeholders early in the process helped them build a more powerful shared vision. They initially thought that those who held opposing points of view would not be able to come together, and instead would push a preformed agenda and plans that would derail the conversation. They believed that excluding them would create a more productive conversation,

and that they would later be able to persuade them to come on board. But they were wrong. Early inclusion of diverse voices, coupled with careful structuring of the conversation to encourage honesty and build trust, allows groups to find a common path forward by inducing members to step away from their roles and parochial focus, attend to those they are all designing for, and learn from each other's perspectives.

ANTICIPATE EMOTIONAL SWINGS. Acknowledge how hard this work can be. Innovation teams experience a roller-coaster ride of emotions throughout the innovation process and some may experience a low point in the journey to Alignment. Some may never reach it. Planning for this emotional oscillation and taking preemptive measures to temper potential lows helps maintain individual and team energy. This is the time to celebrate team progress or encourage random acts of kindness. We have our students fill out weekly journal reflections so that we can support their learning and get ahead of any frustrations before they erupt within the team. We also love good stokes. Stokes are warm-up games, usually borrowed from the world of Improv, that help teams become mentally and physically active. They can also build trust and camaraderie and are great for increasing team engagement. And of course, you can always bring donuts!

PROMOTE PERMISSION TO BE PRODUCTIVELY WRONG. Cultivating a mindset of continuous learning leads to better decision making and, when separated from a group's performance outcomes, motivates the kind of collaboration that leads to a greater experience of Alignment. It lessens the stakes of being "wrong," and allows us to grant others the luxury of trying something we may be skeptical of. While many organizations talk of "continuous learning," a sense of pressure from stakeholders and current performance review criteria incentivizes the opposite behavior. Keeping a mindset of continuous learning front and center reminds people that learning is progress even when they can't see the end result and things might not go the way they had anticipated. Being productively wrong is still learning.

PUT A CAP ON TEAM TIME. Long team sessions are neither productive nor engaging. They are energy killers. Put a limit on the amount of time the group spends together and think carefully about how they spend it. Make sure that everyone has enough time to process the data individually before the group discusses it. Members will stay energized and ready to work.

VISUALIZE DATA USING POSTERS, ORGANIZERS, AND ONLINE TOOLS. As it did in Sensemaking, visualizing data accelerates Alignment, helping to make sense out of complex relationships and connections. One innovator described visualization's ability to transport their team "out of their comfort zone and away from the standard, mundane meetings they were used to, allowing us to draw much deeper insight from them." Visualization also helps remove emotional tension by taking the focus off of individuals and placing it on the problems of those for whom the team is designing. Another innovator told us it allowed them to be "hard on the problem as opposed to the people involved. It removed the emotional tension and the difficulty that we have to push through." Rehashing ideas from previous meetings creates tension. One innovator shared that visual data "helps keep the conversation moving forward instead of getting stuck on a single point over and over again."

CREATE A CULTURE OF TURN TAKING AND ENFORCE CONVERSATIONAL NORMS. Practices like turn taking may seem elementary and obvious, but are highly effective at ensuring that all voices in a group are heard and dialogue is fostered. One innovator who craved authority in groups told us "this might be my personal 'inconvenient truth' and it's something I constantly try to keep top of mind—I need to actively work to engage all of my team in the conversation, and avoid trying to force my opinion too early."

KEEP A POSITIVE ENVIRONMENT. Working across difference benefits from reducing the anxiety involved whenever possible. Recent psychological research has shown that positive emotion increases our tolerance for and openness to taking in discordant data. Positive emotion is best maintained in a positive environment that is protected, familiar and playful. It is not simply the absence of pessimism but the presence of optimism that matters.

FOR VERY RISK-AVERSE TEAMS, TRY USING A GOVERNANCE STRUCTURE THAT ALLOWS VETO POWER. Depending on the nature of the relationships of the stakeholders you are engaging, a governance structure that allows veto power may be a positive way to engage and align otherwise reluctant stakeholders and reduce the stakes involved in moving forward. Here is what one of our innovators had to say about this technique:

> *With the criminal justice system, you've got a lot of tough players. The key to that governance structure was anyone can veto anything we're working on at any time. . . . That's how the district attorney and the courts, which are independently elected or appointed, became comfortable with innovating. Essentially, they said, "Okay, this seems like a good idea and as long as I know I can back out whenever I want to, I'm on board. And I'll bring resources to the table." Nobody yet has exercised a veto, but just knowing that they have that governance structure to do so is what gets them to innovate.*

WHAT'S NEXT?

During Alignment, our focus is on translating current reality into a set of design criteria that specify the qualities of a new future, giving all a shared sense of the problem or opportunity to be addressed and what it suggests about the qualities that any new future should aspire to. Having accomplished that, a group of stakeholders is ready to move to the ultimate expression of collective intent—actually envisioning together a range of new futures more powerful than any one of them could have imagined on their own. On to Emergence!

IMMERSION   SENSEMAKING   ALIGNMENT   EMERGENCE

CHAPTER 6
EMERGENCE

GREGORY

As a new leader faced with a deteriorating botanical garden beset with financial woes, Gregory decided to set in motion a nontraditional approach to revitalizing the organization. He gathered employees from all over the organization—botanists, horticulturalists, gardeners, educators, visitor services, business managers, and custodial and physical plant managers—and invited them to a widely inclusive process to envision a new future for the garden. The emphasis was on creating an open forum of discussion in which participants were invited to share their hopes and dreams in a structured format, and to listen to their colleagues present theirs. All were told to put aside the constraints of funding the new ideas and to share their "blue sky" ideas. The degree of consensus that emerged surprised everyone. As Gregory described it, "When the day came in the process to set priorities, they just fell out in a way that made sense to everyone in the room." The strategy that emerged not only drove the garden's restoration, it built community and together they discovered new possibilities that cut across organizational silos. One example of the shared vision was the idea that emerged to create a garden specifically for children, designed to encourage exploration and adventure. One of the managers involved shared his experience as he worked with colleagues from areas like horticulture, education, and visitor services, which had rarely interacted before:

In the past, we had mostly been concerned with how to restrain that child. You know—don't pick, don't climb, don't roll, jump, or swim. From entirely different sides of our world, a theme started to emerge that had not been talked about before, that became a united goal of this institution—to develop and to put new emphasis on the involvement of children and families at the garden.

Five years later, the garden was an entirely different place than the one Gregory had arrived at, with a committed staff, more sustainable funding, and a revitalized physical landscape. The garden employees' excitement and vivid image for their future attracted other stakeholders who wanted to help them achieve, including major donors. Most of the dreams expressed had been realized. The shared commitment to families led to the establishment of the Children's Adventure Garden, which become one of the garden's most popular attractions and a source of pride to all. ■

A t last, we've reached the point most innovators have been waiting for—they finally get to generate ideas! Welcome to Emergence. This is the phase that many see as the true heart of innovation. We agree—but not for the usual reasons. Most innovators think of this phase of DT as being about the activity of brainstorming—getting what is in the heads of individual innovators out on the table (or onto a sticky note). We disagree. The *best* new ideas,

like the Children's Adventure Garden, become visible *during* the process as it unfolds and are co-created with other stakeholders. The real magic is not in the activity of brainstorming, it is in the creation of the conditions that foster the experience of *Emergence*— when a group of people see together, in real time, the kinds of new, higher-order possibilities that none could see alone or even anticipate at the beginning of the process.

So brainstorming is just the *doing* part. But even the best-structured brainstorms won't automatically trigger Emergence. The most critical preconditions for Emergence happen well before brainstorming starts. Innovators' experiences of Immersion and Sensemaking lay the groundwork for new and better ideas by uncovering deep insights into user needs. Alignment assures agreement on problem definitions and culminates in a joint intention, expressed as shared criteria the new designs aspire to meet. These prior experiences prepare innovators to enter Emergence, where new possibilities are co-created and combined to reach higher-order solutions.

For Emergence to succeed, innovators must trade their ambition to come up with the "winning" idea in order to be, instead, part of a process of collaborative creation. Rather than seeking to compromise when faced with difference, stakeholders must stay in the possibility space and build on one another's ideas to create new and more powerful concepts.

The power of diversity has been a recurrent theme throughout the experiences we have discussed so far. In Immersion, it helped us develop empathy and allowed us to escape our own egocentricity. In Sensemaking, it forced us to unpack and address our assumptions. In Alignment, it gave us superpowers, allowing us to form an alliance committed to positive action. Now, in Emergence, the nature of that action is given substance in the form of specific ideas. The goal is to identify new and better concepts that are superior to what any individual stakeholder could have brought into the conversation.

EMERGENCE ACTIVITIES[49]

- Brainstorming techniques that intersperse individual and group work

- Concept-development tools like Chili tables

- Using analogies for inspiration

- Mashing up/combining ideas

- Creating "How might we" statements

- Completing napkin pitches

- Future visioning though scenario creation[50]

- Experimenting with buy, build, bring

- Using trigger questions like "worst idea" and "explore the opposite"

WHAT IS A HIGHER-ORDER SOLUTION?

We talk a lot about higher-order solutions in this book. But what exactly are they? For us, they represent the Mt. Everest of ideas—the pinnacle we aspire to reach. Higher-order solutions break rather than make trade-offs. In doing so, they make reality out of possibilities. We are taught to believe that trade-offs are inevitable. So long as we keep that mindset, they will be. Accepting trade-offs leads us immediately to compromise. In our view, the urge to compromise is a siren song—luring innocent innovators to watery graves. Even when the compromises reached appear "good," we see them as a failure to reach DT's transformational potential. As Jim Collins famously noted, "Good is often the enemy of great." Premature compromise needs to be vigorously resisted if breakthrough ideas are a goal. Let's look at the difference between higher-order solutions and compromises:

Higher-Order Solutions	Compromises
Break trade-offs	Make trade-offs
Coherent, integrated, and holistic solutions created together	Pieces of different solutions cobbled together
Focused on best outcomes for those we design for	Focused on accommodating political differences in group
Ownership by the entire group	Ownership by no one
Capable of eliciting engagement and commitment	Likely to engender detachment and compliance

WHAT DOES AN INNOVATOR'S MINDSET SHIFT LOOK LIKE DURING EMERGENCE?

As innovators move into the experience of Emergence, our goal is to help shift them from a state of individualized, isolated problem solving to a collective state of possibility thinking.

EMERGENCE MOVES US . . .

FROM A MINDSET THAT . . .	TO A MINDSET THAT . . .
Believes that there is one solution	Understands the value of multiple potential solutions
Fights for "my" idea	Is open to ideas built by many owners without ego attachment to own ideas
Doubts their own ability to be creative	Confidently offers solutions as equals
Withholds their authentic self	Is willing to share their authentic self, driven by possibility, not constraint
Is driven by constraints	Is driven by possibility and patient in the search for higher-order solutions
Satisfices and compromises early	Is suspicious of early compromise and "least worst" solutions
Avoids those who think differently	Recognizes the importance of diversity and requisite variety

THE SCIENCE BEHIND IT

FROM CHAOS AND COMPLEXITY COMES EMERGENCE. Though Emergence is a foreign concept to most of us, it's a well-recognized phenomenon in studies of chaos theory and complex adaptive systems.[51] In these fields, emergence is the spontaneous appearance of order out of apparent randomness. Psychologist G. H. Lewes, one of the first to identify the concept in 1875, observed: "There is a co-operation of things of unlike kinds. . . . The emergent is unlike its components . . . and it cannot be reduced to their sum or their difference."[52] Research at the Santa Fe Institute on complex systems extended thinking on the subject.[53] Though the diverse disciplines participating in the Institute used different terms, the scientists recognized that they were all focused on the same unusual experience, which they viewed as a form of change, terming it *emergent complexity*. What they observed went beyond just integrating old ideas with new ones—it was something different than the assemblage of pieces. Something more. The concept of emergence also appears in philosophy, systems theory, and art as well, wherever there exists the phenomenon of a whole that possesses properties its parts lack on their own that emerge only when the parts interact. In this work, Emergence is often closely related to the principle of self-organizing. Science writer Steven Johnson, examining ant colonies for inspiration, notes that unintelligent individual ants, with any organizing direction from the queen, produce intelligent systems: "Agents residing on one scale start producing behavior that lies one scale above them: ants create colonies," he observes, and relates this to human systems: "Emergence in human systems has produced new technologies, towns, democracy, and some would say consciousness—the capacity for self-reflection."[54] Emergence is also linked to biological evolution and adaptation through the concept of requisite variety, which tells us that the specifics of the particular parts assembled really matter.

NOT JUST ANY VARIETY. The Law of Requisite Variety is one of the fundamental tenets in the field of cybernetics, and is a fundamental precondition for Emergence. First identified by W. Ross Ashby, it asserts that "the variety in the control system must be equal to or larger than the variety of the perturbations in order to achieve control."[55] Extended to the field of evolution, this means that a system is able to adapt successfully to the diversity of challenges in its environment *only* if its range of experience is as diverse as the challenges it faces (that's what makes it "requisite"). Thus, adaptation relies not only on variety but on a particular *kind* of variety—one matched to the nature of its challenges. As Professor Michael Lissack explains: "In order to deal with the diversity of problems the world throws at you, you need to have a repertoire of responses which is (at least) as nuanced as the problems you face."[56] As we bring these two principles of Emergence and requisite variety together, the message for innovation is clear: the diversity of the experience base of a problem-solving group must match the complexity of the problem it faces, in order for higher-order solutions to emerge. But that alone is still not enough. The group must ask itself the right kinds of questions.

> DIVERSITY OF THE EXPERIENCE BASE OF A PROBLEM-SOLVING GROUP MUST MATCH THE COMPLEXITY OF THE PROBLEM FOR HIGHER-ORDER SOLUTIONS TO EMERGE.

WHAT IF ANYTHING WERE POSSIBLE? The final ingredient to be added to this mix is possibility thinking, which asks the question, "What if *anything* were possible?" Such a positive focus, psychologists argue, motivates a group to see more creative alternatives because it frees them from the constraints of existing limitations, as the "blue sky" thinking did at the garden. This creates a larger space for envisioning truly creative solutions—the ones that *break* rather than *make* trade-offs. Positive thinking is essential to creativity. Psychologist Barbara Fredrickson[57] explains that positive emotions affect our brains differently than negative ones. Whereas negative emotions limit our perspective and cause us to narrow our views to what we already know, positive emotions encourage exploration and expand our worldviews (and how we view ourselves). They broaden and build. The "broadening" effect allows us to override automatic (mostly negative) responses and instead look for creative, flexible, and unpredictable new ways of thinking and acting. Positive emotion allows us to "build" more creative cognitive processing—making a wider array of connections accessible for future use. Additionally, practicing positivity today increases

TRANSLATING EMERGENCE TO THE ORGANIZATIONAL WORLD

In her book *Engaging Emergence*,[58] organizational consultant Peggy Holman translates the science of emergence into practical behavioral advice for organizations. She defines emergence as "higher-order complexity arising out of chaos in which novel, coherent structures coalesce through interactions among the diverse entities of a system." This often happens in "an unexpected, almost magical leap," she asserts.

Her advice to leaders is to:
1. Welcome disruption as an opportunity for breakthroughs.
2. Be willing to pioneer and "jump into the mystery and learn from feedback."
3. Encourage random encounters.
4. Seek meaning.
5. Provide simple rules.

our ability to be positive tomorrow, making us continually more open to explore and accept what emerges. It also creates a safe space that encourages participants to bring their own best selves into the conversation.

But getting to breakthrough ideas takes time—the group needs to stay in the ambiguity of the possibility space and continue to explore. This means resisting retreat to the comfort of compromise, often the easiest path to quick, collective decision-making. In Immersion and Sensemaking, DT holds innovators in the *problem* space to yield better (and shared) definitions of the problem. To achieve Emergence, we must first assemble the requisite variety, and then hold innovators in the *possibility* space, if we want transformational solutions.

INVITING THE WITHHELD. We talked in Chapter 1 of Heidegger's notion of the "withheld." This concept is part of a long tradition in philosophy. Scholars of both Western and Eastern philosophies herald the importance of "letting go" to "let come" higher-order solutions. In order for new possibilities to "come" to individuals, physicist W. Brian Arthur argues that they need to observe, reflect, and be patient.[59] They must find the quietness of a deeper place to access a deeper source of knowing. Arthur advocates a set of practices: First, totally immerse in the places that matter most and "observe, observe, observe." Then, retreat and reflect, a state that requires going to a place of silence to allow new knowledge to make itself visible.

WHAT IF ANYTHING WERE POSSIBLE?
The Story of George Washington Carver

At the turn of the twentieth century, formerly enslaved botanist-turned-inventor George Washington Carver witnessed a challenge: cotton production was declining, and its overproduction had left many fields barren, making it impossible for newly freed enslaved people (now sharecroppers) to pay off their debts. Additionally, farmers' diets consisted of what they could afford. Carver set out to find new crops that met four design criteria: (1) regenerated the soil, (2) grew plentifully and cheaply, (3) provided diverse nourishment and (4) were in high demand.

His research at the Tuskegee Institute led him to focus on four crops—peanuts, sweet potatoes, soybeans and pecans—that met all of the design criteria but one: there was little to no demand for them. Rather than accept this constraint and abandon these crops as solutions, Carver stepped back and asked a possibility question: How could they *create* demand by finding other uses for these crops? He and a diverse team explored all possible uses, generating hundreds of product ideas, including 300 from peanuts (including paints, dyes and ink) and 118 from sweet potatoes (including postage stamp glue, synthetic rubber and even a type of gasoline). They had successfully used possibility thinking not only to find higher-order solutions but to redefine the needs they addressed.

(This is the same "quiet brain" that neuroscientists believe is the best state for divergent thinking.) Otto Scharmer[60] describes a similar journey to "presencing" in his work on Theory U: presencing involves the inner work of letting go of biases, assumptions, and ownership of ideas, so we can "let come" new concepts. As an individual, Scharmer claims, each of us must listen with an open heart and an open will to connect to the higher future possibilities, letting go of all nonessential or counterproductive biases and thoughts. As a team, presencing involves collective creativity and flow, generating the rules and parameters of exploration as we go. With a heightened level of energy and a sense of future possibility, individuals and groups cease to force or try to control outcomes. Like Heidegger's withheld, they invite them.

SATISFICING TO THE "LEAST WORST" SOLUTION. Anchoring a very different end of the continuum, we find a concept that economist and Nobel Laureate Herbert Simon[61] called "satisficing," a process that involves selecting the "least worst solution" to which everyone will agree. Though Simon saw satisficing as a productive individual activity that utilized rules of thumb and hardwired mental shortcuts to deal with our brain's cognitive limitations in processing large amounts of data, satisficing can pose a significant obstacle to innovation when practiced by groups. Like Max Boisot's principle of "least action" (when decision-makers select the option that will lead to the least expenditure of effort),[62] left unmanaged,

this leads groups to settle on options that avoid arguments and save resources, time, and energy. These are rarely the most creative or value enhancing solutions for those being designed for. Because it encourages prematurely accepting compromise and negotiating less-than-optimal solutions, satisficing is lethal for the creation of truly creative higher solutions. These are achieved when a group finds *higher* ground, not common ground. Satisficing short-circuits our ability to explore possibilities and brings everyone's creativity down to the lowest denominator.

WHAT MAKES EMERGENCE SO HARD?

While Emergence is full of exciting possibilities, meeting the conditions that foster it can be challenging to pull off in practice for multiple reasons:

LETTING GO IS HARD. Despite the continuous call for teamwork, we see constructs for competition laid out in every inch of society. To experience Emergence, an environment of openness and co-creation must exist, yet individuals often struggle to break free from the old world of competition and let go of "their" ideas. This provides an uphill climb for collaborative co-creation.

ASKING THE WRONG QUESTION. Our brain filters, primes, and frames portions of the world for us, to which we react. We remain in single-loop learning mode, where the norms, values, and goals of the problem space remain unquestioned and therefore remain surface level. Advancing the kind of double-loop, possibility-driven thinking that questions both problems and their solutions, and co-evolves the two simultaneously, can be a mind-blowing challenge.

LEAVING IDEAS "UNFINISHED" FEELS UNCOMFORTABLE. When sharing ideas for the future, our natural inclination is to present a fully fleshed-out idea for others to react to. Presenting less-formed ideas, we worry, will invite criticism for a job left unfinished and reflect badly on our capabilities. It puts our egos at risk and leaves us open to critique. But yielding to these fears and creating such closure will stop co-creation in its tracks.

OUR DEFINITION OF DIVERSITY MAY BE FLAWED. In some cultures, "diversity" has come to be defined as only being about sex, race, gender, etc. These all may, in fact, be requisite for many challenges, but are likely an incomplete list of sources. The diversity of the team we assemble must together aggregate to a repertoire of experiences capable of meeting the complexity of the challenge faced. One of our innovators offered a story about how requisite variety on a team helped them learn together about how to improve the batteries in medical devices:

Putting a medical device manufacturer, a nursing health care provider, a health care technology manager who works in a hospital, and somebody who maintains the batteries in a small group and asking them questions—they feed off of each other's ideas and perspectives and they engage in a dialogue in a way that moves the conversation forward. In a typical workshop, messages are formed before the meeting, then there's an outcome but not a lot of engagement. Being human centered allows us to bring people together and engage them and they learn from each other in a way that we hadn't seen as even possible before.

Another important dimension of requisite variety can involve accessing local intelligence. Using DT as a set of simple rules, local teams can be invited to define their own problems as well as solutions, while sharing their learning.

Barriers may also come from within. Many of us have been taught that we are not the "creative" ones. It's often difficult to coax individuals who have internalized these beliefs about who is creative to take part in the conversation. Building a space of trust and anonymity and refraining from judgment is critical. A key assumption of Emergence is that everyone has the ability to be creative because everyone has a perspective that can be valuable—but helping people recognize their own latent creativity can be challenging.

WE ARE BORN TO DEBATE. Shortcomings in communication can derail Emergence, which calls for dialogue to boost understanding between different stakeholders' perceptions of the system and propose joint creations. Yes—the right diversity of participants is essential, but equally as necessary is their willingness to share their knowledge and experiences and listen to those of others respectfully with an open mind. This is stymied if differences become the basis for debate rather than dialogue.

CTAA: THE POWER OF LOCAL

Allowing people in different parts of a system the freedom to take advantage of local intelligence to identify and solve their own problems, while still maintaining a centralized discipline and capability for sharing what each locality learns, is a strength of DT. One nongovernmental organization we studied, the Community Transportation Association of America (CTAA), focused on the transportation needs of low-wage earners by using DT as the backbone to foster grassroots problem identification and solutions in local communities. Rather than defining the problem centrally from Washington and recommending the implementation of broad transportation initiatives, the emphasis in CTAA's use of DT was on selecting and empowering a diverse set of local partners to frame and continually reshape both problem statements and solutions in response to the unique and changing circumstances within their community. The partners shared their learnings across geographies, getting the best of both local and global knowledge. Best of all, the local partnerships endured after the project ended, creating new capabilities for ongoing innovation.

WE HAVE TO INVENT THE FUTURE—WE DON'T JUST "FIND" IT. Learning theory tells us that in a fast-moving and volatile world, we won't have relevant facts, so meaning must be made through participatory dialogue aimed at *inventing* the future. But the dogma that there is one "right" answer out there just waiting to be "found" is pernicious. Equally exasperating, we expect the one right answer to be a silver bullet. We want to be awed by the stunning creativity of that single right answer. And when nothing so perfect appears, groups become discouraged and lose faith.

WHY DOES EMERGENCE MATTER SO MUCH?

IT ALLOWS US TO PRODUCE HIGHER-ORDER SOLUTIONS INSTEAD OF COMPROMISING AND SATISFICING. When idea generation is rooted in a reframed understanding of the problem and curated design criteria that are focused on what matters to stakeholders, the likelihood of breakthrough ideas appearing during Emergence is much greater. Who among us has not suffered through painful ideation episodes that involved problems like the "boss effect," where team members wait for the highest-level person in the room to pronounce a solution, or the "shout-out" issue, where loud voices overwhelm the conversation and contributions from introverts are lost? These human dynamics often block creative engagement, preventing Emergence and stalling true co-creation. Practices like turn taking, listening first to understand, writing privately before sharing, and using Post-It notes (in all their neon glory) to preserve anonymity all contribute important assistance to creating the conditions under which superior solutions can be crafted together.

EMERGENCE BREEDS A SPIRIT OF SHARED CREATIVITY AMONG TEAM MEMBERS. No "creativity gene" has yet been discovered in our DNA. The ability to form new concepts using existing knowledge develops from passion, persistence, and problem-solving—traits all people can acquire. So everyone can be creative, despite the pervasive myth of the lone genius, and the process of Emergence, by building on diverse perspectives via dialogue and co-creation, allows everyone to take part. There is not one "right answer" (though some are better than others), so the stakes of winning or losing at creativity are diminished. A successful experience of Emergence really helps innovators to see both the power of the collective and that they can contribute to it. As one of our innovators commented:

> *I never considered myself a creative individual. I spent my entire career in corporate finance, in which creativity is often a difficult skill to exercise. Without a doubt, the "What if anything is possible?" mindset that I have developed will be useful throughout my career.*

EMERGENCE MAKES FOR ENDLESS POSSIBILITIES. Researchers agree that there are infinite future possibilities that result from the combination of previous solutions, but certain actions generate more future possibilities than others. Remember the adjacent possible? Experiencing this can be challenging but exhilarating, as described by one innovator:

> *We're good at building ideas from others' ideas and lifting them higher. We're getting better at offering bold and crazy ideas. We have to nudge each other a little, but when we do, some great ideas come out.*

When you are able to stay in the possibility space, brilliance can ensue. Another innovator reflected:

> *Fortunately, I did not give up in the middle of this process, but restructured the way I approached the situation. Instead of looking through the narrower window in front of me, I stepped back, turned around, stepped aside, and looked above my head—I ended up having fun and interesting ideas.*

PARTICIPATING IN EMERGENCE BUILDS OWNERSHIP. Architect Michael Benedikt[63] talks about the power of "emptiness": leaving room for others to create *what could be* instead of being told *what will be*. There is a magic in the *not* knowing, the wondering, the interpreting, he argues, an exhilarating sense of discovery that something significant is about to take shape. These are the conditions for Emergence.

WHAT DO THE MVCs COMING OUT OF EMERGENCE LOOK LIKE?

Again, as in Alignment, the relevant question in Emergence is not "Am I?" but "Are we?"

ARE WE . . .

- ☑ Pursuing multiple possibilities?

- ☑ Avoiding allegiance to particular solutions during the process?

- ☑ Actively engaging in co-creation, looking for opportunities to build on the ideas of others?

- ☑ Taking an active role in working positively, constructively, and collaboratively with the group?

- ☑ Focusing on "What if anything were possible?" in idea generation?

- ☑ Exploring nontraditional and unexpected ideas?

- ☑ Staying in the possibility space despite time pressures and discomfort?

- ☑ Controlling the urge to compromise prematurely?

- ☑ Demonstrating appreciation for the diverse perspectives represented within the group?

HOW DO WE BETTER GUIDE AND SUPPORT OUR OWN SHIFT AND THAT OF OTHERS?

GUARD THE CONDITIONS FOR EMERGENCE WITH SPECIAL DILIGENCE. Think about the requisite variety the challenge requires. Make sure that all voices are heard, with special attention to the introverts. Try to work in small groups where possible. Enforce turn taking and the idea that everyone participates. For example, in preparing to welcome stakeholders who have not participated in earlier Discovery activities, we first invite them to tour a gallery of posters that familiarize them with the stories from our research. This carefully structured process assures a robust conversation between equals, regardless of personality, professional background, or position in the hierarchy. We are also big fans of visualization (yes—again!). Groups that express and share ideas with imagery as well as words lessen the risk of misunderstanding and make it easier for other members to build on each other's ideas. When groups of stakeholders are engaged in a fruitful conversation with simple rules, and are able to focus on the needs of those they are designing for, and use easy-to-learn DT elements like ethnography, storytelling, Post-Its and turn taking, new possibilities will emerge.

PRIME AND TELL A STORY. As mentioned earlier, we can only address what we pay attention to, and we can't pay attention to everything. Priming can manipulate our attention: neuroscience tells us that when we activate an emotion node, the activation spreads through all memory structures to which it is linked. Priming can trigger an emotion to connect the cue with the present system. Stories and personas guide behaviors by evoking experiences. Most stories are set in a context that reinforces the images of place and time while also letting the listeners' imaginations roam. Meaning emerges from the combination of what the storyteller supplies and what the listeners add. One of our favorite ways to prime is through the use of metaphor (more on this in Chapter 7).

POSSIBILITIES FIRST, CONSTRAINTS LATER. It can be a tough challenge to keep things like resource concerns at bay until after possibilities are surfaced and developed. Sadly, many of us are trained to pull apart solutions, not create them. However, only possibilities really excite people enough to do the hard work of working around constraints and crossing the difficult boundaries that divide us. In our experience, it is the energy and creativity generated by user-focused, possibility-driven discussions that power breakthrough thinking. DT's back end, with its careful attention to assumption surfacing, prototyping, and testing, gives analytically focused and skeptical minds plenty to work with later on. Producing something *worth* testing requires protecting the up-front investment in asking "What if anything were possible?" This requires setting rules for the conversation. As one innovator noted:

> *It is incredibly difficult to think outside the realm of what we know. The best brainstorming often came not from the brainstorming activity itself, but from the discussions that our initial thoughts inspired.*

The magic comes alive when you assemble a group of creative people who honor the rules.

THINK BROADLY ABOUT WHO YOU INVITE INTO THE CONVERSATION. We have already talked about the importance of requisite variety to innovation. Requisite variety requires thinking beyond the usual categories of gender, age, race, or even expertise—it's also about the way humans think, about localized versus centralized control, and about levels of hierarchy.[64] In forming groups, think of composing the network of people needed to fully implement any solution created. A group with truly diverse repertoires optimizes our ability to think and work across silos. DT tools like stakeholder mapping can help you figure out who needs to be in the room. And by *room*, we mean an actual space where human beings physically congregate, if at all possible. Sure, you can accomplish a lot online these days. But there is no substitute for face-to-face conversations if you want to build trust across difference. And be sure to invite some beginner minds, as well.

BEWARE OF HIERARCHY. Escaping the limitations introduced by hierarchy is critical for co-creation. One scientist at the National Institute of Allergy and

Infectious Diseases, who designed a new approach to identifying and contacting qualified reviewers for potential grantees, highlighted how the program he had participated in, Ignite, bypassed the barrier of hierarchy:

> *Most of the really good ideas are sequestered in lower levels where people are trying, but where the giant bureaucracy can get you overwhelmed. Ignite links us all up. Instead of going through executive committees at a grand level, you're working on the ground with other people who have buy-in and skin in the game. It's a way of breaking through walls quicker.*

FIND MULTIPLE PATHWAYS TO INCLUSION. In our research, we see many pathways to creating the kinds of inclusive conversations we are talking about. The U.S. Department of Health and Human Services (HHS) uses their Ignite accelerator program (mentioned above) to end-run the hierarchy in Washington, DC, and invite their 80,000 employees throughout the country to tackle self-identified opportunities for positive change. The United Cerebral Palsy Foundation created traveling workshops that they called "Design-athons" in different cities. The Institute without Boundaries (IwB) at Toronto's George Brown College combines DT with a process from the architecture and urban-planning world—the charrette. Adapted from a century-old architectural practice, a charrette is an intensive collaborative process that aims to bring the entire system of stakeholders physically into a room together to create a range of new solutions for a given challenge. The emphasis is on moving between small work groups and the entire collective in fast, iteration-focused, and feedback-driven cycles of idea development. The U.S. Office of Personnel Management founded innovation labs like The Lab@OPM in Washington, DC, that provide support for the engagement of new voices. More than a physical space, the Lab@OPM offers instruction and mentoring and brings together prospective change makers from across a diverse set of federal agencies. Its graduates have built a robust grassroots community of practice around DT that reaches across government silos, while they continue to support each other in making a difference amid the often frustrating bureaucracy of federal government.[65]

WHAT'S NEXT?

When the magic of Emergence happens, innovators usually find, to their surprise and delight, that they have far more great ideas than they can possibly use. Time to start winnowing and move into the activities of Testing.

PART THREE
THE TESTING PROCESS

INTRODUCTION TO TESTING

When the time comes to take the ideas generated in the Discovery process and move the best of them into Testing, innovators face a new set of experiences every bit as profound and transformational as those they faced in the first part of their journey. Many find the experience of transitioning from Discovery to Testing to be one of the most challenging in the entire DT process. DT's front end is well documented and supported by powerful tools; the back end has few recipes (and fewer tools). Innovators now face new kinds of challenges—making their ideas tangible, sharing them with their prospective users, listening nondefensively to their feedback, and using that feedback to improve their design. The choices are no longer in their own hands, but in the hands of those they have designed for. And this is all happening in real time: innovators must iterate quickly in the moment based on what they learn. To add to the pressure, a misguided definition of speed often kicks in, and innovators want (and are urged by their organizations) to minimize this kind of exploratory testing and go straight to creating minimum viable products. Resisting that urge is tough but critical if we want better solutions. As one experienced innovator explained to us:

> *There's lots of iteration, work spent, taking a different direction, coming back to some earlier work, changing, and never a one-and-done until the very end. The closer you get to the end, the more you want it to be finished, but that is the sweet spot for bringing in innovation.*

It is not that speed doesn't matter (it certainly does) but it is *speed of learning* that we are interested in. Learning, either alone or collectively, is never easy, as we've already discussed. It is even harder under these conditions. The barriers to learning in Testing are deeply grounded in one of the most basic human desires: to be *right*. Surmounting them requires fundamental shifts in who we are and how we think—shifts of an entirely different nature than those in Discovery.

Getting people comfortable with *trying* something in the real world is a critical first step. People in action talking to users are likely to learn something; people debating each other in conference rooms are not. One of the leaders we interviewed gives his people only five days to act on the ideas generated. He described his logic:

> It doesn't have to be perfect but they have to take responsibility for actually doing something within the five days. . . . The key is not to get into task force or committee zones where it just goes on and on and on. You've got a week to knock something out.

Innovators must now think more like scientists and investors than entrepreneurs or idea creators. Instead of passion and emotional involvement, they need detachment and steely objectivity. Investment guru Warren Buffett once said, "What counts for most people in investing is not how much they know, but rather how realistically they define what they *don't* know." This stage is all about inviting the people we are designing for to illuminate all that we don't yet know about meeting their needs.

In the next two chapters, we will look at two discrete elements of DT's Testing practice, and the innovator's experiences that accompany them. The first is Imagining, a hallmark of DT. The ability to imagine any new future—so vividly that it becomes real to those whose feedback we need—is the first step to successful Testing. Experiencing the power of making ideas come to life dramatically impacts the innovator's journey. Its key tool, visualization, is used throughout the DT process, and serves many purposes, as we have already noted. In Chapter 7, we will drill down on a focus of creating *mental* as well as physical imagery. In the same way that we found that Immersion involved much more than just doing ethnographic interviews, and that Emergence was about a world beyond brainstorming, we will find that Imagining is about more than making prototypes.

In Chapter 8 we turn to the experience of innovators as they learn in action, focusing on experimentation—the most ignored, but in our view one of the most critical, elements in the DT tool kit. We will use the same format we used in the Discovery chapters: a look at the activities and their intended impact on innovators' mindsets, the science behind them, the challenges and opportunities involved in doing them well, what the MVCs look like, and how these can be facilitated.

It's Testing time.

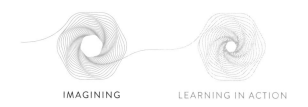

CHAPTER 7

IMAGINING

A CFO'S LIFESAVER

Having already been through two mergers, the CFO in charge of integrating two Australian financial-service firms was nervous. The challenge of retaining the best of both organizations' very different cultures and keeping momentum going while pursuing a new collaborative strategy was keeping him up at night. His integration team wanted to do a metaphor exercise to kick off the conversation between the newly merged department heads. The financially oriented leadership group was skeptical and the CFO himself was especially hesitant, explaining, "As a finance guy, the visualization techniques aren't naturally appealing to me." But the team persisted, and got the go-ahead.

After a few practice sessions, the team chose the metaphor of a "thriving city," with the assignment to fill in a map. Early on, they noticed a few interesting dynamics in the sessions. When they started with maps that had too much detail, it restricted creativity and the conversations were stilted. Maps that were almost entirel+y blank, however, created an identical effect. "It was as if too much detail and too little detail were equally bad," one of the team members noted. Ultimately, they found what they believed to be the "emptiness sweet spot"—creating 10 separate neighborhoods within the city, to allow each area to share the city but also design its own spaces within it. Each department was charged with designing their neighborhood in a way that explained their role in the new strategy to others. When the designs were completed, the departments gave each other a tour of their neighborhoods.

The CFO's own team almost immediately hit on a life-saving theme to characterize their office, patterning it on their personal experiences with Australia's famous surf clubs. They made "swim in between the flags" the banner for their neighborhood, emphasizing their role as lifesavers. "Our job is about rules and guidelines, but we don't want to be thought of as cops chasing 'criminals,'" one explained. "It's about prudential control. But as conditions change, you need to move the flags in a proactive way. Set the boundaries. Keep people out of trouble—and save their lives if they get into it."

A year later, with great momentum behind the strategy and significant increases in staff commitment to it, the CFO talked about his change of heart regarding visualization as a tool:

> *We stumbled across this metaphor of lifesaver and it has really stuck. When I talk about lifesaver or moving the flags, people know what I mean—it makes the strategy more tangible. . . . At the end of the day, the real value was having a grassroots conversation. The leader's challenge is always getting everyone engaged, aligned, and committed. Everyone could develop their own neighborhood— we set boundaries but still allowed engagement. Our team accomplished cultural change and could talk about it in a fun way. It was a way of communicating differently.* ∎

Using a metaphor with financial-service managers to help them work together to understand and buy in to a new strategy? It seems far-fetched—but its success is a testimony to the power of imagining. Visualization tools are key drivers behind the transformational potential of DT. As we have talked about in earlier chapters, they help us make sense of our data, build engagement, align around a common purpose and foster co-creation. Metaphor is among the most powerful tools for Imagining. But metaphor triggers a different kind of experience than building a physical prototype. It utilizes mental imagery and pushes us beyond visualization in this narrower sense (in the form of physical prototypes) to think more broadly about creating an experience through the use of mental as well as physical images. In this chapter, we talk about an innovator's experience of *Imagining* as a critical step in successful Testing. It is where innovators learn how to make a new future *manifest*, to embody it with a vividness that brings it to life.

Many of us think that the act of Imagining is about the invention of new ideas. It's not. It is about making an idea come alive. Derived from the Latin word *imaginare*, it means "to form an image of." The kind of images that we want to talk about in this chapter are as much about the *mind's eye* as the physical eye. Imagining is the bridge between Discovery and Testing, between an innovator's experience of Emergence and that of Learning in Action. It is where we make the future *feel real*.

We seem to be in the midst of a fevered pursuit of things that *feel real* today. It shows up in the seemingly insatiable appetite for "reality TV" and docudramas and the growth of the "historical fiction" genre in literature. We want to live in towns that seem real—even if urban planners create them from the ground up. We want to go to museums to see the "real thing"—even if copies that are indistinguishable to the untrained eye abound. In an environment that bombards us with media messages, tweets, and spin—we yearn, not surprisingly, for what seems authentic.

But *feeling real* is a subjective perception, a personal judgment that each of us makes. What makes anything—an idea, a strategy, a building—feel *real*? One answer to this question takes us back to the work of architect Michael Benedikt, whose concept of "emptiness" we talked about in Chapter 6. Benedikt offers a prescription for what he calls "an architecture of reality"[66] that includes three other components, in addition to emptiness, that contribute to creating a sense that something is real: presence, significance,

> ### IMAGING ACTIVITIES [67]
>
> - Storytelling
> - Sketching
> - Using metaphor
> - Role-playing
> - Lego Serious Play
> - Videos
> - Paper prototypes, journey maps, charts and storyboards

and materiality. "Presence" is used here much as we would use it to describe an individual who possesses a quality that draws our attention—like an actor with presence, for instance. Research suggests that the dominant characteristic of the winners of this attention competition are *interesting* to us. Writing as early as 1890, psychologist William James noted that, in order to be seen as real, something must first attract our attention.[68] Success in accomplishing that task, he argued, was a function of an idea's "liveliness"—its ability to arouse our emotional interest and "active impulses." Almost 100 years later, sociologist Murray Davis discussed the same issue when he noted that the most attended-to theories in his field of sociology were valued not because they were *true*, but because they were *interesting*.[69] Probing further, Davis noted that what made them interesting was that they combined the *familiar* with the *novel*—that's where presence comes from.

But just getting people's attention, while an important precondition, isn't enough. Having attracted our attention, a concept must have *significance* in order to feel real. Benedikt makes an important differentiation here between significant *to someone* rather than merely symbolic *of something*. Once again, it's the personal that counts—*we* find it important, worth caring about—not *Architectural Digest*. As James suggests, something with significance arouses an emotional attachment. Even more so than presence, this moves us beyond the realm of the cognitive to include feelings. Things that feel real arouse our emotions. These aspects

WHAT DOES AN INNOVATOR'S MINDSET SHIFT LOOK LIKE DURING IMAGINING?

As innovators move into Imagining, our goal is to help them move from a position of holding ideas in fuzzy form in their own heads to visualizing that new future in rich detail, in ways that energize and inspire others to bring these ideas to life.

IMAGINING MOVES INNOVATORS . . .

FROM A MINDSET THAT . . .	TO A MINDSET THAT . . .
Leaves ideas abstract	Gives ideas life by moving from the abstract to the particular
Tells with words	Shows with visuals and stories
Thinks of images as "dress rehearsals" for a finished concept	Thinks of images as provocations to engage others in a rich conversation
Makes complicated creations that capture all elements of an idea	Simplifies to essentials to test critical assumptions
Waits for perfection	Moves into action despite incompleteness

of presence and significance are built into the front end of the DT process—Immersion, Sensemaking, Alignment, and Emergence experiences all contribute to that. Benedikt's third category, materiality, takes us straight to the heart of Imagining. Materiality is about substance rather than abstraction. To achieve it, we need to pay attention to the details, to more than words on paper or a PowerPoint slide. Compared to other fields, design is fundamentally grounded in the material world, in translating abstract thought into something tangible. Imagining is perhaps design's most significant superpower—and is almost entirely unfamiliar to most of us. That's why adding it to our repertoire of skills creates so much value.

THE SCIENCE BEHIND IT

SEEING WITH THE MIND'S EYE. The power of seeing with the mind's eye is profound when we are trying to create something new. As Imagineer Walt Disney proclaimed: "The future is a place that is created. Created first in the mind, and only then in the activity." Playwright George Bernard Shaw echoed a similar sentiment and drew the linkages between imagining and creating: "Imagination is the beginning of creation. You *imagine* what you desire, you *will* what you imagine, and at last, you *create* what you will." When Stephen Covey advised us to "begin with the end in mind," he was talking about the power of imagining our future before we set out on the path to reach it. The province of top-caliber athletes and performers

(since the Russians popularized it in preparation for the 1960 Olympic Games), conjuring rich, detailed mental imagery of future success has been used to motivate high performance. Like flow, it works for both individuals and collectives.

Researchers have found that visualizing images ignites similar pathways to actually seeing the real thing. Think of a cat driving a car. First, check yourself—you (hopefully) have never seen a cat driving a car. Yet you likely are currently seeing Fluffy the tabby cat shifting into third gear with paws at 10 and 2. How is this possible? Our brain has separate neural pathways that explain the color, spatial, physical, and tangible aspects of a car and a cat, respectively. Our prefrontal cortex makes the magic happen by coordinating simultaneous firing of both pathways so we see them together. It's all in the timing. Such mental synthesis allows us to build visualizations of things that we have never actually seen.

Imagery is powerful—Belgian researcher Beatrice de Gelder and her colleagues used electromagnetic scans to look at brain imaging and discovered that actually being in a particular place and just visualizing being in that place created similar physical responses. They found that, when prompted to imagine a tree, our frontal cortex triggers commands to form the image. The medial temporal region, the gatekeeper to our memories, sifts through and finds the most relevant stored information, which, beyond the physical "tree," might include the emotions of climbing a tree, the whistling of branches in the breeze, and all the different names of trees. At this stage, the floodgates open, as signals are sent to the parietal lobe for sensory and spatial memory (how rough was the bark?) and to the visual cortex for more detail (leaves, branches, buds, blossoms, etc.). All of this knowledge and information comes rushing back to the frontal cortex for meaning making.[70] The most incredible finding in her research was that even in blind individuals whose visual cortex was damaged, all of the same brain areas were activated.

A PICTURE IS WORTH A THOUSAND WORDS.

Our brains are wired for images. Though vision is one of five senses, our brains disproportionately favor it—75% of our brain's sensory neurons are dedicated to visual processing.[71] The occipital lobe, where most visual processing occurs, takes up 20% of our brain capacity,[72] and neurons responsible for visual activity take up 3 times as much real estate as touch and 10 times as much as hearing.[73] When we see something, we create neuropathways that span our brains like roads, conjuring color, space, physical characteristics, and emotions; and when we visualize it, that intricate mental highway system reignites. Retention also benefits—pictures are retained at far higher rates than words. When we read text alone, we remember about 10% of the information three days later. If we read text *and* see relevant images, we're likely to remember 65% of the information.[74]

Weldon and Roediger[75] assert that pictures elicit more conceptual processing—we encode pictures faster and more uniquely, and so we recall and retrieve meaning more quickly from them. When you read this, your brain has a shortcut loop to understand what we are writing. Your optic nerve receives the visual cues of our words, they are identified as recognizable words in the primary visual cortex, and then they are off to the left temporal lobe, where a special area—Wernicke's area—interprets them. If you want to respond with your own speech, the words are crafted in a neighboring area—Broca's area—and then you speak. This is a pretty simple loop, but it takes time to process and produce words.

On the flip side, our brains completely and immediately activate when we process pictures. When we see an image, the optic nerve sends the signals to the primary visual cortex, which reconstructs the image into basic lines, and then it spreads it far and wide. The parietal lobe notes the space, texture, and other sensory information associated with what we see, the premotor cortex processes any movement, and the temporal lobe forms visual memories including colors. Essentially, processing a visual engages our whole brain, helping us boost understanding and create deeper meaning from what we take in.

EMOTIONALLY ENHANCED VIVIDNESS.

Imagery engages our emotions and ignites a deeper sense of empathy and familiarity. According to researcher W. J. T. Mitchell, images act as "go-betweens in social transactions" that structure the way we interact with others and the world.[76] Images identify and categorize items by characteristics (or schema) that ignite instantaneously in similar situations, creating emotionally enhanced vividness. But vividness benefits from more than just the one sense of seeing. At its best, Imagining engages all five senses—smell, taste, touch, and hearing, as well as sight. A scholarly field known as "embodied philosophy" argues for moving beyond cognition to embrace a full-body-based perspective.[77] Even more so than seeing, the other senses are intensely personal and subjective—and evocative. An important part of Immersion, for example, encompasses the direct sensory experiences. Think back to our Kingwood Institute designer in Chapter 3, mirroring the experience of Pete, a person with autism. The vibration of an ear against the wall, the touch and sound of ripping paper—all enriched her understanding of Pete's needs and pleasures. Or think of babies (or puppies if you prefer). Reading the word "baby" may not evoke much, but imagine large eyes, small noses, chubby cheeks, and little toes. Now add their soft skin, dewy scent, and a baby belly laugh, and an involuntary hormonal response is unleashed. Dopamine, in this case, makes us feel happy and completely captivated by these small wonders.

THE MAGNIFICENCE OF METAPHOR. Though words and text have less of an impact neurologically than images do, there are exceptions—one is metaphor (the other is storytelling—more on this later). When we create metaphors or think analogously, we shift part of our neural processing to transform

words into visuals to make sense of the description. Going back to babies, I could say, "This baby weighs ten pounds and has 10 toes and a big head." I would be accurate, but your response would likely be flat. But if I said, "This baby is a ten pound bundle of joy with a smile as bright as the sun," you'd be lying if you said you didn't get a little bit of a warm, happy feeling. That's because since our minds cannot make literal sense of the description, it turns to visuals. What would a bundle of joy look like? How would it feel? Just questioning the brightness of the sun inspires feelings of warmth, blinding brilliance, and the visceral desire to soak it all in. Think back to our CFO's team and the metaphor of the lifesaver rather than the police as a way to think about their role in the newly merged organization. Remember combining the familiar with the novel? That's what metaphor does.

Metaphors connect words to prior knowledge, experience, and memory, and translate concepts from abstract to concrete, making them easier for us to comprehend.[78] In coaching aspiring authors, psychologist Melissa Burkley advises them to enrich their writing by using metaphor to "take the abstract and hard to understand and compare it to the simple, concrete and well-understood." Bestselling author Stephen King is a fan as well, arguing that metaphor allows us to "see an old thing in a new and vivid way," likening it to "a kind of miracle between a writer and a reader."[79]

Take the light bulb, a simple object at first glance. Researcher Alex Marin and his team found that when focus groups were given visual stimuli that was either conducive or not conducive to creativity, like a light-bulb going on or off, those who received metaphors for generating creativity yielded a greater creative output.[80] Additionally, Michael Slepian and his team at Tufts University found that "exposure to an illuminating light bulb primes bright ideas [because it] activates concepts associated with achieving insight and facilitates performance on spatial, verbal and mathematical insight problems."[81] Simply put, visual metaphors create a shortcut around the normal language processes that aim straight for how people think and feel.

WHY STORIES WORK. It is well recognized that storytelling is another powerful way to engage and motivate. But why? When the brain sees or hears a story, neural coupling happens. Yes—it's the same mirror neurons we talked about that play a role in Immersion, back at work, firing the same patterns in the listener's brain as in the speaker's. We retain stories in memory much more than abstract thoughts—we remember the scenes that stories create and details they contain that we would otherwise forget. The most compelling stories engage all of our senses. Far more than when facts are shared, they transport us into the experience described. And they keep us focused, while our brain produces oxytocin, which enhances our empathy and increases our ability to detect cues in our environment. While we think of Sherlock Holmes (yes, him again!) as having superior *thinking* abilities, architect

João Ferreira[82] argues that the detective's skills depend as much on his ability to *see* and tell a compelling story of what he sees, as on his famous reasoning skills. Sherlock, he asserts, "observes something no one has yet noticed and presents it with sufficient detail for others to see it too." When his faithful sidekick Dr. Watson asks, "How did you know?", his response is "I did not *know*, I *saw*."

Finally, research demonstrates that compelling stories can actually cause us to alter our behavior. Professor Michael Lissack explains the magic of stories:

> *Storytelling helps us to consolidate our experiences and to make them available in the future to ourselves and others. The power of a story is that it allows listeners to recreate an experience. . . . The storyteller carves out a canyon for the listener to supply a river of meaning to run through it.*[83]

EUREKA! Albert Einstein's greatest breakthroughs came from thinking in pictures. His thought experiments started when he was just a teenager, when he pictured in his mind what it would be like to ride alongside a light beam. For the rest of his career, he would visualize how math equations were reflected in reality, giving birth to some of the most influential scientific discoveries of all time. When he died, neuroscientists jumped at the chance to study the brain of a genius; what they found reflected the power of

<table>
<tr><td>

WHY WE NEED MORE STORIES

Andre Martin, director of people development at Google, talks about the "3 Cs" of storytelling: make it clear, compelling, and consequential. He explains why business today needs more stories:

> As I look at the world we live in, there's some basic challenges that leaders face. One is that they only have about 20% of the attention of the people they lead. Storytelling allows you to get them to pay attention for just a little bit longer, with a little bit more diligent energy. I think that's important. If you can raise the level of engagement in your business, you will do wonders for your performance. And storytelling allows you to create energy and passion and excitement around something. Most business leaders are honestly bored with 90% of the conversations they have in a day. They sit there through PowerPoint after PowerPoint, meeting after meeting, to-do list after to-do list. They are looking to be inspired.

</td></tr>
</table>

Imagining. Researcher Marian Diamond discovered that Einstein's left inferior parietal cortex was 15% larger than usual, with even more glial cells (the glue that speeds up signals and connectivity between neurons).[84] The enlarged areas have nothing to do with IQ—they are linked to mathematical and spatial ability and become highly active when making unusual associations of imagery and abstraction—conceptual gymnastics, as some researchers term it. Research over the past decade supports the theory that the parietal lobe flexibly recombines stored information in memory into novel mental representations and future thinking. Einstein's commitment to creativity, inquiry, and imagination constantly flexed this brain area like a muscle, regularly activating neural circuits that, over time, may have changed the physiology of his brain.

WHAT MAKES IMAGINING SO HARD?

THE URGE TO TELL INSTEAD OF SHOW. Despite the power of imaging through stories, metaphors and images, for those of us raised on PowerPoints and spreadsheets, the proclivity to "tell" is deeply ingrained. We live in environments that emphasize verbal interactions and, often, debate. We are taught to look decisive; after all, if we don't stand up for our ideas, who else will? But nobody experiences anything by being *told*. Such telling, though it may seem more efficient, actually slows down collaborative work. When members spend more time telling each other about their ideas instead of showing them, they risk losing momentum or getting stuck. They mistake conversation for progress. The majority of innovators learning DT find the idea of "showing" baffling, having rarely worked with anything but words and numbers. This can cause a range of reactions from reluctant innovators, from "this feels too artsy-craftsy" on one end of the spectrum to "we need to leave this to professionals" on the other end.

BUT I CAN'T DRAW! One of the most prevalent pushbacks comes from confusing visualizing with drawing. Yes—most of us can't draw, but that really doesn't matter. The key skill in Imagining is conceptual, not artistic. We need first to conjure in our minds a vivid sense of the new future—how it gets translated to paper is less important. One innovator exclaimed:

> *Yes! My favorite part! Just having a working idea (in the form of storyboards) is surprisingly powerful. . . . I was super skeptical of my crappy stick figures, but with dialogue bubbles and some context clues I drew into the frames, my test subjects actually understood the solution with limited context. All the inferences and insights, assumptions and leaps that I watched my test subjects process through were so stunningly real—they were aspects we never considered, a few we had tried to anticipate, and in general an incredibly valuable and "fresh" take on the solution.*

But because they can't draw, we find novices to DT offloading this responsibility to others, and missing the opportunity to develop this powerful ability themselves. In our classes, we have learned the hard way that pairing business and design students together in teams, left unmanaged, almost always results in a "divide and conquer" strategy: the designers do the visualizing and the business students do the "business" stuff. What a loss to both.

DRESS REHEARSALS OR PLAYGROUND? In his book *Serious Play: How the World's Best Companies Simulate to Innovate*, author Michael Schrage asserts that a core problem is that most of us think of prototyping as staging a dress rehearsal for an idea. Prototypes are meant, instead, to be *playgrounds*, he argues. They are conversation starters, not mimics of the end product—*provocations*, in designer talk. That is a very different way to think about prototyping. In traditional R&D, we produce the "thing" as it is supposed to be, and then we test the "thing." In DT, we use the "thing" as a vehicle to a better conversation and to get better feedback. We leave it rough *and* we want it to feel real. Leroy Grumman, cofounder of Grumman Aerospace Corporation (now a part of Northrop Grumman) used to say, "It is better to have a rough answer to the right question than a detailed answer to the wrong question." So we need a prototype to help us get feedback that is as accurate as possible. The popularity of Lean Startup, with its emphasis on creating a workable minimum viable product (MVP), further confuses would-be design thinkers. In DT, our early visualizations have no ambitions to be MVPs. Instead, they are low-fidelity tests of critical assumptions, not high-fidelity conceptions of the entire concept.

IT'S HARD TO FIND THE BALANCE BETWEEN "EMPTINESS" AND "VIVIDNESS." Innovators often run into trouble finding the right level of detail. Living in the abstract is comfortable. This is how we are used to talking about a new future—in general, rosy terms, and in a kind of "one-minute elevator pitch" format. This is simply not enough detail for reliable testing because our users just project what they would like to see to flesh out the skeleton we have given them. For accurate feedback, the little picture matters as much as the big one. But moving from the abstract to the particular takes courage and a lot more thought. We associate materiality with implementation, not creation. But experiments require sufficient detail to make an idea consistent to all users, as well as vivid.

But we also see problems at the other extreme. We need detail that matters, not detail that is superfluous to testing our assumptions. When innovators try to create a complete and "perfect prototype," it overwhelms those we are trying to get feedback from. The details included have to be the appropriate ones. But how do we know which ones are essential versus extra? This is where careful attention to surfacing assumptions becomes key, to tell us exactly what hypothesis we want to use our visuals to test. Those are the vital pieces to detail. Imagining the essentials of ideas in a simple way reduces complexity and invites co-creation.

WE DON'T REALLY UNDERSTAND OUR IDEA. It is often when innovators begin to prototype that they have an unpleasant realization: they and their teams lack a shared view of what the concept they have created really entails. Because they lack this shared concrete understanding, they tend to postpone using visualization until they can sort out the details in their own minds. Couple this with a lack of confidence in their perceived drawing abilities and the task feels daunting. One innovator told us:

> *I felt terrible and overwhelmed when my concept was positioned as the "preferred" direction. This made me feel like I had to answer all the questions—but I hadn't even thought through the whole idea. I'm lacking confidence and clarity in any of the tasks and struggling to comprehend prototyping.*

WHY DOES IMAGINING MATTER SO MUCH?

Despite how unfamiliar working with imagery is for nondesigners, it is essential to managing the risks and reaping the rewards of innovation efforts. Why?

THE POWER OF MAKING SOMETHING "FEEL REAL." Luigi Ferrara, dean of Toronto's IwB, explained to us why pushing people out of theoretical debates and abstraction and toward action and concreteness is so important:

> *It is easy to stay safely in the debate space and never have your hypothesis interact with reality to get feedback about whether or not it is true. This is what makes everything slow down. It's what paralyzes bureaucracies. You can debate forever. This is where design gets interesting. You have to*

translate your sentiment into an embodiment that others can see. A fundamental part of design is making things sharable in the world.

In making something concrete and tangible, you make it real and open it to others. It acts as a catalyst for understanding. One innovator described how the process engaged even skeptical colleagues:

We were dealing with a range of stakeholder groups and departments, each having their own agendas and opinions. Some were completely opposed to the project, others were major proponents, and others were completely indifferent. We could have just held a group meeting to discuss the project or administered a survey. Instead, we used visuals and did a lot of hands-on exercises with these executives. . . . They were clearly skeptical when they first arrived in the morning, but by the time they left the session in the afternoon, they were raving about how great it was. It allowed us to draw much deeper insights from them.

IMAGINING FORCES DEEPER DEVELOPMENT OF AN IDEA. It is not only those we are designing *for* that visualization helps—it helps those we are designing *with* as well. During a recent debrief, one innovator shared a refrain that we commonly hear: "We realized that we didn't know exactly what our idea was until we had to start building it." Exactly! Innovators struggle often with identifying assumptions before prototyping

MAKING STRATEGY REAL

Consider the experience of a frustrated group of strategists at a large software company trying to engage their colleagues in a strategic planning process, which the managers considered a waste of time—those who needed to fill out the forms just didn't see the point in taking their precious time to do what seemed to them to be an exercise in bureaucracy. Design colleagues suggested that the strategists try *visualizing* the new plan. Desperate to build enthusiasm, the strategists worked with the designers to create a multifaceted story of the future they faced. The results turned even the most hardened ex-strategy consultants into believers.

Once I saw that even a rough prototype was really changing the conversations we were having with people, it became very easy to get behind that. You have to see it to believe it! It's far more concrete and open than the traditional "I'm going to walk you through my PowerPoint" approach. Once I started experiencing that, there was no going back. . . . The conversation was entirely different. It was such a different starting point. People got excited as we walked them through this experience. That took the classic process of filling out the forms and all the usual stuff that we still needed them to do and put it into context.

because they don't have a clue what their idea is really about until they begin fully Imagining it. As they build it, it becomes real. Not only that—at a very personal level, each sees the power of making an idea feel real, and starts down the path of developing their own competency to do this important work. In an increasingly diverse workforce, using imagery instead of words has the power to remove communication barriers between individuals, aligning information and ideas more effectively. One innovator we talked to said:

> *Certainly, it makes it easier for our audience to understand ideas and concepts. But much more important, it makes us think a lot—when we are drawing, all our senses go into a creative mode that produces more and deeper ideas. That is something that I haven't experienced before.*

Coming out of Emergence, ideas are high level and abstract. In Imagining, we further develop those ideas, as well as present them. Images can provide clues to our brain to make further connections, so seeing rudimentary sketches can trigger a deeper concept or understanding that is "hidden" (think Rorschach images).

IMAGERY SIMPLIFIES AND INVITES. Like Pinocchio becoming a real boy, things *become* more real over time as we interact with them—they are not made that way. We don't want our ideas to remain fantasies that only we can appreciate—they are meant to be handled, pulled apart, questioned, and iterated. So motivating this interaction is critical. This phase sets the basic framework for the coming set of interactions, especially with those we are designing for. "What designers do is take complex and unrelated information and turn it into something original, useful, and understandable," architect João Ferreira[85] argues—so they

VISUALIZING THE STO-WING

Leading into World War II, the U.S. Navy desperately sought to stock aircraft carriers with more planes. With wide wingspans, storing planes and raising them to the flight deck limited the number of planes on any carrier, but if wings were hinged and folded to shorten the wingspan, they crumpled under flight pressure, especially in a dive. Leroy Grumman had a hypothesis that pivoting wings in storage could provide the structure to withstand even the immense stress in climbs and dives while saving significant space. To help himself figure out the concept, and explain it to his engineers, he captured it simply, using an old-fashioned rubber eraser as the plane's fuselage and bent paperclips for the wings. By bending the paperclips in multiple angles, he discovered and demonstrated that the wings needed to fold back (pivot) on the body of the plane like the wings of a bird (there's that metaphor again!).

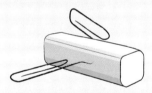

In engineering parlance, Grumman's Sto-wing was based on a "skewed axis," and this style of wing was instrumental in the tide-changing battle of Midway, when the U.S. Navy sank four Japanese aircraft carriers while losing one of the capital ships. Although the Japanese pilots were highly experienced—and outnumbered the less-experienced American flyers—the American Navy had more planes on each carrier as, due to Sto-wings, American holds contained up to five planes in spaces which previously held only two.[86]

need to communicate ideas both visually and verbally. This dual approach allows the designer to represent an idea as something fluid and malleable, yet vivid. Sketching can be an especially powerful medium for accomplishing this. Designer Praveen Sidyal spoke about the power of the sketch:[87]

> *Sketches have an amazing ability to foster discussions about ideas. With colleagues and especially clients, I've found sketches give everyone involved the permission to consider, talk about, and challenge the ideas they represent. After all, it's just a sketch. Because sketches are unfinished and loose, they invite commentary. There is a latitude inherent in a sketch that seems to magically open the door for others to offer ideas—often thoughts you couldn't come up with from your singular perspective. When I've presented conceptual ideas in finished form, colleagues and clients often hesitate to be as honest as they are with sketches.*

SPECIFICITY GIVES US BETTER FEEDBACK. Remember bias Category 2, which we talked about earlier—the old "say/do" gap? One of the obstacles to reducing innovation risk is how bad people are at accurately predicting their reaction to a new idea. But we don't want to make the investment needed so they can react to the real thing. The more we can Imagine a vivid image of what this new idea is—a product, service, or strategy—the more we can postpone our investment in actually building it. Visualizing done

THE GUGGENHEIM BILBAO

Architects, we are told, think with their pencils. In describing this century's 100 greatest designs, *New York Times* architecture critic Herbert Muschamp included, at number 100, the only building designed in the last decade: Frank Gehry's Guggenheim Museum in Bilbao. This master work started with "fast scrawls and mere annotations" on pieces of stationery at his hotel in Bilbao. Later, as he worked on the plane home, the design evolved, and the sketches began to capture the basics of his scheme for the site. Later, he described the process through which the museum's design evolved from sketches to models and back: "I start drawing sometimes, not knowing where it is going. . . . It's like feeling your way along in the dark, anticipating that something will come out usually. I become a voyeur of my own thoughts as they develop, and wander about them. Sometimes I say 'boy, here it is, it's coming.' I understand it. I get all excited and from there I'll move to the models. The drawings are ephemeral. The models are the specific; they then become like the sketches in the next phase." Throughout, Gehry's process remains iterative, with both sketches and models playing a key role. "Often the models take me down a blind alley, and I go back to sketches again. They become the vehicle for propelling the project forward when I get stuck." He described his process "unfolding": "I put a bunch of principles down. Then I become self-critical of those images and those principles, and they evoke the next set of responses. And as each piece unfolds, I make the models bigger and bigger, bringing into focus more elements and more pieces of the puzzle. . . . And those evolve, and at some point I stop, because that's it."[88]

well is really about creating a pre-experience. A vivid pre-experience activates the same part of the brain that an actual experience does, leading to much better feedback. Whether in the form of storyboards, journey maps, user scenarios, or business concept illustrations, two-dimensional prototypes offer specific tools to make new ideas more tangible and allow us to solicit more accurate feedback.

MANAGING THE RISK OF FALSE POSITIVES. Reducing risk was high on the innovation wish list we talked about in Chapters 1 and 2. The risks of inaccurate feedback are not evenly distributed. False negatives are errors of *omission*. They cause us to forfeit future gains. This is unfortunate, but since we often don't know what we *might* have achieved, they are usually not personally costly to the innovators involved. False positives, on the other hand, are errors of *commission*. They lead to painfully evident personal failures by encouraging us to spend money *today* investing in ideas that will later fail. Many a head has rolled due to false positives. Yet, we know that if you ask people in a focus group if they will buy a product, 50% of the people will deliver a false-positive response, saying yes but never actually buy it. We call those people the "customer's evil twin"—they look like the good customer right up until the point where they don't buy. The value of a good pre-experience is to create a set of conditions in which people can access a deeper reaction and share their truth about it—especially the negative truth.

IMAGINING ENERGIZES. The shared meaning that visualization makes possible provides the momentum to keep going and to iterate and improve an idea. Any idea is only as good as its champions and their motivation to support it. Without shared understanding, there is no source of energy to push on. Imagining is the key to unlocking surprising new possibilities and deeper understanding. New meaning is created, which leads to more effective refinement of the idea.

JESSICA MEETS WALT

My (Jessica) son Oliver has a sweet friend named Walt. He bounds across the yard with him on the greatest adventures. He joins us for family dinner. He splashes around with Oliver in the bath and when both are tucked in, we give Oliver and Walt each a goodnight kiss.

Walt is my son's imaginary pet whale. From what my son describes, he is massive, blue and green, and has legs to help him run. He has likes (reading), dislikes (thunderstorms), and strong opinions (like how dessert should happen before dinner).

It is tough interacting with something we can't actually see, yet it is magical to experience the type of friend my son values. Walt is adventurous, fiercely loyal, gets hurt but gets back up again, and loves deeply. My assumptions are often wrong when I try to interact with Walt ("No, Mom. We can't put suitcases in the trunk. Walt will get squished." Or "Mom—Walt's favorite food is chicken nuggets!"). But as Walt remains in our lives, he becomes real enough to give me a glimpse into the way my son sees the world and the type of friend he wants to be.

In Chapter 6, we told the story of the inclusive planning process at the botanical garden to demonstrate Emergence in action. An important element of the garden's success, however, was its ability to attract new stakeholders, particularly donors, to help them make their dreams real. This outcome came from Imagining, not Emergence. Imagining takes the ideas that Emergence produces and realizes them, making them real to others, not just their creators. The vividness with which the staff had imagined what the new garden would look like in the *future* changed the way important stakeholders interacted with the garden in the *present*, as one garden employee described it:

> At the time it was created, the plan was better than the institution. The plan was a view of what we wanted to be. As people came to understand and accept the plan, they came to embrace the garden that they saw through the plan, rather than the garden as it actually was, even though not much had actually been accomplished yet.

WHAT DO MVCs COMING OUT OF IMMERSION LOOK LIKE?

If Imagining is not about being able to draw well, what is it about? What are the competencies we are looking for? Here are some questions to ask yourself:

AM I . . .

- [x] Capturing, in my mind's eye, a vivid image of the experience a concept will create for users?

- [x] Translating what I see to others in ways that make a concept come to life for them?

- [x] Building artifacts that allow users to "pre-experience" my idea?

- [x] Transitioning in a clear and compelling way from text to image?

- [x] Developing immersive prototypes that facilitate feedback conversations?

- [x] Surfacing and prioritizing assumptions to be tested?

- [x] Embodying those specific assumptions in a prototype?

- [x] Finding the optimal trade-off between emptiness and vividness, using the right level and kind of detail?

- [x] Actively inviting co-creation with users and partners?

HOW DO WE BETTER GUIDE AND SUPPORT OUR OWN SHIFT AND THAT OF OTHERS?

GET HANDS ON! Move into action—try building instead of talking. Imagining is working at the edge of understanding, where information is often scarce or nonexistent. The purpose of using visuals is to help us make meaning where none currently exists, and provide clarity where ambiguity reigns—it is an avenue to resolve some of the fuzziness all new ideas have. As we gain more confidence in the idea and move down the risk curve, we will invest more time and more resources in the visualization—but early on, we just want quick sketches and storyboards that make what is in our head available to others.

IMAGINE A SCENE AND INHABIT IT. Creating mental imagery and traditional prose writing are perhaps not so disconnected as we might believe based on our discussion thus far. Imagining is fundamentally about an innovator seeing another world and then describing it so that others can see it as well. The critical skill here, as with compelling prose, is in *conceiving* and *describing*. Architect João Ferreira argues that designers have much to learn from writers as they approach their visualization task. In both imagining and writing, Ferreira advises that designers focus on creating a scene: "the best way to master the principles is to understand that they are contained in the classic scene, and then practice inhabiting that scene."

"When a writer inhabits a scene," he continues, "he shows the reader something in the world. . . . There are things in the world that the writer can notice and point to. . . . The reader is there with the writer and is capable of noticing the same things if offered a clear view."[89] This goal of setting a scene is to allow readers to *notice* for themselves rather than pronouncing the writer's truth. That is what showing rather than telling looks like.

MOVE FROM THE ABSTRACT TO THE PARTICULAR. One of the primary jobs during Imagining is to give form to ideas, to render the abstract concrete. While we want to generate lots of ideas, and so start off abstract, these must be translated into something concrete if people are to pre-experience them. By making the abstract concrete in a believable way, you link your intentions to meaningful elements of reality. Don't forget to use all five of your senses wherever you can to make the particular emotionally engaging. Remember our baby—soft, cooing endearingly, smelling sweetly, and laughing that baby belly laugh.

EXPERIMENT WITH DIFFERENT APPROACHES. To short-circuit possible debate, have people build. Building to think is usually far more effective than talking to think—and a lot more fun as well!

Using multiple mediums—a journey map, a storyboard, and a flow chart—can help to unlock the details of a concept. Work individually first and then bring the team back together to share ideas once they have created their own initial images.

FIGURE OUT HOW TO SHARE YOUR IDEA IN A WAY THAT MAXIMIZES QUALITY FEEDBACK. Don't limit yourself to literal prototypes. Look for imagery that helps express an idea at a personal level. Start with the assumptions you need to test. Name the person you are designing for and walk in detail through their experience. Visualize multiple options and build these in. People are more accurate in their feedback when you ask "Do you like A or B?" than they are when you ask "Do you like A?" and they have to say "Yes" or "No." Multiple options help you move from interaction to genuine participation, whether you are in an information-gathering phase with potential users or a meaning-making phase with team members. Choice creates opportunities for co-creation.

REMEMBER SIMPLICITY. Often, the simplest methods like charts and diagrams can be more powerful in clarifying ideas and eliciting feedback. When faced with the seemingly daunting task of creating some sort of artifact, people tend to go into complex mode. Instead, make an effort to stay simple. The right details are important, but an overly complex prototype will make testing particular assumptions difficult and provide less useful feedback.

INVITE CO-CREATION. It's important to deliberately build empty spaces into prototypes to give people enough structure to have a coherent conversation *and* enough room that they feel like they can really bring themselves into your scene. Prototypes that look too finished discourage people from sharing openly what they truly think and feel. Instead, they are encouraged to make us feel better by telling us what they think we want to hear—that they love it (even if they don't!).

JUST DO IT! For those trained in traditional business methods, Imagining does not necessarily feel like a natural act at first. Our deeply ingrained habits and beliefs when we talk to customers and even colleagues, about the efficacy of telling people things versus showing them, even about the idea of "playing" with a prototype, really get in our way. Get ready to get nervous, and then go do it anyway. Here is some parting advice from our strategic planner who saw the power of making strategy real:

> My one piece of advice would be just to start. And have fun with it—especially for people who spent most of their careers in more structured analytical approaches to problem solving, this is a huge breath of fresh air. Embrace the quirkiness of it and use that as an excuse to break people out of their shells. If you're having fun, it leads to successful outcomes.

WHAT'S NEXT?

So now we have created our vivid and multisensory images of some exciting new futures—what do we do with them? We use them to Learn in Action.

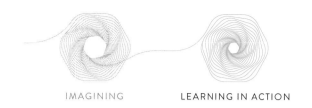

IMAGINING   LEARNING IN ACTION

CHAPTER 8

LEARNING IN ACTION

MICHAL

Michal was not sure what to do at this point. As his team reached the Testing stage, they were not finding it to be the same kind of inspiring experience that Discovery had been. The team had created and prototyped what he was sure was a winning product. At his design colleagues' insistence, he had dutifully taken his rough prototypes out to a few customers, despite his concerns about protecting the intellectual property at stake. To his surprise and dismay, the feedback they were getting did not seem to be validating the value of the new concept. The customers they talked with did not see the concept as a good fit for how they used the product. Michal believed that these users were being irrational—they just didn't understand and appreciate the value delivered. His design colleagues urged him not to be discouraged, to be curious about the data, rather than reject it outright. But the data was murky and inconclusive, and making a major pivot at this point was just too painful to even think about. He just wanted to move forward with his concept and get the job done. ■

As we arrive at the final experience phase of the innovator's journey—Learning in Action (LIA)—innovators experience what can be the most challenging of the six phases for managers like Michal. The *doing* part of LIA sounds reassuringly straightforward: the activities that make up this phase, like the design and execution of experiments, are well recognized and form the backbone of other popular methodologies, like Agile and Lean Start-up, as well as DT. The mantra "fail fast and cheap" is accepted dogma in many industries. Yet in no other aspect of DT do we see the tension between rhetoric and reality more obvious than here—and nowhere are the necessary transitions in innovators' mindsets more pronounced.

The enemy of learning is not ignorance—it is already *knowing*. It is impossible to both learn and know simultaneously, argues Tom Chi, cofounder of Google X. To make the necessary transition during the LIA experience, innovators must swap a lifetime of rewards for acting like they *know* the answer for the uncertainty and lack of ease associated with acknowledging that they *don't*. Fear, ego, discomfort and identity all get in the way. We love knowing we are right and hate risking being wrong: trading in the comfortable "allure of certainty" for the emotional costs of living in the uncertainty of what Kathryn Schulz calls "investigative doubt" is not for the faint of heart.

LIA is where the full force of what it means to *test* our own creations really hits home. We see Michal struggling with the most natural of feelings—attachment to the "baby" that he has nurtured throughout the DT process. Will he be able to "call his baby ugly," as one of the managers in our research described? Innovators face a challenge for which most of us are unprepared: detaching our egos from our ideas. Faced with the need to combat some of the most pernicious biases we talked about in Chapter 2, designing and conducting quick and inexpensive experiments in the real world turns out to be devilishly difficult for most innovators and their organizations. It requires profound changes not only in how they think and behave, but in who they are. It requires becoming a *learner* rather than a *knower*.

We also suspect that those most likely to be drawn to DT's human-centered front end may be the *least* likely to be drawn to testing—confidence in their ideas, a lack of time, and a desire to help as many people as possible all combine to make testing less appealing than creating. As one dedicated but harried government innovator explained to us:

> *In the optimal world we would do testing. But you're one person, working on a very specific case, and you're already convinced by the evidence that you generated so far. So you want to make sure*

that you maximize the outcome of our particular piece of work right now. And to say, "Let's take a step back and use it as a testing opportunity"— that's really a tough sell.

As a result, innovators are often tempted to bypass this final stage. Our research shows experiments to be the least used DT tool. Time and time again, we see well-intentioned but overworked innovators, thrilled with the ideas they have generated and already exhausted by what it took to get this far, moving into implementation rather than experimentation. That, we believe, is a very big mistake. In order to avoid making it, it is important to understand what the challenges in the journey to becoming learners look like and the obstacles they present to LIA.

LIA ACTIVITIES

- Surfacing assumptions behind ideas
- Prioritizing assumptions to be tested
- Identifying data needed to conduct tests
- Specifying disconfirming data in advance
- Designing experiments
- Using learning from experiments to iterate solutions

INVESTIGATIVE DOUBT

"Investigative doubt" is Kathryn Schulz's term for the attitude of doubt fueled by curiosity rather than cynicism. The doubt of cynicism kills creativity at birth, the doubt of curiosity fuels it. She defines "an active, investigative doubt" that challenges our beliefs and "inspires us to wander onto shaky limbs or out into left field; the kind that doesn't divide the mind so much as multiply it, like a tree in which there are three blackbirds and the entire Bronx Zoo. This is the doubt we stand to sacrifice if we can't embrace error—the doubt of curiosity, possibility, and wonder."[90] Without the humility of this kind of doubt, how can we hope to learn?

WHAT DOES AN INNOVATOR'S MINDSET SHIFT LOOK LIKE DURING LEARNING IN ACTION?

As innovators move into LIA, they must overcome the obstacles posed by fear and discomfort with ambiguity that accompany the transition from *knowing* to *learning*. Let's look at this shift in more detail.

LIA MOVES INNOVATORS . . .

FROM A MINDSET THAT . . .	TO A MINDSET THAT . . .
Needs to be right and avoids failure	Is willing to be wrong
Passes judgment	Adopts investigative doubt that seeks out disconfirming data
Looks for "proof"	Seeks directional guidance by triangulating data points
Thinks like a creator	Thinks like a scientist or investor
Has a deep emotional attachment to ideas	Attaches emotionally to meeting the needs of those they are designing for
Seeks to test the concept in full for "proof"	Treats ideas as hypotheses and tests assumptions

THE SCIENCE BEHIND IT

For most of us, as documented by volumes of research on human decision-making, none of this comes naturally.

FACING THE FEAR OF FAILURE. The fear of failure is deeply rooted in many of us, from our earliest days as school children. Stanford psychologist Carol Dweck identified "fixed" versus "learning" mindsets in the children she studied. She delineates the ways in which many of us have internalized the insidious belief that being smart means having the "right" answer.[91] As a consequence, we spend much of our lives avoiding new situations where we might make mistakes. Other psychologists offer similar findings. Professor E. Tory Higgins at Columbia has identified a preference for what he termed "prevention" (avoiding action to prevent the possibility of error) versus "promotion" (taking action to seek something better).[92] Kathryn Schulz also chronicles a litany of reasons why being right is so important to us.[93] She warns that the negatives associated with such certainty of rightness go far beyond just being proven wrong. They result in the loss of imagination and empathy. In fact, learning requires unlearning first.

HOW DO WE UNLEARN? Psychoanalysts have studied the phenomenon of "unlearning" for decades, believing it to be foundational to successful therapy. Unlearning old beliefs and ways of thinking and acting is a critical precondition for learning. As noted psychoanalyst Otto Rank described it, unlearning involves "illuminating the habits of mind and heart" that drive current behaviors, and is fundamental to all deep change.[94] Letting go of aspects of our past is essential to "letting come" a fuller version of ourselves, Rank argued. Organizational theorists, too, have studied what it takes to unlearn, arguing that it can entail a significant amount of emotional work, as individuals are invested in established ways of perceiving. Deep unlearning may surface confusion, anxiety or fear, while other negative feelings like blame, guilt, or shame may be necessary for the process of unlearning.[95] Unlearning is serious business and requires action as well as reflection.

LEARNING AND ACTION OCCUR IN TANDEM. Action, coupled with reflection, provides the most robust form of learning, and educators since John Dewey have argued for the primacy of experiential education. In what is likely the most well-known description of the process, learning theorist David Kolb highlighted a learning cycle with four sequential phases: concrete learning, reflective observation, abstract conceptualization, and active experimentation.[96] He argues that learners must pass through all four. Organizational theorists Kimberly Elsbach and Ileana Stigliani[97] have traced the ability of DT to provide a structured path through Kolb's four stages. Similarly, research on after action reviews (AARs) demonstrates that conducting and then reflecting on experimental results simulates a kind of retrospection which improves future performance. Reviewing both successes and failures is beneficial when understanding *why* events happen as they do. Research also suggests that learning from success happens less naturally and requires more motivation and effort to replicate than learning from failure, and that knowing the *general* cause of any outcome is less useful in improving future performance than knowing a *specific* cause—hence the importance of reflecting on detailed and explicit assumptions rather than general ones. "Effortful" reflection, in conjunction with external feedback, accelerates performance, research suggests. Reflection without external feedback does not, and the depth and focus involved in the reflection process matters to performance improvement.[98] Unfortunately, even reading the feedback signals, much less responding to them, turns out to be no easy feat.

AND NOW FOR THE REALLY BIG BIASES. Coping with fear of failure and successfully unlearning are stymied by an especially powerful set of human cognitive biases. As we discussed in Chapter 2, cognitive scientists (and more recently, neuroscientists) have filled libraries with research devoted to understanding the many flaws of humans trying to test their own solutions. Category 3 biases—the availability bias, planning fallacy, endowment effect, and hypothesis confirmation—are the most powerful (and well-researched) of all. Testing brings the tension between what we want to see (*people love our ideas*)

and what is actually true (*not so much*) into full relief. The source of this tension is surprisingly simple: we seek pleasure and avoid pain. Being right feels great, while being wrong feels awful. So our brain obliges by not upsetting us with disconfirming data—it quite deliberately tricks us into *not* seeing things that would create dissonance with what we *want* to see. Though helpful in surviving our children's teenage years, this creates big challenges for innovators trying to manage risk. We need help! Fortunately, we have it in the form of the scientific method.

THANK YOU, SIR ISAAC NEWTON. Sir Isaac Newton is known as the "father of science" for a reason—he first promulgated the scientific method. For many of us, the scientific method is likely just a hazy memory from around the fourth grade and is rarely discussed in organizations other than universities and research labs. It advocates problem solving through a formal process of hypothesis generating and testing. We have discussed the value of being hypothesis-driven in earlier chapters, but it really comes home when Learning in Action is your goal. But the kind of hypothesis testing done by scientists is different than that done by designers: scientists *discover* and designers *invent*.

SCIENCE VERSUS DESIGN. The scientist and the designer have many characteristics in common. Both have a repertoire of tools suited to the kinds of questions they tackle. Both are skilled at decomposing problems into manageable subcomponents without losing sight of the interactions among them. Both are adept at pursuing a sequence of "what if" and "if *x*, then *y*" loops, moving between the global and the local, managing the tension between the concrete and the "big picture." Both develop, over time and with experience, a sophisticated and selective search process that pays special attention to disconfirming data. But designers deal primarily with what does not yet exist—*what might be*—while scientists deal with explaining *what is*. While both methods of thinking are hypothesis driven, a design hypothesis is *prescriptive*—suggesting what does not yet exist, what we might do, rather than scientist's *descriptive* hypothesis about what is currently going on. Descriptive hypotheses can be demonstrated to be true or false based on data from the present. Prescriptive hypotheses about the future can never be "proved" true in the present in the same way that scientific principles can—until we build the solution and introduce it into the world. But managing risk requires *not yet* building the solution. So the best we can do to test design solutions is to surface the descriptive hypotheses that underlie the prescriptive ones. This avoids having to even build a minimum viable version of it. Instead, we first embody the assumptions about why we believe this solution should work, and test those—especially the most important "make or break" ones. This allows us to marshal evidence to convince important stakeholders that our particular "story" about the future is worth investing in.

STEPS IN HYPOTHESIS-DRIVEN DESIGN

1. Define the problem.

2. Gather preliminary data to make sure that the problem definition is robust and to allow construction of initial hypotheses about the causes of the problem (the descriptive hypotheses).

3. Develop a set of competing hypotheses about the causes of the problem (what if) and their associated solutions (prescriptive hypotheses).

4. Select the most promising hypothesis pairs for testing.

5. Identify the data needed to test them and design the study to collect it.

6. Collect the data.

7. Using the data, test the hypothesis. Is it supported or rejected?

8. Resolve any anomalies or disconfirming data by gathering additional data and reformulating hypotheses, or move to an alternative hypothesis to begin new testing, as necessary.

WHAT MAKES LEARNING IN ACTION SO HARD?

A FALSE SENSE THAT THIS FINAL STAGE IS OPTIONAL—WHEN THE DESIGNING IS DONE, THE IMPORTANT WORK IS OVER. This ties into the myth that the hard part of innovation is generating good ideas. But often, we see great design work that goes nowhere. As one of our interviewees reported:

> We did an IDEO project. It showed potential for application, maybe to do in four months what normally takes a year or more. It expanded our perspective and engaged a much broader group of stakeholders. But at final briefing, we just didn't know what to do with it.

DESIGNING AND CONDUCTING EXPERIMENTS IS HARD. Another myth is that idea generation is also the really creative part. But the design of experiments takes every bit as much ingenuity and creativity as the design of the idea itself. Resilience, discipline, persistence, flexibility and focus are all key. It is not easy to do, even for those committed to trying. Most of us simply have no idea what it means to design a real experiment. When we work with management groups, it is not unusual for half of the teams we are working with to fail to produce even the most basic competent experimental design on the first try. Instead, they produce partial pilots suffering from confirmation bias that are likely going to give them the findings they *want*, not the data they *need*. Or they create tests that take six months and cost five figures. Designing experiments that help us "fail fast and cheap" is a lot easier to say than do.

WHO GETS TO DECIDE? We talk about the importance of listening to the voices of those we serve. That comes pretty easily for most innovators during the Discovery phase, when users provide us with the raw materials to develop deeper insights and inspire new ideas about how to serve them. But when the time comes to let them actually decide *which concepts to move forward* and which to kill, it can feel like a whole different ball game. Honoring user voices instead of our own convictions, as Michal learns, gets a lot harder. Add in some hierarchy in the form of a boss who controls the purse strings and believes that he or she has the right to decide, and things get really sticky.

DETACHING OUR EGO FROM OUR PROTOTYPE. Designers are raised in studios and learn by critique. They design something and then make it public for everybody else in the class, including the faculty, to examine for flaws. Design students are trained to actively seek negative feedback. Over time and with practice, this enables them to detach their egos from their creations so that they are able to listen nondefensively to criticism. What matters, they learn, is understanding the underlying source of the criticism in order to make the decision whether to advance, iterate, or table the concept. Unfortunately, very

COLLEGE COFFEE CUP EXPERIMENT

One of our MBA students described his experience when a team of student leaders, searching for a replacement for disposable coffee cups for use by their classmates, set out to design and conduct an experiment:

I was blown away by the amount of thought that goes into conducting even the simplest of experiments. Our goal was to distribute 16 cups to volunteer users and collect their feedback on them over the course of two weeks. Once we had worked out the myriad logistics (Who is picking these up? At what time? Who will we drop them off with in the kitchen? Which of these are dishwasher safe?), we barely had energy left over to think about how we were going to collect direct feedback and observe the participants for the juicier ethnographic insights.

*It really is quite amazing to see the variety of feedback we got, even from such a concentrated group of receptive users. We began to see what attributes of the different products were spiking, both positively and negatively, with our participants. For example, we were unsure about how users would respond to lids, and it turned out the type of lid used greatly affected the way people use them. If the lid was awkward to drink out of, they removed it and set it aside. But then they complained when their coffee got cold more quickly and the puddle of condensation the lid left behind only further worsened their experience. Lids that were easier to drink from remained on the cups and the users were more content with the overall experience because their coffee stayed warmer for a longer period of time. Who would have known? I thought the most important thermal insulation was on the **side** of the cup. It looks like having a lid on top is more important. You wouldn't have learned that from a market survey.*

*We also learned firsthand about the importance of properly communicating **what exactly prototyping is** to **nonparticipants**. It turns out that many peers who weren't involved in the experiment were immediately cynical because they believed that we had to choose from one of the eight cups. We explained that we were merely using the cups to uncover the most desirable (and undesirable) attributes of a coffee cup. Amazing how that shifted people's mindsets. Isn't that often half the battle?*

*This kind of rich data would simply not have been possible if we went out and asked people, "What would the ideal coffee cup look like for you?" I have gained an acute appreciation for the importance of **making small bets** and **questioning your assumptions**. Can you imagine how disastrous it would have been if we had simply selected a cup and moved ahead on our own?*

few of the rest of us get this kind of training, so our ideas quickly become tangled up with our ego. I *am* my idea and my idea *is* me; when someone criticizes it, they criticize me—and make me look less competent. Inevitably, defensiveness creeps into the conversation and learning loses out to debating and defending. Detachment is hard to achieve. This is a well-repeated refrain among our innovators. As one offered: "I assumed that we'd be comfortable spitting ideas out and tossing them away, but it's been a bit more challenging since people are more attached to their ideas than I expected."

Ego involvement leads innovators to become passionate about their own ideas, rather than the needs the idea is meant to address. Having the support of shared and explicit design criteria, as we discussed in Chapter 5, becomes very important to achieving detachment. As another innovator noted:

> *This process of giving feedback to your own teammates is really difficult. Everyone came to the table with their ideas and many verbalized and indicated through body language that they were really attached to their ideas. So it was really challenging to say, "Maybe, that idea doesn't totally fit." In many ways, at those moments, having the design criteria really helped decide whether we should keep an idea or veto it.*

LEARNING IN ACTION IS OFTEN A DIFFICULT EMOTIONAL TRANSITION FOR INNOVATORS. This is not just because of bruised egos. At DT's front end, interviews open doors full of new possibilities that energize and inspire. In Testing, however, the work we do is just as likely to close doors, surfacing data that suggests we abandon or at least change cherished options. Confirmation feels good, and disconfirmation feels disappointing, no matter how much we try to focus on learning. Our heartwarming emphasis on the human beings we served in the front end must now accommodate more prosaic issues like execution and value capture. We must attend to other stakeholders, like value chain partners. The picture gets more complicated as constraints reenter the equation. The feel-good vibe that is so empowering during Discovery is simply not sustainable as we move into Testing. Having gotten so excited about immersing ourselves in the subjective human experience, innovators often feel they have been baited and switched when we pivot abruptly to the unemotional, detached process of experimentation.

SECRECY IS IMPORTANT TO PROTECTING THE VALUE OF INNOVATIONS. Most senior managers today, like Michal, have deeply ingrained perspectives on the importance of keeping information about any new invention proprietary. The idea of publicly sharing your great new idea—even with just a small number of trusted customers and value chain partners—makes them very nervous. Secret is good, public is not. In the networked economy, this way of thinking has been turned on its head, but old habits die hard.

WE LACK THE RIGHT METRICS. The data that innovators *have* is not necessarily the data they *need*—the metrics that are easily accessible are often not the ones that allow true testing of their hypotheses. Instead of simple measures of activity (how many did we sell?), we need deeper, mushier measures that test our assumptions (why did they sell? or not sell?). Frequently, they simply don't exist. As a result, innovators find themselves undertaking the taxing work of constructing bespoke measures and thinking carefully about *what* to measure *when*. It is a mistake to underestimate just how big a challenge this can be. Creating new measures is well outside the experience base of most people. Throughout their careers, managers are told to look to the "numbers" people when new metrics are needed. They are the only ones granted the privilege of making up numbers. Whereas front-end activities like ethnographic interviewing usually feel good after the initial awkward introductory period has passed, there is no similar corollary to constructing and working with bespoke measures. That feels like a risky and thankless task.

Even worse perhaps, whatever measures we use likely will give us data that remains inconclusive, as no single approach yields the kind of ironclad "proof" we are looking for. When we try to test the validity of something that does not yet exist, the best we can usually hope for is data that is *directionally* encouraging.

ONE STRATEGY ISN'T ENOUGH. It's already hard enough to set up an experiment, but to fully understand the depth of our users' feelings and experiences, we must triangulate our data. Researchers John Creswell and Dana Miller define *triangulation* as when experimenters "search for convergence among multiple and different sources of information to form themes or categories in a study."[99] Simply put, we need two or more sources of data to fully understand the "how" and "why" of our data. While this increases our confidence in our findings and allows us to go beyond surface-level results, data triangulation is time consuming. It can also create the daunting task of organizing and making sense of large amounts of data (remember Sensemaking?).

VALUING IDEAS OVER ACTION. Though we use the term design *thinking*, much of the power of DT lies in design *doing*. But so much innovation attention and energy—from crowdsourcing to hackathons—is about idea generation. This is a mistake, as one innovator explained:

> One of the things I've had to coach folks on a lot around here is we don't actually want your idea. For years, administrations have said, "We really value our employees, so give us your ideas." And then people would give the ideas and nothing would happen. . . . So then people would become frustrated—"You asked for my idea, I gave you my idea, but you didn't do anything with it." I coach

leaders not to do that, not to ask for ideas, but ask for the innovation—to act as opposed to just having an idea.

THE PURSUIT OF PERFECTION. The good may be the enemy of the great in theory, but in the reality of an uncertain world, moving people into action with a work in progress has many merits. Seeking perfection before actively experimenting is a bad idea. As one of our interviewees pointed out: "It's better to go through the process imperfectly than to spend all your time debating it. . . . You take what works and leave the rest, right? That's what's so lovely about it."

Inevitably, we must expect that some of this action will result in failure, as another noted: "We're trying to teach folks that it's okay to fail, and that we'll catch you when you fall."

WHY DOES LIA MATTER SO MUCH?

Despite the challenge they face, innovators need to persevere—for without the ability to iterate and learn in action, they will never achieve the kind of transformational outcomes DT is capable of.

LEARNING IS ABOUT MORE THAN PROJECT SUCCESS. Learning to learn is about a way of life, and deeply personal. It is the path to ongoing adaptation and change in our crazy world. The experience of LIA equips us with the motivation, structure and tools to make the difficult transition from knower to learner. Success in your project is valuable, yes—but learning to learn is priceless—a gift from DT to you that will keep on giving for the rest of your life. As longshoreman turned poet Eric Hoffer noted in one of our favorite poems:

In a world of change, the learner shall inherit the earth,
while the learned shall find themselves perfectly suited
for a world that no longer exists.

So press on!

YOU NEED DATA TO SUPPORT YOUR STORY ABOUT THE FUTURE. We work in organizations that demand justification for investment. The skeptics will not be convinced by anecdotal data, no matter how compelling. When we said that the purpose of data gathering at the front end of DT was inspiration, not proof, our intention was to free innovators to focus and go deep with ethnography rather than broad and superficial with surveys. But it wasn't a pass to ignore proof forever. We are not talking about absolute "proof"—we are talking about marshalling evidence in a rigorous way to support further investment. Without real-world experiments, the risk of scaling solutions that simply don't work—regardless of how good the front-end research was—is very real. The possibilities for error, even in a well-executed discovery and generation process, are multiple:

- Maybe we misinterpreted what we heard in our interviews as we mined them for insights.
- Maybe we interpreted correctly and got the insights right but then addressed them with solutions that failed to trigger the satisfaction of user needs in the way we thought they would.
- Maybe our solutions worked great for the small group we co-created with, but don't work as well for the larger group we want to address.

Discovery was about inspiring, not proving, but with so many potential sources of error (inspirational though they still may be) in Discovery, we need Testing.

LIA BUILDS CHANGE READINESS. Our research suggests that many of the most valuable outcomes DT is capable of producing—beyond just higher-quality solutions—rely as much or more on Testing than on Discovery. Foremost among these is facilitating implementation and change. Involvement in experiments does important work below the surface, actively managing the levers that accelerate change readiness. "Active experimentation builds community," Fred Kofman and Peter Senge note.[100] One of our favorite theories of change makes clear why involvement in experiments creates critical change readiness when we engage implementers. It focuses on just four factors: dissatisfaction with the status quo, the clarity and resonance of the new future, and the existence of a pathway to get there, all balanced against any perceived loss associated with the change.[101]

AMOUNT OF CHANGE = LEVEL OF DISSATISFACTION WITH THE STATUS QUO × CLARITY OF THE NEW FUTURE × PATHWAY > LOSS. During experiments, engagement triggers dissatisfaction with the status quo (as testers interact with users and experience their unmet needs, as they did in Immersion). It also forces them to clarify the new world—prototypes make the future feel real. Conducting real-world experiments requires translating abstract ideas into concrete action and insists that innovators specify the details of implementation in ways that focus on the pathway, not just the end point—What resources will be needed? What training? What are the way stations along the path? Cumulatively, these actors all encourage implementers to focus on the opportunity that the new concept represents, rather than the loss involved in making it, by highlighting its contribution to meeting the needs of those they serve.

It also changes the nature of their conversations with their colleagues. At Monash University Medical Centre, one of the physician leaders there described what he observed about the unexpected benefits of involvement in experimentation:

I am more and more convinced that the value of prototypes and learning launches is that they make concepts tangible and create a conversation space for engagement. Language is about the creation of shared meaning. This is achieved through conversations that establish trust, and that lead to commitment. . . . Design tools work on the conversation, and embody the nature of the commitments that bind us.

WHAT DO MVCs COMING OUT OF LEARNING IN ACTION LOOK LIKE?

As with previous aspects of their experience, as innovators become more comfortable and competent with experimental methods, they exhibit specific behaviors. We ask the following questions during LIA:

AM I...

- [x] Listening nondefensively to critique?
- [x] Able to recognize when my knowing is interfering with my learning?
- [x] Actively seeking feedback on new ideas from critical users and partners?
- [x] Exploring disconfirming data with curiosity, rather than rejecting it?
- [x] Able to detach my ego from my ideas?
- [x] Accepting imperfect data and moving on?
- [x] Designing rigorous experiments?

- [x] Using what I learn to refine ideas?
- [x] Identifying and gathering the data needed to test?
- [x] Clear on what kinds of experiments to do at different stages?
- [x] Thinking creatively about how to triangulate data sources?
- [x] Practicing a hypothesis-driven approach?
- [x] Focused on testing critical assumptions?

HOW DO WE BETTER GUIDE AND SUPPORT OUR OWN SHIFT AND THAT OF OTHERS?

KEEP THE STAKES SMALL AS YOU START OUT. The place to start overcoming the fear of failure and make unlearning safe is not giving pep talks about how important it is to take risks—it is reducing the level of risk within your control. Aspiring jugglers start with bean bags, not flaming torches. Stress and anxiety interfere with learning. Don't bring it on yourself. In order to practice LIA, find a real issue that matters but also creates a safe space to learn through trial and error. Tim Ogilvie, founder of Peer Insight, agrees with the advice offered by our occupational therapist to find a "just right" challenge, urging novice innovators to use the Goldilocks rule: "Don't choose something too big or an opportunity so small that people will just shrug and say, 'Why bother?' Aim for something just right."

START WITH EXPLICIT SURFACING OF KEY MAKE-OR-BREAK ASSUMPTIONS. Get clarity on the key assumptions to be tested first, then prioritize and test individual components (the likely failure points) before you even consider testing the end-to-end experience. Pay attention to identifying disconfirming data in advance. The true test of the presence of the new mindset is what happens when a test produces data that contradicts what you believe. Do you dismiss the disconfirming data? Rationalize it? Or say, "This is something I need to pay attention to"?

ALLOW TIME FOR IMMERSION IN THE NEW WAY OF THINKING. Ideally, teams need to sit in the same room together for a few hours every day. The people who do this for a living tell us that if 90% of an innovator's time is devoted to business as usual, it's unlikely to achieve the kind of mindset tipping point that successful LIA requires.

BUT KEEP MOMENTUM GOING! *Create a sense of urgency and need for speed.* Momentum is a precious commodity in innovation—hard to get and easy to lose. Set deadlines, however artificial, that require quick action. And then—*just do it!*

HOW FAST IS FAST ENOUGH?

Peer Insight, a thought leader in Testing, suggests creating a 100-day road map that moves through alpha, beta, commercialization/pilot, and scale. They believe that speed requires joint action on the part of an interdisciplinary team. PI frames the process as a team journey—a "path to enlightenment" and hosts two-day "frame storming" workshops to encourage teams to arrive jointly at a plan for what needs to be done. Assembling the needed decision-makers, usually 10 to 15 people, in the room together, they begin by circling back to the concept's job-to-be-done in the morning, then proceed to assumption surfacing. Following this, they take assumptions one at a time, and drag each to a test plan that focuses on "What do you know?" and "What don't you know?"

FIND SOMEONE WHO CAN MODEL THE NEW BEHAVIORS. This is a role that more experienced design thinkers can play. First they show, then they do it *with* you, then they coach you to do it by yourself. Expecting inexperienced innovators to succeed on their own without help offers few prospects for success. Leverage the people who *thrive* on experimentation to help those who are struggling.

CONSTRUCT THE RIGHT KINDS OF MEASURES EARLY IN THE PROCESS. Preparation for success during LIA doesn't start when the prototypes are ready for testing. It needs to start early in the DT process—as early as the creation of the design brief itself. If innovators devote attention to specifying what success looks like and how to measure it when they create their design brief, before even creating a research plan, good things happen—like gathering the necessary pretest data to compare to outcomes as experiments are conducted. As one team leader described the benefits:

> There's value in thinking about measurement sooner rather than later, in asking, "What does success look like?" When discrepancies in the definition of success are stark—this frames what is important to work on.

Emphasizing the importance of effectiveness rather than activity measures is also critical, as a leader at CTAA offered:

> We have to develop performance measures. You can't just say, "I predict 10 people will ride my bus." Instead, you ask, "What's my indication that something is desirable? What's my indication that something can be operationally feasible? And what's my indication that there's some buy-in from funders?" We adapt all that to our work.

Creating a scaffolding of a plan for what gets measured when is important. Doing this requires developing the ability to zoom in (be tactical) and zoom out (be strategic). Innovators must face the challenge of demonstrating the specific impact that sponsors desire and understand. Encourage broader views of what measurement means. Sometimes teams can even use a simple Likert scale with questions like "How frustrated was I before?" versus "How frustrated am I now?" or "How did this change my ability to help my team?" Assessing ROI often requires multiple components.

LOOK FOR SYMPATHETIC PARTNERS TO EXPERIMENT WITH. Because the objective is co-learning, it is critical to find a partner who is open and engaged in the idea of joining you in experimentation. Eventually, in order to perfect the recipe, you must figure out how to roll out the concept to a group of people who aren't trusted advisors anymore—but early on, you really benefit from a sympathetic partner. One way to do this is the creation of skunkworks, or finding partners in key areas like IT, in order to get to speed.

WHAT'S NEXT?

Perhaps the most pronounced shift in how innovators think comes as they finally abandon what the folks at Peer Insight call "the search for the gladiatorial thumbs-up or down" in favor of asking the question, "Have we learned enough to move on to the next cycle of experimentation?" Absolute proof is hard to come by when your goal is creating a new future. You will never know for sure until a new concept is scaled. But at some point experimentation ceases and implementation begins. You batten down the hatches and your idea moves from a work in progress into a work in practice, with a single-minded focus on implementing the new fully formed concept. Andy Grove, former CEO of Intel, described the cycle of divergence and convergence that successful innovation required as "periods of utter chaos punctuated by periods of intense single-minded focus."[102] The chaotic world of invention followed by the focused world of implementation. Those are the conflicting worlds that innovators inhabit, whether we like it or not.

CHAPTER 9
PUTTING IT ALL TOGETHER

Having completed our journey through the six experiences in depth and in sequence, let's review the path our innovators have followed, looking at how these experiences build on each other to reshape who they are as well as what they do, encouraging the development of new ways of thinking (mindsets) and behaving (MVCs) along the way.

IMMERSION lays the foundation for the journey, preparing innovators to think and act in new ways by raising awareness of the extent to which we all view the world, and others within it, through the lens of our own perspectives and experiences. By encouraging a mindset shift from egocentric to empathetic and from detached to emotionally engaged, Immersion motivates innovators to learn new skillsets around active listening, attending to bias, and focusing on opportunity.

A successful Immersion experience sets innovators on a journey of discovery about themselves and those they design for and with. It begins by building awareness of the blinders created by their own life experiences. In doing so, it opens the floodgates to new information and realizations about themselves and others. It brings valuable new data about the needs of those they are designing for and the deeper problems they face, along

133

Mindset

MVCs

IMMERSION	Mindset	MVCs
	Empathetic	Listens to understand other perspectives rather than to test own preconceptions
	Aware of personal biases	Sensitive to own biases and blinders
	Curious and personally engaged	Develops an emotional engagement and empathic bond with others
		Asks good questions
	Patient and willing to invest time to understand current reality before developing solutions	Stays fully present in the moment to the lived experience of colleagues and those being designed for
		Searches for areas of opportunities rather than solutions
	Critical of the obvious definition; treating it as a hypothesis	Probes deeply for root causes, unarticulated needs, and beliefs

with emotional engagement that motivates action in ways that traditional research methods cannot. By reminding them of their own humanity and that of others, it invites them to bring more of their authentic selves to the work.

But the Immersion experience also creates anxiety. Confronting such "otherness," their fear about getting the process wrong and insecurity about their own ability to be creative and collaborative, takes its toll on innovators. They are likely to become overwhelmed by the volume of their new knowledge, are unsure of what to do with it all, and worry that they will not be able to live up to this new-found sense of obligation to improve the lives of those they design

for. Some will get angry as a way of coping with the vulnerability they feel. They have lost certainty about the correctness of their own perspectives, problem definitions and solutions. At best, they emerge from Immersion more empathetic, curious and humble, but now need help figuring out how to translate what they are learning about themselves and others into better solutions.

SENSEMAKING takes over, helping to guide innovators in their search for meaning. By acknowledging the ambiguity of their task, and offering a structured approach to dealing with the cognitive complexity involved, it supports not only the innovators but the

	Mindset	MVCs
SENSEMAKING	Willing to step into ambiguity to achieve greater understanding	Controls need for closure
		Remains patient with iteration and search
		Distinguishes between observations and interpretations
		Summarizes key interview takeaways cogently and clearly
	Treats problem definition as a hypothesis	Gains more clarity on what is the most relevant problem to solve
	Clear around what is important to those they are designing for	Delves beyond the obvious and clearly stated needs to identify tacit ones
	Inspired that problems are solvable	Develops informed inferences that are actionable
	Persistent, willing to stay with their search and dig deeper	Questions the givens—norms, rules, and status quo
	Cognizant of the value of differing perspectives	Treats differing views as an opportunity to understand and learn, rather than debate
		Clearly articulates the "why" behind their own perspective to others
		Listens openly to those who disagree with their interpretations
		Challenges (productively) the perspective of others

collectives within which they work. The mindset shifts Sensemaking encourages equip them to deal more productively with the ambiguity and corresponding discomfort of uncertainty, fostering the persistence to stay with the search for deeper meaning. Meanwhile, new skillsets equip them with the ability to move forward amid the messiness—probing, iterating and challenging both their own perspectives and that of others.

In doing so, Sensemaking builds on the personal awakenings of Immersion to set the stage for the creation of both personal and shared meaning and purpose, strengthening the commitment to collective action. Individual innovators see, often for the first time, the power of leveraging diverse perspectives for deepened understanding.

Confronted with what feels like chaos and challenged to defend their personal interpretations of what the data means, some find it hard to stay present amid the turbulence, and settle for superficial insights. However, innovators who stay with it and successfully experience Sensemaking leave this phase inspired, with a new level of confidence in their ability to do this work and create better futures for those they design for.

ALIGNMENT takes over to cement and formalize the will and direction of the group. Through the mechanism of establishing design criteria, innovators jointly commit to a specific set of user-driven, human-centered aspirational qualities that an ideal design should meet. Innovators better appreciate the value of shared perspective taking, have developed trust in each other, and are more comfortable with surfacing, acknowledging, and leveraging difference. An accompanying skillset in the practice of dialogue equips the group with the tools that operationalize their capacity to learn together.

The source of anxiety during Alignment often relates to concerns about navigating difference, and the sense of threat that can accompany openly acknowledging and addressing it. Without the creation of a

	Mindset	MVCs
ALIGNMENT	Sees value in shared perspective making	Gives careful thought to structuring collaborative conversations
	Welcomes different perspectives	Attends to the rules of dialogue, like turn taking
	Candid and comfortable with productive disagreement	Focuses on issues that really matter, as expressed in the design criteria
	Feels connected and trusting	Listens heedfully and respectfully to others, ensuring that each feels heard
	Motivated to co-create and solve problems together	Able to make different perspectives visible to each other
		Willing to let go of own perspectives to be open to those of others
	Believes in the power of the collective as well as the individual	Works to achieve a shared definition of the problem that the collective has agreed to solve
		Aligns on a prioritized understanding of the qualities of the ideal solution, expressed as design criteria
		Contributes to the process of learning together

safe space and the development of trust, individuals may interact with each other, but not fully participate in co-creation—coordinating but not collaborating.

When successful, the cumulative effects of successfully navigating Immersion, Sensemaking and Alignment are transformational to both the individual and the group. They produce what Otto Scharmer has described as the three conditions for presencing powerful futures: shared reflection (on the needs of those they are designing for and with), shared will (with individuals bringing more of their authentic selves to the conversation) and a commitment to shared action.[103] If these are established *before* any attempts at idea generation, the likelihood of higher-order solutions emerging from the collective in real time is strengthened. They have built an innovation community that is like-minded, engaged and inspired to act.

EMERGENCE is where the careful investment in building awareness during Immersion, individual and shared meaning making during Sensemaking, and trust and a commitment to joint action in Alignment pay off.

Mindset	**MVCs**
Can let go of the belief in one "right" answer and understands the value of envisioning multiple solutions	Pursues multiple possibilities
Open to ideas built by many owners without ego attachment to own ideas	Does not develop allegiance to particular solutions during process
Confident in own ability to contribute	Actively engages in co-creation, looking for opportunities to build on the ideas of others
Willing to share authentic self and be possibility rather than constraint driven	Takes an active role in working positively, constructively, and collaboratively with group
Patient in search for higher-order solutions	Focuses on "What if anything were possible?" in idea generation
Suspicious of early compromise and "least worst" solutions	Explores nontraditional and unexpected ideas
Recognizes the importance of requisite variety	Stays in the possibility space despite time pressures and discomfort
	Controls the urge to compromise prematurely
	Demonstrates appreciation for the diverse perspectives represented within the group

EMERGENCE

Several profound mindset shifts, with accompanying skills, put the final touches in place for the creation of a safe, shared space in which a collective, staffed with the requisite variety of different perspectives and experiences, can see together new and better possibilities that none could see alone.

During Emergence, innovators display a set of mindsets and behaviors that are the product of what has come before:

- the patience and persistence to stay in the possibility space together without yielding to premature compromise or "least worst" solutions
- an appreciation for leveraging the power of difference
- a willingness to let go of the allegiance to one's own ideas
- an enthusiasm for embracing joint authorship of multiple concepts

Taken together, these maximize the probability that the portfolio of high-level concepts that emerge from this stage will be valuable enough to be worth testing, in the next phase of the process. Some innovators will have difficulty letting go of their investment in their own ideas. Others will be disillusioned that the process failed to immediately produce the magic "out of the box" solution they had hoped for. Many will be exhausted at this stage in the journey. But innovators who successfully experience Emergence become comfortable with co-creation and are better able to balance the waxing and waning energy levels of different team members as they explore "What if anything were possible?" together.

IMAGINING has the ability to re-energize the group. Innovators have a whole new set of skills to learn as they take on the challenge of translating their portfolio of abstract concepts into something that feels real—to the group itself, to those they are designing for, and to the partners whose support they need to move forward into testing and possible implementation.

Though aspects of successful Imagining, like innovators' understanding of the power of visualization and comfort with ambiguity and incompleteness, are rooted in their Discovery experiences, Imagining ushers in a very different set of mindsets and behaviors. In the same way that the new mindsets and behaviors cultivated during Immersion, Sensemaking and Alignment set the stage for Emergence, the personal and collective changes essential to successful Imagining prepare innovators for their final experience of Learning in Action.

LEARNING IN ACTION, though seemingly straightforward, challenges innovators at their core. Despite the progress made acquiring new competencies and perspectives, most still see themselves on a path where the ultimate destination is *knowing*. The realization that the process is one of *continuous* learning—that the security of knowing they have the right

Mindset

MVCs

Mindset	MVCs
	Able to capture, in their mind's eye, a vivid image of the experience a concept will create for users
Recognizes need to bring ideas to life by moving from the abstract to the particular	Translates what they see to others in ways that make a concept come to life for them
	Builds artifacts that bring concepts to life and allow users to "pre-experience"
Desire to show instead of tell	Translates ideas in a clear and compelling way from text to image
Sees visualizations as provocations to engage others in a rich conversation	Develops immersive prototypes that facilitate feedback conversations
Aspires to creating low-fidelity tests of key make-or-break assumptions, rather than the entire concept	Able to surface and prioritize assumptions to be tested
	Able to capture specific assumptions in a prototype
Seeks simplicity	Finds the trade-off between emptiness and vividness, using the right level and kind of detail
Willing to risk moving forward despite incompleteness of prototype	Actively invites co-creation, actively enters conversations with users and partners

(Left margin label: IMAGINING)

answer, as they once experienced it, is *never coming back*—can be depressing. The difficulty of the shift in mindset from knower to learner cannot be overstated. Without the preparation of the previous five stages, it would likely be unattainable to all but the rare Geoffs of the world (remember Geoff from Chapter 1?), those who exhibit little, if any, fear of failure.

Though learning has been a constant theme through each phase of the DT process, this phase feels different. Rather than the euphoria that often accompanies the inspiring collective learning of Discovery, learning during Testing is often painful and demotivating. Innovators are confronted with stark evidence that the creative possibilities that emerged from Discovery, and that they built out and captured so vividly during Imagining, are not nearly so compelling to users as they are to the team itself. They must accept being proven wrong.

Without profound shifts in mindset, and the equally challenging development of what are often entirely

	Mindset	MVCs
LEARNING IN ACTION	Treats ideas as hypotheses	Practices a hypothesis-driven approach
		Focuses on testing critical assumptions
	Attitude of investigative doubt that seeks out disconfirming data	Able to recognize when knowing is interfering with learning
		Actively seeks feedback on new ideas from critical users and partners
		Explores disconfirming data with curiosity rather than skepticism
	Seeks directional guidance by triangulating data points	Thinks creatively about how to triangulate data sources
		Accepts imperfect data and moves on
	Willing to be wrong	Listens nondefensively to critique
		Designs rigorous experiments
		Identifies and gathers the data needed to test
	Thinks like a scientist or investor	Uses findings to iterate hypotheses
		Clear on what kinds of experiments to do at different stages
	Emotionally attached to meeting the needs of those they are designing for	Able to detach ego from ideas

new skills around the design and execution of experiments, the investment made in the five previous sets of experiences may not bear fruit in the form of new and better ideas that work. This is a sobering realization during LIA.

STEPPING BACK to look across how the six phases work together, one inevitable takeaway is that, though the experiences cumulate in a powerful kind of gestalt when everything *works*, the consequences of a superficial experience in one stage dogs future success. If Immersion fails to produce openness and empathy,

Sensemaking will be superficial, Alignment is unlikely, Emergence is impossible—all of which will produce nothing worth Imagining or Learning (about) in Action. Sensemaking is similarly fundamental—without deep insights about the needs of those we are designing for, nothing that happens further down the line means much. Without Alignment, only those changes within the control of the individual innovator will happen. And Emergence—the most fragile experience of all—is reliant on the success of the previous stages and the preconditions they create to happen, and on what comes next to bear fruit in Testing.

There is a silver lining, however. Who we are as humans is not nearly so reliant on the gestalt of the cumulative experiences as the quality of solutions is. We change anyway—the *doing* involved in each experience helps us to *become* someone new and better—and each in different ways. Some experiences make us more empathetic and open-minded, others teach us to make sense of complexity and messiness, still others help us to work better in collectives—to value what diverse perspectives bring and to listen more heedfully to each other. Still others teach us how to use mental imagery to engage and inspire others in manifesting new futures or how to accept our own inevitable failures and to learn our way through them. Every one of these is a remarkable gift in its own right.

Each one also moves us in the direction of building capabilities to help us, as individuals and as a community, survive an increasingly complex, diverse, and uncertain world—and maybe even make it a little better in the process. Really, what more could you ask?

At this point in our discussion, we hope that we've convinced you that DT, despite the challenges of doing it well, is something worth investing in—whether personally just for yourself or on behalf of your organization or community. If we have failed at this basic assignment, you can close the book now and find some more pleasurable reading. Because it is time to layer in the complexity of real human beings (at least a simplified version of them) to explore more deeply what it takes to get ourselves and our colleagues literate in these powerful tools and methods.

And what it takes, we have learned, is different strokes for different folks.

PART FOUR
DIFFERENT STROKES FOR DIFFERENT FOLKS

HOW JOURNEYS DIFFER

In Parts 2 and 3 of this book, we explored how different experiences at each phase of the DT process potentially transformed our innovators, moving them beyond merely *doing* to *becoming*. This metamorphosis is not easy—we examined the obstacles to achieving the mindset shifts and the minimum viable competencies (MVCs) essential at each phase. In this section, we want to complicate the story we've told so far (sorry, readers!) and move beyond the general guidance we offered in those chapters, because different folks require different strokes. (Apologies if Sly and the Family Stone was before your time.)

Our research shows clearly that gaining DT expertise is not one-size-fits-all—our personal preferences play a large role in how each phase is experienced. Take the task of ethnography—connecting with a relative stranger and speaking intimately with them may be exhilarating for some and terrifying for others. Innovators' personalities shape how they approach different phases of DT, creating different starting

DiSC ASSESSMENT

Before we introduce the personas, you may wonder how we determined these four distinct characters. Our process involved hundreds of MBA students and professionals in DT experiences completing the DiSC assessment. For over a decade, we have used the DiSC, a reliable and valid leadership-profile tool frequently used in the business world, in our research on innovation and growth. It has consistently shown statistically significant relationships between DiSC types and the experience (and even success) of the managers and MBAs that we studied. Each of our personas associates with a DiSC behavior type, a "gut feeling" when faced with ambiguity, risk, and change. When we share information on their DiSC type, their responses tend to be amazement at the accuracy of its description of their preferences (Aha!) and enlightenment into how and why they—and their teammates—act as they do.

points and challenges to mindset shifts in each phase. If successful, we hope that design thinkers leave each phase of the process having reached a similar design mindset—but our experience tells us that they start from very different places. Sound daunting? No worries—we are here to help!

We have studied the different paths of four distinct personas: Driver, Influencer, Analyst, and Supporter.

MEET THE PERSONAS

DRIVERS have a preference for action and are comfortable moving forward in the face of uncertainty. They have no problem becoming the leader (even if self-proclaimed). On the downside, they are often impatient, both with the process and with their teammates, and may be seen as domineering—it's their way or the highway. They also tend to ignore disconfirming data.

INFLUENCERS are people people. They are persuasive and good at marshalling support for new ideas. They thrive on consensus—perhaps a bit too much—and may be reluctant to act without it. Analyzing DT's mass of qualitative data can seem overwhelming.

ANALYSTS are conscientious. They revel in data analysis, and can come across as skeptics. Often perfectionists, they find it uncomfortable to act without complete information.

 **SUPPORTERS** are the nurturers. Steady and agreeable, they are great team players. But they are conflict avoidant and sometimes wedded to the status quo.

Over the past several years, we have tracked learners in our classes in real time, asking them to share how they felt during each phase of the DT process, using a scale from 1 (Feeling lost) to 10 (Feeling fantastic). We have also administered the DiSC (usually at the end of class so as not to influence students during the course). When we look across all this accumulated data, at their comfort levels week by week, it reveals no single innovation journey. Depending upon their personality profile, people's journeys were very different. But within a profile, they were usually quite similar. The graph on the next page shows what our accumulated research data suggests about what the journey of each profile looks like.

It is important to keep in mind that these four personas are "pure" types—most of us have some blend of them. But even at a quick glance, you can see profound differences. Influencers (our *people* people) start and stay high, engaged, and enthusiastic throughout. All other personas enter the process with varying levels of discomfort (but for different reasons). For Supporters and Drivers, this evaporates pretty quickly as they get on board. Not so for Analysts, who may struggle mightily throughout DT's front end of Discovery, then rally (even soar) as Testing takes over.

ONE JOURNEY. MULTIPLE EXPERIENCES.

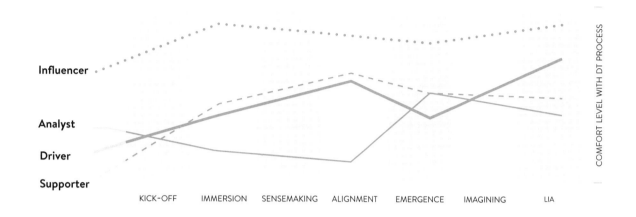

When you combine a mix of these personalities on a team (which we hope you will do), the real fun starts! Using these different preference profiles as our base, Part 4 will explore in depth what each persona feels, needs, and brings to the table. Each will experience peaks and valleys. Each one struggles and thrives, but in different phases. No one holds steady throughout. Acknowledging their differences and honoring their preferences, identifying who might struggle at each stage and leveraging those who thrive, is critical to moving both innovators and their teams forward and maximizing the impact of DT—because another finding from our research is that the more diversity of DiSC types a team has, the higher it performs. Having all four types on a team may not make the shared experience as comfortable, but it will, we know, produce better results—if we can tap into that power of diversity.

In Chapters 10 through 13, we get up close and personal with each of the personas, exploring in more depth the story behind this data—what each one thinks, says, feels, and does—as we track their individual DT journeys. We will examine in depth, by phase, the path of each of the four personas as they advance from *doing* to *becoming*. We will also offer tips on how to support each innovator persona as they go through their DT journey, alert learners on what to look out for in their own behaviors and reactions and suggest what leaders can do to help each type get past their struggles and experience DT to the fullest. Our goal is to provide insights to help individual innovators, their teams, and their leaders overcome the specific mental and behavioral traps that impede mindset change and competency development.

Throughout these chapters, we strive to communicate with different audiences. For innovators, we want to prepare you for the differing journeys you and your teammates might experience and perhaps validate some of the feelings you have throughout the process (in Part 5, we will work with you to create a plan to make DT work for you). For leaders and facilitators, we want to support you with tangible advice specific to each persona to help you to deepen the experience of all team members and reap the full benefits of DT (we will also work to create an organizational plan in Part 5). We will provide examples of coachable moments to give you the feeling of being a fly on the wall to otherwise very personal conversations, hoping that you might find them useful in discussions with your own team members. We will also share real-life quotes from the journals of our own learners.

Let's look behind the curtain to see what is going on in the lives of a fictional project team: meet Ana, the project leader, and her team members: Diana, Aman, Inez and Sam. We will follow them as they collaborate on a project journey, encountering the ups and downs of each innovator's experience.

Journey in Action

Ana gathered her team to discuss a new opportunity using the DT process to find ways for their nonprofit to better inspire a sense of community, engagement and loyalty among donors and supporters. A DT enthusiast herself, Ana hoped for more than just new ideas—she wanted to transform the culture of her team. Thrilled with the diversity of backgrounds and experience she sees when she looks around the table, Ana knows that this diversity makes teams stronger, more creative, and more successful. Paired with an innovative process like DT, her optimism for great outcomes is high. What Ana doesn't know (and can't see) is how each individual around the table will experience DT. As the team members—managers from donor-relations and communications departments, a client-relations manager, and a volunteer coordinator—introduce themselves, each is thinking and feeling very different things.

The manager from communications, Aman, an Analyst, is quiet and pensive. If he shared his thoughts, they might look like this:

> *I confess—this kind of ambiguity makes me nervous. I'm the "devil's advocate." I doubt everything and everyone except good-quality data. When someone wants to move forward, just know that I will likely demand proof. I mildly dread talking to strangers because empathy does not come naturally for me and I worry that these conversations will waste our time, so we have to be very methodical and careful. Is now the time to ask the 15 logistical questions I jotted down before our meeting?*

The client-relations manager, Inez, a natural Influencer, is beaming, sitting on the edge of her seat with muscles tensed like a teacher's pet who can't wait to raise their hand with an answer. Her hidden thoughts:

YES! We are getting the time and resources to really explore this issue with no boundaries and therefore endless opportunities for innovation. We have such a short timeline—we'll have to just jump in and adapt as needed. Hopefully we don't spend too much time on initial questions so we can start diving into the deliverables. We are going to rock this!

The donor-relations rep, Diana, a definite Driver, smiles smugly and ever so slightly rolls her eyes every time "design thinking" is mentioned. She is thinking:

Well, this is uncomfortable—no one around this table seems to know what our goals are for this project. How are we going to succeed when we don't really know what success looks like? If we are trying to boost contributions, we know how to do that already—just do what I tell you to do! Design thinking seems to take a lot of time, and I want to get moving. The rest of the team just doesn't seem to have any urgency.

The final member, Sam, the volunteer coordinator, smiles amiably as each member talks. As the Supporter of the team, he makes eye contact, but almost looks through the person, as if meticulously trying to "read" them. His thoughts:

I'm nervous about all this—this is a big responsibility that requires group cohesion, but these people seem unlikely to get along with each other. I predict some sticky points of conflict on the horizon. The donor-relations person seems awfully competitive and the other two may butt heads at some point. There are definitely some strong personalities here. If we all disagree, nothing will happen. Would an icebreaker help?

Sadly, Ana cannot read minds, so she is not privy to the radically different thoughts in her team members' heads. She selected them because each person brings strengths to different issues involved in the challenge, but she needs to figure out how to surface and leverage their differences in productive ways. In what is likely to be a roller coaster of a ride through the design experience, harnessing such difference is essential to the team's success—but challenging to pull off. Where to start?

Let's dive into the magic and misery of *difference*.

CHAPTER 10

THE DRIVER

DEAR ANA,

How well do you think design thinking will serve this project? Because I'll be blunt—I think it is a big waste of time. I agree that talking to donors is important, but it's always been my job to talk to them—what else are we hoping to learn? I don't under-stand why we need to drag this out over weeks when we could have conversations and move forward with some ideas (I already have a few) by next week. We've had two working sessions and the team still doesn't think we have properly "scoped" the problem. I know I'm not the most patient person, but the inefficiency is killing me. Can we speed up the pace?

— DIANA

t only makes sense that the Driver is the first persona we mention. Drivers are competitive, figurative "captains" who are driven by achievement and recognition. Comfortable acting in the face of uncertainty, their focus is on the end result, not the process, so sitting in the problem space collecting and analyzing data deflates them. They tend to be very direct, much to the discomfort of their teammates, and only trust others who are straightforward as well. In fact, if they had their way, they would work alone, or with subordinates to whom they could delegate tasks toward a specific goal set by them.

What they FEEL

Drivers approach DT apprehensively, with lower comfort levels. They question the need for such thorough investigation, likely already have solutions in mind, and somewhat dread the "team" aspect and fear that the pace will likely be slow because of it.

What they SEE

They see a way forward (note: their way) and are ready to act—now! This sense of urgency is often motivating to others, but in the early stages of design, where patience and a spirit of inquiry are required, they find it hard to contain their frustration.

What they HEAR

Drivers tend to hear themselves before they hear outside influences. The loudest sound they hear is their own internal clock ticking loudly, which never really quiets down—they have concerns about the pacing of the team throughout the entire project.

What they SAY

"I can have difficulties sticking with the pace of the team and need to be more patient when people require additional time to make a decision."

"I think a few of us were pretty adamant about doing that topic. . . . It was hard for me and others to divorce from our original idea."

A DRIVER'S JOURNEY THROUGH DT

Immersion

Drivers have a hard time getting through Immersion. They start DT confident in their own abilities and the wisdom of moving into action, and often consider themselves the leader of the group (even if no one asked them to be). When faced with a problem or opportunity, Drivers are adept at drawing on prior knowledge and sizing up the challenge based on what they already know. Since they believe they have already got a solution in hand, they tend to discount the need to listen with a beginner's mindset. Drivers fail to recognize that challenges have many layers to uncover, and are at risk of solving the wrong problem. They also prefer environments with a clear direction and a plan of action. Asking them to dig deeper into a problem with no defined end is daunting and uncomfortable.

Drivers are always concerned with pace. They define success by efficiency and action. Sitting in the question generates an underlying tension and anxiety that the team is losing momentum. Discovery takes more time than Drivers want to invest, tempting them to do "fast" research that validates their own thinking. They also harbor doubt that they will learn more by listening to others than what they already know. Lastly, Drivers find it hard to suppress the urge to think about solutions. When they see a problem, their natural instinct is to solve it immediately, often failing to appreciate how much they can learn from others—if only they listen.

What Drivers Say During Immersion

"I learned that it's OK that we don't know where we are going."

"The speed is glacial—really slow to me. I feel like it is lost time."

FACILITATOR TIPS

Keeping the start-up of a project moving briskly is critical to maintaining a Driver's interest. Their teams keep them engaged when they:

Avoid debates about vocabulary. Teams can spend precious early team time debating whether the process they are about to begin starts with a problem versus a challenge versus an area of opportunity. All that matters is that whatever the starting point is, it is not a solution masquerading as a problem.

Don't spend an extraordinary amount of time crafting a design brief. The design brief is a living document that can be changed over time. Cautious members of a team who want to perfect a design brief before diving into the project will frustrate a Driver.

Identify success metrics before diving into the project. Measurement is a significant challenge and can be tough to figure out. You may not know what the solution looks like, but defining success for the process is motivating to a Driver.

Coachable Moment

DEAR ANA,

I'm having doubts about this process. The problem we are trying to solve seems fairly obvious—it's not really that different than challenges we've faced before. Do we really need to spend more time hearing about the problem? Seems like a waste of time to me.

— DIANA

DEAR DIANA,

I know it is tempting to want to jump right into solutions. My guess is that you probably already have a plan for how to inspire our donors and volunteers and would rather go off with a small team and start working. It may seem inefficient to broaden the conversation when you see a clear solution. Am I right? The fact is that you have a unique ability to see the big picture, which is always valuable to our team. However, I think it is important that we pause and explore differences in the way team members see the problem. The reality is that we each are in our own box, shaped by the set of experiences we've had with our donors and volunteers. The way we escape our own boxes is to get a peek into someone else's. Through that glimpse, through pushing each other, we just might discover a possibility that maybe none of us saw. I know it feels ambiguous and maybe even unsettling now—but the diversity of our experiences ultimately holds the seed of real creativity. I am confident that we will learn something valuable that will change our understanding of the needs and dreams of our donors and volunteers. We need to slow down now to speed up later. Let's touch base during research to be sure we are probing deeply enough to uncover interesting nuggets of knowledge.

— ANA

Sensemaking

During Sensemaking, Drivers struggle with mindset shifts. Carrying over strong conviction in their initial assumptions and prior knowledge, Drivers struggle not to "hand pick" data to tell the story they want it to tell. It seems daunting and counterproductive to them to continue to explore and search for deeper insights. While they can recognize their prior assumptions and shift their thinking, they face temptation to find data to support ideas they brought into the process (even if interviews did not mention them or discounted them).

What Drivers Say During Sensemaking

"I can't believe out of all of our interviews, no one mentioned funding issues!"

"The more I look at the data, the less I know to be true."

"I realize that I made a lot of assumptions up front that aren't true."

Coachable Moment

DEAR ANA,

I'm not sure this is really leading us to the right answers. Most of what we expected to hear was barely talked about in the interviews. But I KNOW it is a challenge. Maybe we just didn't interview the right people? Or ask the right questions? Either way, I still think it's a critical point we should include.

— DIANA

DEAR DIANA,

I appreciate how difficult this new way of working is, so let's focus on what the tools of design thinking can do for us, what they are meant to do, and how to use them appropriately. We are using these tools to inspire better and more creative ideas—not to prove what we already know. And here's the rub. There is a steep learning curve. The more we do it, the better we will get. It's hard to let the data talk to us if we think we already know everything there is to know. If we are not learning anything new or inspiring, then we are probably not digging deep enough into the data. If we are not hearing things we didn't know before, then we have more work to do. That may be a problem with the team's level of curiosity and exploration, not the tools. Creative ideas don't come from mundane insights. We need to develop deeper, richer, more interesting insights about the donors and volunteers we're trying to serve. Those insights will open the door to more creative solutions.

— ANA

Alignment

Drivers fare better during Alignment. They begin to be more comfortable learning from others and value the deepened sense of understanding. Their challenge here, however, is their natural drive to debate. They love to compete, to find the "right" answer, and to feel confident about defending their perspectives. This can backfire, as their forceful nature may cause others not to share—debating a Driver takes energy and conviction others may not have.

What Drivers Say During Alignment

"I'm intrigued by the different ways my team interpreted the data, but there are so many ways we can go from here, and I'm still worried about what the solution will look like."

"I wonder if I drove the process too much."

FACILITATOR TIPS

Drivers need help managing their desire to debate while supporting their desire to learn from others. To help, facilitators can:

Establish trust and psychological safety on the team. Help Drivers avoid being so forceful that they deter teammates from voicing their thoughts. Talk through the difference between dialogue and debate, and encourage inclusiveness by creating group norms that stress that the purpose of sharing conflicting views is to gain perspective, not to win.

Shore up active participation by all members of the team. Drivers take up a lot of space in a conversation. Left to their own devices, they push the group forward, and they will do so . . . forcefully. Setting up protocols to ensure all opinions are heard will mitigate the pressure to lead (read: dominate) the conversation. Practices like turn taking are essential.

Coachable Moment

DEAR ANA,

This is the first activity I feel prepared for. While it still feels somewhat obvious what our path forward should be, I'm looking forward to learning from others, sharing my own thoughts, and then debating until we all agree. I just hope my team isn't turned off by my "direct" style of discussion.
— DIANA

DEAR DIANA,

This is the moment where all of our hard work in Discovery will pay off. I imagine you feel like a racehorse in the starting gates, ready to move forward and sprint to the finish line. The team will benefit from your leadership and your ability to leverage our team diversity. The most important thing to remember as we enter Alignment conversations with the rest of the team is that these conversations are fragile. It only takes a few cynical exchanges to shift the conversation and destroy the goodwill we have worked hard to establish. Let's try to keep the conversation grounded in the current reality of those we are designing for. Keeping their needs front and center will lead to a productive conversation.
— ANA

Emergence

Drivers can have a tough time during Emergence. Throughout the first three phases, Drivers have been collecting tidbits of facts and formulating relevant solutions in their minds. Their take-charge personalities have pushed the team forward with a plan and a goal, which can lead them to falsely believe that the rest of the team shares their priorities, attitudes, and beliefs. They come to a brainstorm with "surefire solutions" and expect quick agreement so the group can move into action. However, all members get an equal voice and often fail to rally around the Driver's solutions. This catches them off guard and can be deflating, causing them to lose enthusiasm.

Fully experiencing Emergence requires Drivers to relinquish strong attachments to their own points of view and let go. This is quite a challenge for them. Reminding themselves that they don't know everything and focusing on the value in learning from others on the team becomes key. Otherwise, their attachment to their own ideas can be viewed as domineering or even manipulative. There is no longer *my idea*, just *our solution*. Additionally, they must learn to accept that the best ideas are not the first ones generated, but that later ideas, in combination, can be more impactful.

FACILITATOR TIPS

Drivers run low on steam during Emergence. They can be defensive of their ideas and impatient to go with early ideas and move into action. To help, facilitators can:

Inject energy and fun into the ideation process. Drivers will bounce back quickly if the ideation process is energetic, fun, and positive. They will be drained if the team takes an overly long time to get organized or insists on engaging in unnecessary discourse.

Utilize a clear structure for brainstorms. Drivers like to work efficiently and don't have a lot of patience for excessive explanations or tedious details. Agree on a clear structure so that the activity is productive.

Brainstorm quickly and go for volume. By keeping swift and strict time limits to each round, Drivers will avoid attachment to just one, or early, ideas.

What Drivers Say During Emergence

"The design process is great, but it invites a lot more outside chatter than I expected."

"My 'focus and get things done' personality rubs some people the wrong way."

"I feel this is the most difficult part of the whole process."

Coachable Moment

DEAR ANA,

This process is really getting to me. The initial brainstorms sent us off in so many different directions, it's hard to know which way is up. And it didn't seem to produce the home-run kind of idea I was hoping for. It seems overly complicated to keep pushing to combine ideas for something better, when really it is just creating frustration. I thought I was creative, but now I'm not so sure.

— DIANA

DEAR DIANA,

I know you are eager to converge on solutions (and we are so close!) but you need to hang with it for just a little bit longer. Brainstorming starts with generating lots of ideas and not narrowing down to solutions just yet. Inviting others into the conversation helps our search for more-creative ideas. Otherwise, we may miss identifying new possibilities. We benefit as a team if we don't censor ourselves, if we don't worry about the quality of our initial ideas, and just get in there and generate lots of them. We can worry about sorting through them later—when we will be able to prioritize the great ideas over the not-so-great ones. Maybe we should even spend some time thinking about what we would never do? Kicking around some really terrible ideas may free us from worrying about what is a good idea and what isn't and help us invent a new future experience with our donors and volunteers that we can't even imagine today. Try not to worry about hitting that home run yet. Combining multiple ideas into concepts provides the magic that will get us somewhere we could never have predicted. So hang in there—we are getting there.

— ANA

Imagining

Drivers are usually excited to enter this after the discomfort of Emergence, because creating visualizations feels actionable and productive. While other personas may actively avoid or delay at this stage, Drivers appreciate the importance of managing risk and the role of prototyping in accomplishing this and illuminating the value proposition. They see the finish line in sight and are motivated to cross it with a successful outcome. The spirit of inquiry and learning from others is rekindled for Drivers during this stage. They may still doubt whether their solutions can actually solve problems, so they are interested in getting out into the world to learn from others' perspectives, share their own, and iterate as necessary. However, they fear running out of time (and the quick turnaround of testing) and their drive to complete the process may cause them to keep prototypes superficial in nature, limiting the depth of user feedback and causing the team's unsurfaced assumptions to remain hidden and not tested.

FACILITATOR TIPS

Drivers struggle with the need to be "understood" and the desire to be finished during Imagining. To help, facilitators can:

Prototype multiple options: Drivers may feel immense pressure to design the one correct prototype. However, exploring multiple solutions relieves some of this pressure by removing the all-or-nothing expectation and inviting a comparative and exploratory test of different concepts.

Provide structure: Drivers may resort to selling concepts to users rather than listening for accurate feedback. By providing templates, multiple options for prototype design, and clear direction on how to show rather than sell, facilitators can help Drivers actively listen and observe.

Reiterate a judgment-free zone: Drivers need feedback from managers, coaches, teammates, and users to validate their choices or spur a different direction, but they may feel apprehensive about receiving it. To get Drivers primed to accept such feedback, set group norms around framing hypotheses, discussing results without judgment, and celebrating good and constructive feedback. Practicing giving and receiving feedback will also lessen the Drivers' anxiety to "deliver."

What Drivers Say During Imagining

"It's very inspiring to see how real customers can immediately add value to your solutions by proposing concrete suggestions."

"Prototyping is a hard step. Don't overthink the process and keep it simple."

Coachable Moment

DEAR ANA,

I like the concepts we are developing, and I want clear validation that they are the solutions we should take forward, but I'm worried. Every time I try to make our idea real, it seems cheap and amateur instead; I don't think it does justice to what our solution could do. I catch myself talking on and on about it instead of actually building, and the person who is supposed to be exploring and reacting to the prototype is just focusing on my words. I don't think I am effectively prototyping at all.

— DIANA

DEAR DIANA,

I appreciate your desire to create the perfect prototype, but I don't think we have to have a perfect prototype. Remember—the feedback is precious but the prototype is not. We have a good idea of what it is we think we should create, so this is our chance to make something concrete and start engaging in conversations with our donors and volunteers to experience key elements of the idea so that they can provide us with meaningful feedback. Our job right now is to find out if we are interpreting our donors' and volunteers' needs and values correctly. We can bring that experience to life pretty simply with some great storyboards, which are just paper sketches. The storyboards will allow our donors and volunteers to imagine themselves in our new donor experience. We don't want to distract them with too many unnecessary details. Remember—we are still testing our assumptions about the value of this idea right now, and the storyboards will get us better feedback from our users exactly because they are rough—the roughness gives them permission to critique. Later, when we are trying to prove feasibility and viability, we will ratchet up the fidelity (I promise!) but right now, with so much learning to do, we have to keep it simple.

— ANA

Learning in Action (LIA)

With LIA comes new challenges for Drivers. As we discussed earlier, they struggle to detach from their own ideas and can get defensive when receiving critical feedback. During experimentation, when a solution "fails," it can be difficult for Drivers to let it go and start again. They are frustrated and see the process as a waste of time, and more importantly, see failures of solutions as personal failures. As a result, they may be tempted to "cherry-pick" testing subjects that will yield favorable reactions or "sell" rather than listen to feedback.

What Drivers Say During LIA

"I struggled to stay detached from ideas and show no preference from one to another, even as I tried to present them objectively."

"Had I not jumped into this role, I believe my group would have continued to discuss and never agreed on a final deliverable."

Drivers can see the end in sight and can be so focused on getting there that they stop learning. To help, facilitators can:

Insist on a minimum number of experiments: While the ideal situation would be to test solutions on as many subjects as possible, enacting a minimum creates a "task" that is not optional. Drivers need to feel that this is a required component of the process.

Put "learning" first: When analyzing and discussing results from experiments, Drivers may get caught up in whether a hypothesis "failed" or "succeeded." Instead of such all-or-nothing language, frame the conversation as "What did we learn?" and provoke discussion on more granular discoveries. If an idea does meet with user enthusiasm, dissect why to capture possible learning that can help shape future ideas.

Engage leadership: Drivers may be scared to pivot if they feel it will reflect poorly on them with the boss. Whether it is building no-risk experimentation funds into the budget, inviting leadership into the testing process itself or finding other ways for them to publicly champion the team's testing efforts, Drivers will appreciate the attention from leaders while also feeling permission to learn from what works and what doesn't.

Discuss plans to pivot up front: Drivers have difficulty letting go of failed solutions partly because they cannot imagine starting over. Take some time before LIA to discuss what the team will do if solutions are not supported. Providing a blueprint for the pivot will make it easier for the Driver to let go.

Coachable Moment

DEAR ANA,

Today we pulled the plug on one of our solutions. While some results were positive, it's not compelling enough for an investment long term, which is beyond disappointing. This solution felt so right to me. To say I am frustrated is an understatement. What do we do now? Was this all just for nothing?
— DIANA

DEAR DIANA,

*It is frustrating to pull the plug on a favorite idea—one that seemed so good, but that our users just didn't like. It might surprise you to hear that I take this news as a win for the team. Why? We avoided a potentially very expensive investment in the wrong idea. Failure is an inevitable part of innovation, but **expensive** failure doesn't have to be. The process worked. This one wasn't a good bet. But it is just one possibility in our portfolio of opportunities. Did you know that the most successful venture capitalists in Silicon Valley only have a success rate of 1.7 investments for every 10 investments they make? To find a few great ideas, we need to have an inventory of options. The lessons that we learned will not be wasted—they will be taken to our next project. We led with confidence and curiosity and found out what didn't work. That is a positive step forward to figuring out what does work, which is success in my book.*
— ANA

WRAP-UP

Drivers face a set of challenges they experience that can persist throughout the process—fighting their own forcefulness and egos and testing their patience. But Drivers bring great value to the team as well. They are confident and goal-oriented, motivated to find great solutions, and willing to act in the face of the unknown. They test their peers and strengthen everyone's voices in the process. Their debates provide necessary challenges to teammates' assumptions. When others lose steam, they provide a pick-me-up for the Testing process. DT would not be the same without Drivers, and Drivers have so much to learn from DT. In our experience, they come to appreciate and value DT as a new way to solve problems.

The next persona seems more of a "natural" with DT, but still faces struggles of their own. Let's get to know the Influencer.

CHAPTER 11
THE INFLUENCER

DEAR ANA,

I have to say, I am so excited we are taking this approach to solving our problem. Numbers don't lie, but they don't tell the full story either, and I am ready to fill in the gaps between what we think we know and what the donors actually feel. I think the greatest strength of our team is how different we are—I have never worked with a team with such diverse representation and backgrounds. This will be a valuable asset as we steer toward new ways of thinking, with the bonus that they are all great people. I'll concede that it is challenging not to jump to solutions, but I keep telling myself that sticking to the same knowledge will yield the same results, and we need change. I've found the premise quite freeing—where normally I am expected to have all the answers up front, design thinking flips the expectation to forget what I know and relearn. I'm ready to take it all in.

— INEZ

nfluencers are the quintessential *people* people. Less focused on the task and more focused on human interaction, they are the most naturally inclined of all personas to the DT process. They are talkative and social, interactive, empathetic, and generally agreeable. They can carry a conversation with anyone and create a bond of trust quickly with relative strangers. They thrive in the exploratory stages of design (where connecting with stakeholders is key) but they struggle with more analytical tasks (and would rather choose gut feelings over data analysis).

What they FEEL

Influencers are the most comfortable members of the group throughout the whole journey, but their confidence ebbs and flows. Influencers are excited initially by the promise of deep human interaction and sense of purpose. For this journey, they are ready to go!

What they SEE

Influencers see the possibilities for change and their optimistic mindset drives innovation forward. Their affinity for people extends to their teammates and they truly see the value of diverse perspectives.

What they HEAR

Influencers are energized by the users they serve and could talk to them for hours trying to understand all the nuances in their lives that might result in better insights. They are equally energized by team discussion as a way of deepening their understanding. They like external praise (from teammates, leadership, or anyone, really!) to know they are positively impacting others' lives.

What they SAY

"It's great to see that we can work well together. If people disagree, we do a good job talking it out, agreeing on a decision, and moving forward."

"Something I really appreciate is how passionate my teammates are—they genuinely care!"

"I learned that many times I interpret things differently than others, and I can very much benefit from working in a group, hearing others' perspectives and sharing my own."

AN INFLUENCER'S JOURNEY THROUGH DT

Immersion

Influencers embrace Immersion more naturally and enthusiastically than others because they already start in the most optimal states of mind: they are curious, optimistic, and, above all, excited to learn from the experiences of others. In a phase where others are hesitant, dubious, and fearful of the unknown (and of talking to others), Influencers can provide the nudge to *just start*. They are enthusiastic and can be counted on to quickly assess a problem space, set a big-picture vision, and guide the team into an appropriate scope. Conversely, Influencers are so ready to jump in that they may not recognize the struggles their team-mates may be facing and therefore may not recognize

What Influencers Say During Immersion

> "I actually love the pace—being 'forced' to just make a decision and keep moving works well with my style."

> "Interviews with target consumers are incredibly insightful because they help you reframe a problem in a way that is customer-centric and more tangible."

the necessity for their leadership. Giving them the permission (and the responsibility) to informally lead the team during data gathering will elevate all team members to get past personal barriers and get closer to the mindsets needed to experience Immersion.

FACILITATOR TIPS

It may seem unnecessary to coach Influencers during Immersion, but there are still ways they can improve their own experiences and those of their team. To help, facilitators can:

Leave space for interpretation: Influencers need space to explore and dig deeper into the problem space. A strictly defined problem will stifle their perceived permission to push boundaries.

A defined research plan: Influencers have a natural curiosity and affinity for people. Without a defined scope and plan, their ethnography can follow tangents that are not aligned with the project.

Offer templates to share processes: Influencers move swiftly and may lose the attention of those who cannot keep up. Providing structure to document processes will allow them to bring others along for the ride effectively.

Coachable Moment

DEAR ANA,

After deciding the scope of our challenge, it is so re-freshing to speak with those who can bring it to life. It is fascinating to hear the emotions, the experiences, the burdens, and the motivations they express. At first, I was worried about getting all the interviews set (because they could have all said no . . .) but the first interview felt just like a conversation, and the rest have been the same. If I could, I would do all of the interviews. It's really interesting to me how hearing their accounts surfaces the many biases my team and I brought into the project. We are lucky to learn from them.
— INEZ

DEAR INEZ,

I love your energy and enthusiasm for the project. I bet you could do all the interviews for the entire team and do them with a depth of understanding that would be incredibly valuable to our work. And . . . I think the other team members would probably let you do all of them if you offered. But our goal is not simply to conduct great interviews, it is for everyone on the team to experience a deeper immersion into the lives of our donors and vol-unteers. I want our team to be more aware of their own biases and blinders, to truly listen to understand and to develop an emotional and empathetic bond with our supporter base. The team won't achieve that if they don't try to do some of the research themselves, even if it is not done as well as you might do. Now, is research going to come as easily to others as it does to you? Not likely. But that's okay, because we are bringing an enriched way of working into their world. Perhaps you can partner with team members who are less comfortable and serve as a role model. I think it will be important to recognize that as we begin to incorporate this way of working, we're all moving in the right direction and that is enough.
— ANA

Sensemaking

Influencers maintain their optimism and empathy from Immersion, creating the greatest initial opportunity for transformative experiences. They continue to be driven by the shared experiences of the interviews—the feeling, the emotion, the shared perspectives, the vulnerability—and recognize that there is much more for them to learn. Influencers actively let go of prior assumptions and prioritize users' pain points to drive decisions, even if they're in uncharted waters, and they are excited about the many directions the data could lead them in. Their biggest struggle is deciphering which data is most relevant or most meaningful; it is hard for them to "cut" any of the users' experiences, especially independently from their teammates. They also are inclined to keep interviewing, not out of fear of not having enough data, but because they are gen-uinely interested in hearing the experiences of others.

FACILITATOR TIPS

Generally, Influencers appreciate ambiguity and seek the stories the data may tell them. However, they run the risk of getting overwhelmed by the sheer volume of data to decipher. To help, facilitators can:

Use human-centered tools to help frame insights with emotions: Influencers are motivated to catalyze change when insights are led from the heart, not the mind. They need to feel very familiar with the deep needs of the people for whom they are designing. Tools that include the users' challenge, the struggles they face, and potential sparks or themes that emerge, such as personas, journey maps, and story frameworks, motivate Influencers even when the interviews end.

Don't skip the solo act: Influencers carry over so much energy from Immersion, and may want to skip the independent exercise of finding insights and go straight to the group chat. This is partly because they are drawn to conversation with others, but it also masks their discomfort of sitting with the data and deciphering its meaning on their own. However, Sensemaking requires all members to sit individually with the data and create their own perspectives first before meeting with their team. That is how we ensure divergent thinking. Ensuring integrity in this phase using explicit processes and norms will help Influencers work with their team to find deeper meaning in the next step.

What Influencers Say During Sensemaking

"How do we know when we have enough data? Too much data? Do we really have all we need to move forward? Right now, this data overwhelms me a bit."

"The insights exercise is incredibly helpful because it forced me to take the time to more critically assess the results of the interviews and think about their implications."

"The interviews really brought to life the journeys of our clients. There were so many parts of their experience that remained concealed until now."

Coachable Moment

DEAR ANA,

After hearing all of the personal strengths and struggles of people, it is hard to consolidate that down into neat little insights. However, it's such an exciting puzzle, sorting through the many conversations and finding the ways people are connected in their strengths and struggles. I love that every time I read a note, I can remember exactly what it was like in the interview, the emotions felt by the users. My notes still seem to come alive, and only the insights can tell us how to move forward. I wish more of my teammates felt the same way. They seem to want to argue over every point!

— INEZ

DEAR INEZ,

I know that you can see the next horizon in front of us and you are eager to align on crisp, neat insights. I am looking forward to that moment myself. But we are not there yet as a team. Some of our team members have a low tolerance for ambiguity and the smallest doubt can stop them from seeking out new lines of inquiry. They may find it hard to explore new places and new questions when they lack the creative confidence to do that. They find it difficult to concentrate when there is a possibility that the process seems inefficient. But slowly, we are changing the nature of our team conversations. It is easy to fall into debate mode as a team—am I right? Someone has an interpretation of the data, they pitch it to someone else on the team, that person has their own idea, so they then pitch that new one back to the first person. Everyone listens with their own desire to find faults in everyone else's ideas so that they can establish the superiority of their own idea. We get locked in this kind of paralyzing debate where no one is able to do what they're supposed to do, which is to figure out how to find a higher-order insight than anyone brought into the room. And that's what I think some of the design tools can allow us to do. I think, ultimately, that the most strategic impact will be a shift in the conversation itself. We are peeling back from the politics and the competing priorities that everyone has and finding out what is real that we have to deal with as a team. We are still aligning on the important questions we should be asking. But the investment we make now in grounding people in the current reality will increase the likelihood that we align on a new experience for our donors and volunteers. The team needs your help to work through all that!

— ANA

Alignment

Influencers fare pretty well during conversations around convergence, though their comfort level drops from the high levels they experienced in Immersion. They love conversation, so as long as the conversation doesn't get too argumentative, they are excited to participate. However, teams often face their first struggle here, and Influencers can feel challenged by team dynamics and others' need to clarify details and data. Since the insights created in Sensemaking are directly correlated with the lives and emotions of the users, they may feel especially challenged "letting go" of certain insights about which they feel strongly but that may not be deemed pertinent by the group. Fortunately their resilience and the value of insights produced keeps them motivated and encouraged. Alignment is a team sport, and no one gets more excited by team synergy than Influencers. They are the motivators, placing priority on encouraging and involving all team members and bringing energy and fun, which helps take some of the stress off other team members when the conversation gets heated or engaged in debate. Their relative comfort with ambiguity makes them more willing to trust their intuitions and make the creative leaps required during Alignment, and in the process, they increase their teammates' capacity to jump as well.

What Influencers Say During Alignment

"I love my team! Absolutely positive. I mean, the effort each one of us puts in to understand each other and where each person is coming from is really great."

"Though we did have some dominant personalities, getting everyone to eventually agree was possible."

FACILITATOR TIPS

Though Influencers are naturally inclined to the mindset shifts necessary for Alignment, they still face struggles in this team-based activity. To help, facilitators can:

Organize data so that it yields more team discussion: Influencers place high emphasis on learning from their teammates and they could get overwhelmed trying to digest all the diverse perspectives of their teammates. Making data concrete using Post-It notes, frameworks, and gallery posters helps Influencers capture the various perspectives of the group in a way that ensures team participation and visually maps the team's thinking.

Welcome questions: Influencers will be the first to acknowledge that the process of Alignment may actually yield more questions, not less. They may be torn between further exploring the problem space and appeasing their team members who want to move on. Encourage the exploration of such questions by restating the nonlinear nature of DT and the need to properly determine the problem for any solutions to work.

Coachable Moment

DEAR ANA,

I'm excited to hear the insights that resonated with my teammates. I know my mind is going in a million directions already, so it will be nice to hear others' thoughts as well. The pain points of our users are so intense. . . . I really hope we are able to agree on how to most effectively meet their needs.

— INEZ

DEAR INEZ,

Philosopher Isaiah Berlin wrote an essay more than 50 years ago titled "The Hedgehog and the Fox." In the essay, he described the world's greatest thinkers as either hedgehogs—people who saw the world through the lens of a single idea—or foxes—people who gathered as much information as possible and combined it and recombined it to get to useful insights. I think you know where I am going with this, which is to say you are a powerful fox on our team. Your ability to sniff out useful nuggets of knowledge and combine that with things you already know takes your thinking to a higher order of understanding and the entire team benefits. You are able to spot patterns and make meaning where other members of the team are struggling to make sense of the data. As we start to dig deep into the data and align as a team on our insights, it will be important to remember that curation of the data will keep the conversation on track. We have a lot of great data, but it can become easily overwhelming to the rest of the team with too much data.

I know all of the data is interesting to you (it's interesting to me too) but we will lose the rest of the team in all the detail. We want to manage a healthy creative tension on the team between too much optimism and too much anxiety. We can't respond to all of the data, so I recommend that we figure out how to curate the data so that clear priorities emerge.

— ANA

Emergence

Again, Influencers tend to thrive in this phase. Never one to turn down a good brainstorm, Influencers can't wait to finally share their gift for idea generation. To them, each and every solution is an opportunity to improve the lives of their users, so they are open to all ideas that could make that happen. They do not push their own ideas for the sake of competition, especially when others are better fits for meeting the design criteria. A challenge, when unchecked, is that they get so excited about their initial ideas that they rush to move forward, leaving minimal opportunity for higher-order solutions or co-creation to occur. This occurs unintentionally because Influencers are likable and easily build rapport with the team; they are valuable leaders because they are quick to improvise and know how to motivate team members to take action. This ignites a more rapid pace, but sometimes teams need to slow down the process to allow stronger solutions to emerge.

What Influencers Say During Emergence

"I loved hearing everyone's unique brainstorm ideas—it's crazy how different people took the prompts different ways, ways I would have never imagined on my own."

"We seemed to be hitting a creative wall for concept design, so I turned on some hip-hop and the mood in the room transformed."

Coachable Moment

DEAR ANA,

I find I have to restrain myself in ideation. It's so fun to let my creative juices spill out all over the table. However, I felt the other members of my team didn't share my enthusiasm. Some barely participated, which I suppose is fine because we have a surplus of ideas covering the wall. Still, it felt a bit one-sided.
— INEZ

DEAR INEZ,

Ah—to be so creative! I know you have probably already come up with lots of new ideas. You can't help yourself because idea generation is so natural to you. But I think we are just getting started. I usually expect the first few brainstorming rounds to be a data dump of obvious ideas

---

FACILITATOR TIPS

For Influencers, the environment of ideation is fun and familiar—so much so that they may speed through and miss out experiencing. To help, facilitators can:

Use brainstorming to build trust and engagement: Generating ideas is so natural for an Influencer that if not careful, they will brainstorm alone for the team. While other team members might initially be happy to let them take the brunt of ideation, the co-creation required for all to experience Emergence doesn't happen. Additionally, allowing Influencers to dominate ideation misses an opportunity to build trust and creative confidence among all members.

Move swiftly from brainstorming to concept development: Ideation is high energy, so if too much time lapses, Influencers lose energy and enthusiasm. They also might get distracted and run with early ideas before higher-order solutions can form.

Utilize forced-connections exercises: Influencers come up with great ideas right from the start, but if they are not forced to reach for higher-order solutions, they likely won't. Forcing the combination of otherwise disconnected ideas pushes their creativity.

before we get everyone comfortable with brainstorming. The key to keeping our team motivated in brainstorming is speed, so I think we were smart to cut the session short when it looked like some of the team was starting to fizzle. Brainstorming is exhausting (not for you, I know!) and I think we risk getting diminishing returns as fatigue grows. The real magic will start happening when we start to shape all of those ideas into bigger concepts. That work is time intensive and does not rely on speed. It's so easy to fall in love with the first few ideas and stop creating, but it's usually the latter concepts that are the best ones. The team will benefit from a little diversion and will come back refreshed and recharged. We are on the right track. Let's not rush the concept building.
— ANA

Imagining

After experiencing Emergence, Influencers risk slowing down (mostly because they have been so energetic throughout the entire process, and it's hard to maintain that stamina). Their second wind comes while getting to really dive into how a solution would transform users' lives. Influencers are driven to create visualizations that elicit deep thoughts, emotions, and physical responses, but they don't need to reach perfection. However, they place a lot of pressure on themselves to create something useful and impactful to the users. Without coaching to guide Influencers in focusing first on key assumptions, they may try to test the whole concept at once, which may overwhelm them. Influencers likely have strong ties to their ideas because they are able to imagine (at a deep level) the impact a solution could have on the lives of the user; this connection may make it initially challenging to invite feedback during LIA. But they give their team encouragement to stay motivated and engaged, even when a concept is complex and ambiguous.

What Influencers Say During Imagining

"It's important to not be married too closely to your ideas—getting feedback on prototypes is a test of will."

"I was defensive, but it taught me to listen better next time."

"Hearing others validate our solutions is so rewarding. Knowing it could really make a difference makes the whole process worthwhile."

FACILITATOR TIPS

Influencers feel deeply connected to the user, potentially leading to overconfidence in their solutions and a heightened sense of pressure to deliver. Inviting space for assumption testing is a critical reality check to ensure solutions truly respond to what the user needs. To help, facilitators can:

Ease in gradually: Imagining is a marathon, not a sprint. Influencers may feel so excited to share their solutions that they combine too many components into their prototype, which ultimately may confound any initial assumption testing. Instead, advise teams to test one or two assumptions per prototype; this will help keep Influencers on target to receive useful feedback to their design.

Level expectations: Influencers may feel pressure to create the most novel, creative solutions. Provide reminders that innovation does not need to be novel to be valuable.

Coachable Moment

DEAR ANA,

I really love our solutions—I think they respond to so many of the needs we heard from users during interviews. However, as I try to think through them in full detail, I realize there is more that I don't know about the user than what I do know. It's neat to see the various ways our team "sees" these ideas become real, but it's also confusing—which way is best for the user? My other concern is, are they real enough? Do they have enough detail to accurately test?

Lastly, I'm worried they aren't really that new or exciting. In fact, many details involve the way things exist for the user right now, just with some minor changes. I just worry that people will question our ability to create something meaningful if it mostly keeps things the same.
— INEZ

DEAR INEZ,

I know you care deeply about the needs of your user, which is so valuable, but you are right—there is a lot more that you don't know. This likely feels like a burden to you, this pressure to be totally in tune with what people need. Luckily, this phase is about recognizing these assumptions to ensure that we are driven by what we know, not what we think we know. Bringing ideas into reality requires many iterations and considerations from multiple viewpoints. No one expects perfection. Speaking of perfection, you likely are thinking: Will a less-than-perfect visualization of a concept give us valuable information? Yes! The most successful prototypes we can build will be somewhat unfinished—they leave room for interpretation by users. We want our prototypes to have enough substance to allow for interaction and reaction, but ones that look too finished or too perfect might have the opposite effect. If we leave them unfinished, our donors and volunteers will complete the story in a way that makes sense to them, allowing us to learn.

— ANA

Learning in Action (LIA)

For the first time in the DT process, Influencers struggle with the mindsets necessary to experience the impact on themselves as innovators. LIA proves challenging for Influencers because they take great pride in delivering results for people, and they have a hard time letting go of ideas of which they take ownership. They can emotionally empathize with the impact such solutions could have on their users, making it hard to separate themselves from the solution. Detachment is not their strong point. They are, however, still focused on ensuring the solutions that move forward have the greatest impact on others, and their genuine curiosity about the experiences of others helps them naturally to test to learn rather than to test to confirm. If the solution is proven ineffective, they may initially mourn its end, but at the end of the day, if the user is happy, they are happy.

What Influencers Say During LIA

"It's challenging to let a solution go, but I have to remember that it isn't for me, or for my team. And if it doesn't address the challenges our users face, then it isn't the right solution."

"Hearing that our solution wouldn't actually work was a punch to the gut."

"It's amazing to think that one of our solutions could actually transform a whole community."

FACILITATOR TIPS

Influencers place a high importance on delivering a solution that successfully impacts the lives of their users, which can create challenges for them in LIA. To help, facilitators can:

Focus on the learning: Influencers may take it personally if one of their ideas yields negative results, mostly because it means they were not as connected to the user as they thought. Remind them that when testing to learn, there is no right or wrong, no success or failure, and that they now are even closer to understanding what the users truly need.

Lean on the team: Influencers feel a giant burden to deliver for their users, which can create unintentional distance from the team. As a facilitator, remind the group that they got to where they are today as a team, and it is further than any of them could have gotten individually. They succeed as a team, they fail as a team, and they learn as a team. Teams are very important to Influencers, so this should lessen the weight they put on their shoulders.

Coachable Moment

DEAR ANA,

So . . . it happened. We tested my favorite solution and got a pretty strong "no" from the results. I'd be lying if I said I wasn't crushed. All I wanted was to make the lives of our users better, and I really thought this was the way to make that happen. I'm not quite sure what to do now. We have other solutions, but I have doubts about how effective they will be. I feel like I failed our client.
— INEZ

DEAR INEZ,

I can see how disappointed you are and how you might think that we failed our supporters, but I don't view this as a failure at all. In fact, I view this as a win for the team. We got a quick and unambiguous answer. That will save us a lot of time, energy, and money to put toward another idea. If we fool ourselves into thinking that we don't need to test our assumptions because we spent so much time up front understanding our donors' and volunteers' needs, we are setting ourselves up for a big surprise. We never know whether the insights we develop during insight identification are actually true or not. In some ways, we almost don't care if they are absolutely true because their purpose is to inspire us. But now that we are experimenting, we do care if they are true. And we can no longer solely think about satisfying the needs of our donors and volunteers. We are looking for the intersection of three critical requirements—what our supporters want, what we can deliver as an organization, and what a sustainable business model might look like that allows us to deliver the entire experience. We didn't meet the criteria for success, so it would be a mistake to keep investing in this idea when we didn't get the support we needed. Let's let go of it and move on to another option in our portfolio. There is a superior idea that is out there. . . . If we push further, I know that we will be successful.

— ANA

WRAP-UP

At first glance, Influencers may seem to be made for DT. The focus on the needs, experiences and emotions of others drives them more than the rest of their teammates, and their optimism and innovative spirit lift up the team during times of stress and struggle. However, Influencers still have much to learn. They are so driven to create impact for others that they risk falling victim to confirmation bias. In fact, they would much rather act off of their gut reactions, so the Testing phases are critical to keeping Influencers in check. Nothing, however, is more valuable to Influencers than a diverse team. On their own, Influencers feel so comfortable with the process that they could move too fast, speeding through opportunities to learn and missing key insights in their blind spots. It is the diverse perspectives and dialogue of the team that keeps them in the moment just long enough to illuminate higher-order solutions that better serve the needs of the user.

Now we turn a complete 180. It's not that the next persona doesn't like people, they just value facts more than feelings and emotions. Now, we welcome the Analyst.

CHAPTER 12

THE ANALYST

DEAR ANA,

We have barely scoped our project and I can't help but think about solutions—partly because I already feel like I know a lot about what drives our donors, but mainly because I can't grasp what additional knowledge my team might have. I have always worked in tandem with my teammates, but everyone stayed in their lanes. Now, we are all muddled together and I'm afraid that I'll have to spend my time either justifying what I know to be right or minding our pace so we stick to the facts and don't wander idly off topic. Don't get me wrong, I respect them and the work that they do. I just have a hard time believing that jumping through the hoops of design thinking together is really going to get us anywhere different than where we are now.

— AMAN

W hen one thinks of the ideal "designer," the Analyst is likely the last person who comes to mind. This objective, analytical and skeptical individual will drive the Influencers and Drivers crazy with their constant demands for proof. Private and often unemotional, they struggle in the exploratory phases when the goal remains unclear and their task is open-minded inquiry. They may become overwhelmed with having not only to explore, but to *feel* as well. But as champions during later phases in the process, their enthusiasm for testing hypotheses will propel the team during DT's final phase. At the start of DT, an Analyst is the one who says little. However, if you look close enough, you can see the gears hard at work as they try to process the tasks at hand, calculate risk and reward, and decide whether or not DT is an efficient way forward.

What they FEEL

Analysts display a similar level of discomfort at the start of DT as the Drivers, but for entirely different reasons. They are concerned with pacing but are more nervous about the ambiguity of the path forward. Avoiding solutions at the start is a real challenge because they enjoy being seen as the experts and doubt their ability to develop empathy.

What they SEE

Analysts see a murky and ambiguous path to innovation full of threats and dangers and teammates who must prove themselves to earn their trust. Analysts deal in the world of facts, so they struggle to see the value of talking to "random people" as research.

What they HEAR

Analysts listen for facts, figures, and quantitative data points. They have strong mental models (some may call them biases or blind spots) and it takes deep, active listening to others' points of view to challenge their often deeply held beliefs.

What they SAY

"I tend to be the most comfortable when in environments where I can ensure consistency, accuracy, and control."

"I exhibited quite a bit of discomfort in the vagueness of the project."

"Initially, I was a little intimidated to go through the design thinking process because I assumed it was meant for people who are 'naturally' creative. . . . I've never perceived creativity as something that can be learned—people just have it or they don't."

AN ANALYST'S JOURNEY THROUGH DT

Immersion

Analysts usually get off to a slow start—they are hesitant to engage and may want to slow down the team's progress in the name of "better research practices." It is common for Analysts to feel that they are not equipped to interview stakeholders for a long list of reasons:

- Lack of personal experience with the problem being explored or the research being conducted
- Not enough time to do adequate research
- No control over the outcome and no preidentified solution
- A lack of cultural sensitivity necessary to engage with particular stakeholders

Analysts naturally doubt the value of qualitative data. They find comfort in quantitative analysis. Empathy is not naturally understood—some Analysts doubt they can even develop empathy if it involves something they have never experienced. This hesitation is exacerbated by their confidence and commitment to finding solutions and their need to be "an expert." They need permission to admit they do not know everything and to dig for deeper understanding. Analysts push for clearly defined procedures and modes of working, and they are skeptical of other team members who seem eager to dive into research. They may even criticize team members who don't meet their standards for working too quickly, or worse, may refuse to begin research until certain operating procedures are in place. All of this comes from a sense of discomfort with the ambiguity of this phase. However, once they get started, interviews have the capacity to dramatically increase Analysts' comfort if the conversation is productive and yields "useful" insights.

What Analysts Say During Immersion

"I struggled with handling the ambiguity surrounding our topic, but once I started interviews, I saw new avenues to explore and felt more comfortable."

"We don't have enough time for us to achieve everything we would ideally want to achieve."

"I don't think I can grasp it fully because I haven't suffered through it myself."

"I learned that a major part of this is relinquishing control."

FACILITATOR TIPS

Analysts need a helpful nudge to leave their perfectly calculated ways behind and dive into the ambiguity of Immersion. To help, facilitators can:

Help narrow the scope of the project: If the problem is too broad or abstract, research can end up being superficial. Every team wants to think big, but it is more advantageous to think smaller than you normally think. This will help an overwhelmed Analyst.

Just do it! Small but deep insights in early interviews can really build an Analyst's confidence and willingness to invest more time in research.

Use debrief tools: Analysts build their confidence with every interview they complete, but this only occurs if they can confirm the usefulness of the data collected. Analysts will be motivated by discussing and validating the small, deep insights achieved, which creates positive reinforcement and builds momentum.

Coachable Moment

DEAR ANA,

The problem we are facing seems somewhat straightforward. I'm struggling to understand why, when we could get some quantifiable data, we would choose instead to rely on interviews. When we only interview five people, I don't feel comfortable overriding real data with such a small sample size. Why not do a survey? I feel like I must be doing the process wrong, but I already have solutions popping around in my brain, and I'm not sure how to ignore them.

— AMAN

DEAR AMAN,

The problem may seem straightforward on the surface, but I think it is important to keep in mind that we are trying to understand the lives of important stakeholders—our donors and volunteers—and not just a set of quantitative data points. I love quantitative data too, but I am afraid if we reduce these people to data points, our solutions may ignore better ways to serve these human beings so vital to our organization. They have unique motivations, attitudes, and behaviors that shape their reasons for supporting us, and those are worth understanding. Relying solely on quantitative data is a choice that I think undervalues the need to create real value for them as humans. That's not an easy shift, I know. Using qualitative data requires the team to behave in very different ways—but data that can be embedded in Excel spreadsheets may fail to capture the complexity of those

we are designing for. The best way we can address their needs is to better understand why they behave the way they do. Remember that we are not trying to "prove" anything at this point—we are looking for inspiration. Collecting qualitative data can help us do that.
— ANA

Sensemaking

Analysts really struggle with developing insights. They tend to avoid emotions and separate them from their decision-making; this emotional detachment may translate into a low level of self-awareness and intro-spection, making it difficult for an Analyst to recognize the emotional needs of others. If interviews were kept at a superficial level, they also likely have not heard

What Analysts Say During Sensemaking

"I know my own personal experiences cloud my ability to create insights."

"My team really helped pull me out of a 'causal logic' hole while trying to craft insights."

"It is challenging to explore what is 'unsaid.'"

enough to disprove the strong initial assumptions they brought into the process. They may be listening for data that confirms what they already think is right. Analysts also struggle with the idea that analysis (an activity of convergence) could actually lead to more uncertainty, more possibilities, and new directions. They appreciate logic and rationale that follows some pattern. Insights from ethnographic data may not afford such luxury.

FACILITATOR TIPS

Processing qualitative data may seem like a foreign language to Analysts. To help, facilitators can:

Focus on the user experience: Analysts have a hard time translating data surrounding emotions into meaningful insights. By providing structured tools that focus on the users, like journey mapping and personas, you can offer Analysts guidance in translating emotional responses into usable data.

Don't give up too soon: Insights are hard to develop and Analysts may be tempted to give up the search prematurely. But giving up too soon will almost certainly lead to superficial insights. Be relentless about putting in the time required to bring an Analyst to a deep understanding of those you are designing for.

Coachable Moment

DEAR ANA,

I've realized a personal blind spot in my burning desire to clarify something ambiguous. I find myself growing impatient with how many layers there are to peel back, and the more we learn, the more questions arise. It seems backwards and highly inefficient, especially when the data doesn't confirm or deny our hypotheses. During the interviews, I found myself jumping to specific questions, so now I wonder if my data tells the full story. I also feel like I am the only one really driven to finding a solution, which is frustrating.

— AMAN

DEAR AMAN,

Doing qualitative research is messy work. It starts messy and ends messy. But ultimately it is our responsibility to examine what we learned, decide what's most important, and reframe our problem to focus our exploration. There is a high-level structure to our analysis, which will make it easier to step into the ambiguity. We are looking for evidence from our observations and interviews that helps us understand why our donors and volunteers have disengaged recently. We know from our quantitative data that they have, but we don't know why. This will get us closer to revealing the real opportunities for change that are actionable. Only then can we create the right experiences for them.

Right now, it's tempting to look at our data as evidence that our donors and volunteers just don't understand what we are doing and should be doing things differently. That kind of analysis is missing the point of our research. It is our job to listen to their needs and be open to their realities, which are obviously different from our own. We have to be willing to step into their values and give them the benefit of the doubt that they are rational human beings making a different set of choices than we think they should make. If we want them to make different choices, then we need to start by understanding why they are making the choices that they are making. This is a time for sensemaking and not a time for solutions—yet.

— ANA

Alignment

The inherent challenges Analysts faced in Sensemaking carry over into the group experience of Alignment. Good collaborative conversations require emotional understanding and engagement, yet Analysts tend to detach. They also have a strong bias toward their own points of view, making it difficult to consider alternative perspectives. Trusting the judgment of others comes slowly, and Analysts aren't quite there yet. They "run the numbers" in their heads, so it seems unlikely that insights brought forth by others will provide new value. Because they put so much effort into their own understanding, they feel confident in what they know and do not overtly look to others to learn more, or to challenge what they know. However, if team members can help them check these biases, they are the first to appreciate and grow from the learning. Discovering the power of the collective is a revelation to them—and very inspiring. Lastly, Analysts may activate only superficial insights because of their insecurity with empathy and the user, who may still feel somewhat foreign to them. Superficial insights result in self-evident design criteria and abstract insights lead to generic criteria—which, ironically, demotivate Analysts, so they rely on the team to bring them to a deeper understanding of the user experience. And they appreciate it when it happens.

What Analysts Say During Alignment

"I realized that I am quick to judge."

"Our design criteria feels way too broad to lead us to meaningful solutions."

"This phase really requires some structure to capture the variety of perspectives. I know it's important to hear how others viewed the data, but sometimes my initial reaction is to tune out what doesn't make sense to me."

Coachable Moment

DEAR ANA,
I'm a bit apprehensive. I haven't really developed trust in my team, which I anticipate will make this part pretty challenging. After going through the data, it seems pretty clear-cut what our path forward should be—the user

issues seem similar to problems we have typically faced in the past, so, to me, it's pretty straightforward. I just hope we can remain focused and come to that conclusion somewhat quickly, and create criteria that actually lend themselves to solutions with substance.

— AMAN

DEAR AMAN,

The value of immersing ourselves in the lives of our donors and volunteers is that it aligns us around a set of reasons why we should be dissatisfied with the status quo. Our donors have disengaged for a reason. It is easy to dismiss their feelings when we hear them second- or thirdhand, but it is much harder to remain satisfied with the way things are today if we sit across the table from them and hear firsthand their pain points and their needs. My hope is that will help us align around what a new experience should look like. We get lots of messages as a team (and individually) about what must change and what is unworkable, but part of the difficulty of stepping into a better experience is aligning on what we are moving toward. What should the attributes of our ideal future be? We have never created space for this kind of conversation, and aligning together on what that ideal future needs to look like will help us create a passion for change that will drive us toward great results.

— ANA

Emergence

Analysts do well during Emergence, not because it comes naturally to them as it does for Influencers, but because they are pleasantly surprised by their own creative output. After struggling in the earlier stages of the design process, Analysts find their creative confidence during brainstorming and embrace collective ideation as a way to get better results than they could have achieved on their own. They appreciate that diversity of thought is a path to superior ideas. They also enjoy the puzzle of concocting higher-order solutions using the building blocks of initial ideas. This newfound creative confidence also brings a personal sense of relief that the team will achieve its goals. Their initial pessimism about having to work with those who may not value their approach is replaced by optimism and a recognition that there could be many possible paths forward.

What Analysts Say During Emergence

"This really opened my eyes to what is possible beyond just my limited experience."

"My Aha! moment was creating bizarre but unexpectedly wonderful ideas."

"I learned how important it is to have multiple perspectives and people from various skills and backgrounds in the group."

FACILITATOR TIPS

Emergence, and its requirement to consider all possibilities, may give trouble to Analysts, who typically stick to what they know will work. To help, facilitators can:

Architect a different conversation: There is an element of stagecraft in a good brainstorming session. Analysts are diligent planners and approach ideation with carefully crafted preliminary ideas, but to ignite their creative confidence, they need to be caught off guard. Asking provocative trigger questions based on what the worst idea would be, or what an unrelated industry did that faced the same problem, can help Analysts shed their preconceived ideas and embrace creativity as it flows.

Manage critiques: There is a fine line between too much critique and not enough. Emergence is about creating something new and valuable together—too much judgment can demotivate a team, but not enough critique can cause innovators to miss opportunities to improve concepts. Analysts need clear guidelines such as "comments must include ways to improve the concept" and "avoid engaging in debate."

Coachable Moment

DEAR ANA,

The ideation session made me feel like a new person. I had so many doubts about this process and its necessity to our goals, and another brainstorm session certainly didn't hold promise in my mind. Today, however, felt new. I eased in apprehensively during the first round, ready to share the solutions I have been crafting for weeks in my head, but the questions were so unexpected, the ideas I walked in with just didn't make sense anymore, and I felt free to respond with whatever came to mind, which led to much more valuable ideas. What surprised me was how good I was at coming up with off-the-wall ideas—who knew I had it in me?! How do I harness this creativity all the time?

— AMAN

P.S.: I'd be lying if I said I wasn't still a bit worried about the impact we can make. There are some amazing concepts we could explore, but so little time. Should I be worried?

DEAR AMAN,

Diversity is perhaps the surest route to creativity. It is one thing for me to tell you this and another thing to see it in action—right? When we started this project, each of us on the team viewed our supporters and their needs in our own particular way and we unconsciously imposed that view on our understanding of the problem. We couldn't help ourselves. But there would have been all kinds of opportunities that we missed because of the narrowness of our framing. When we aligned on the real needs of our donors and supporters, we came together as a diverse team, and now have produced ideas that are better than any of us could have brought to the table as individuals. That diversity made our creativity possible. Thank you for sticking with the process and allowing our curiosity to unfold so that we could get to this breakthrough thinking. We got here because we had better conversations with each other about what our donors' and volunteers' current reality is, and that led us to a more productive conversation about how we can better serve them.

— ANA

Imagining

Analysts are their own greatest barriers to experiencing Imagining. Their perfectionist tendencies kick in and can show up as attempts to delay or avoid putting pen to paper. This can be tough on a team's morale because strong Analysts will pull away from their team in the process. They need lots of permission to fail fast and keep things rough because in their mind, a less-than-perfect prototype might invite unwanted critical feedback, which is hard for them to receive. Emotional connection continues to be a struggle for Analysts. Making ideas real takes them back to Discovery and that uncomfortable feeling of dealing in the emotional world of user needs and values. Analysts are also worried that they might hear something during feedback sessions that they don't already know, and inviting such critique counterbalances their need to be perceived as "experts."

What Analysts Say During Imagining

"I am a good planner, but sometimes I need help from others to take my creative capabilities up a notch!"

"Creating a tangible artifact is not easy. It takes some forethought, research, practice, and a few trial-and-error moments."

"It's hard to get the idea out of your head and onto paper. I want to flesh the idea all the way out, but we don't have time for that. I have to fight the urge to shut down the process, which means shutting down the team. I don't want to do that, but yikes, this is hard."

FACILITATOR TIPS

Analysts hold great promise to experience Imagining if they can get past their greatest hurdle—themselves. To help, facilitators can:

Focus on prototyping as a de-risking process: Give Analysts clear permission to fail fast and keep things rough.

Model prototyping first: Analysts need to see prototyping modeled first and then they will jump in and try it on their own. Simply providing prototyping instructions will result in blank stares. Model it first with an unrelated, universally understood task.

Coachable Moment

DEAR ANA,

I don't get it. I felt such a rush of confidence during ideation, but now I am stuck back in my head again. Imagining our ideas requires vulnerability, and as someone who thinks through things and expects to have the right answer, I don't know where to start. I don't feel particularly skilled at creating drawings or illustrations and I have a hard time believing that someone is going to be able to find my stick figures useful or valuable.
— AMAN

DEAR AMAN,

It sounds like you have the idea figured out in your head, which is the first step toward making it as tangible and concrete as possible. What we are talking about is translating the idea in your head into a very simple storyboard, user scenario, flow chart, and, yes, even stick figures to help make the idea visible to the team, and eventually our donors. We are not talking about a slick and professionally designed rendering. I have a budget of funds for this project and I want to use that money as wisely as possible. These rough visualizations are a really effective, fast, and cheap way to continue to develop our ideas and create our value proposition, so we can save our budget for that moment when we have a much better understanding of the value we are creating.

The alternative is that we just describe the future to them in words. But here's the dilemma—words aren't half as effective as pictures. Pictures evoke all of our senses and create a more immersive experience, so the more we use imagination to create as vivid a picture as possible of what our new donor experience is, the richer and more complete our feedback will be. It is merely a vehicle for better conversations. As long as the prototype feels real enough to allow us to speculate about our future plans, we will get the feedback we need right now. I realize this might feel like you are walking a tightrope, but we are trying to minimize investment in this idea until we are confident that it is a good idea.
— ANA

Learning in Action (LIA)

Once past the initial pressures of testing, Analysts are ready to take their places as the champions of experimentation. Their meticulous nature and desire for objectivity ensure they are capable of designing experiments to prove or disprove hypotheses, not to determine success or failure of themselves or the team. Analysts finally get to find ways to infuse quantitative data into the mix, which is familiar and useful to them. While the rest of the team grapples with emotional biases and fears of failure, Analysts' natural emotional detachment proves valuable in ensuring experiments are not skewed just to confirm their solutions. They are the ones who will remind their team that no matter how the experiments turn out, there is good stuff to be learned. They are also adept at running multiple experiments at once, which also mitigates the pressure to "succeed" felt by their teammates. Analysts clearly see the value that visualization and experimentation, coupled together, deliver: they are quick to realize their blind spots, finding encouragement and creative confidence that helps them become the skilled experimenter their team needs them to be.

FACILITATOR TIPS

Analysts thrive during LIA, but may not recognize just how poised for the job they really are. To help, facilitators can:

Give them the green light: Throughout all earlier phases, DT and its many experiences have not come naturally to the Analyst. They are naturally poised to thrive during LIA, but may fear their feelings of ease may be too good to be true. Draw attention to their strengths during this phase and encourage them to share their methods with the rest of the team. Such encouragement should be just the boost they need to lead the group through successful experimentation.

Stay focused on the learning: Analysts can detach themselves from expectations during experiments. However, when a solution falls short and the rest of the team struggles with the "failure," Analysts may have difficulty refocusing the team on all the great insights the experimentation produced. Keeping the conversation focused around learning will lessen the "distraction" of emotional attachment and will grant Analysts the space to share such learning with the team in a way that pushes the team forward.

What Analysts Say During LIA

> "When a solution doesn't work, it isn't all or nothing. There's always something to be learned, knowledge to be gained, to make whatever we do next more likely to succeed."

> "You can't argue with the data."

> "Whether it's now or a year from now, we'd realize the same thing: our solution was a flop. The only difference is by realizing it now, we saved our time, money, and sanity."

Coachable Moment

DEAR ANA,

I feel so in the zone right now. Developing experiments and staying objective come naturally to me, and I genuinely am curious as to how our solutions will fare at a larger scale. What concerns me is the level of insecurity and pressure evidently felt by my teammates. There are a lot of opinions on how we should design each experiment,

and each one seems biased and safe. I fear in focusing so much on "being right," we are going to miss out on really understanding if our solution works in the real world. That should be the focus, right?

— AMAN

DEAR AMAN,

Absolutely. I think you can expect that the rest of the team may feel defensive if we don't get the traction we want with this idea. Try as they might, it will be very difficult for most of the other team members not to justify the choices they made if criticism starts coming back. At this point, our idea feels very real. We are no longer in the rough-prototype stage. Our prime concept seems ready for testing and possible scalability. And we want our donors to say "I want that!" Everyone is excited. But this is where the rubber meets the road. Measurement matters (I know that is music to your ears!). We need some sort of quantitative proof before we can loosen the purse strings on this idea. I have had sidebar conversations to remind the team that our job is to get donors to ultimately increase contributions. It's really just like being back in the research phase. This is your time to shine. Let's get some analytics and make our testing as rigorous as possible. I have a fixed amount of money and I want to be able to preserve as much of my budget as possible so I can shift resources to something else if we don't get the results we need.

— ANA

WRAP-UP

Much like Drivers, Analysts experience highs and lows during the DT process, but the reasons for their roller-coaster rides are different. The human-centered nature of DT is foreign to Analysts (some of our Analyst clients have been known to say they "don't do emotions") and qualitative data seems unreliable and weak. However, they bring so much value to the process. Their insatiable need for proof keeps the rest of the team from moving forward prematurely, and their meticulous attention to detail and steadfast commitment to being objective and skeptical prove invaluable when testing solutions. The beginning stages of DT go against every natural inclination of our Analysts; in fact, our research suggests that Analysts often don't truly see the value of DT until idea generation. However, if we can get them to *experience* each phase instead of going through the motions, they have the potential to emerge as creative, empathetic listeners who don't have to know everything.

It only seems right to have this last persona rounding out our team. More concerned with the comfort of others than their own, this type focuses the majority of their effort on mitigating conflict and keeping the team running smoothly. Meet our final persona, the Supporter.

CHAPTER 13

THE SUPPORTER

DEAR ANA,

I know you said that the diversity of our team will be its greatest strength . . . and I believe you. I just worry about how much time it is going to take for our team to "gel," especially with the tight timeline we have for the project. It takes me a while to get familiar with everyone's type and feel comfortable putting myself and my ideas out there. I don't know if we will have the team dynamics figured out by the time we have to interview the donors, and I'm worried our solutions will miss the mark because of it. Should I be nervous, or is it all part of the plan?

— SAM

Supporters take deep and personal owner-ship of the team as a unit. They make a point to be in tune with the feelings of their group members and work relentlessly to keep the peace. They bring the cookies. Friendly, predictable, em-pathetic, and collaborative, they prioritize psycho-logical safety, trust, and camaraderie. Supporters create a family-like feel to the team and become uncomfortable if the team doesn't feel cohesive.

Such team qualities come at the Supporter's expense. Supporters are not direct or forceful and therefore can easily be shut down by teammates, especially the Drivers. Fearful of being wrong or creating conflict; they compromise accuracy to spare hurt feelings, and are willing to redo inaccu-rate work instead of confronting others who did it wrong. They struggle to find their voice.

What they FEEL

Supporters are the least comfortable members of the group. Early on, DT makes Supporters panic (just a bit)—not due to the process so much as to concerns about keeping the peace during what could be a very tumultuous team journey.

What they SEE

Supporters see no clear path forward to a solution and lots of room for error, which makes them anx-ious, hyperaware, and less willing to assert their opinions.

What they HEAR

Supporters hear everything. They are active listen-ers when engaging with users and are motivated and inspired by others' stories. They strive to be in tune with the feelings of their group members. This can be exhausting if other team members are not self-aware enough to recognize how much space they take up in conversations.

What they SAY

"It's great to see that we can work well together. If people disagree, we do a good job talking it out, agreeing on a decision, and moving forward."

"I learned that many times, I interpret things dif-ferently than others, and I can very much benefit from working in a group and hearing others' per-spectives and sharing my own."

"I selfishly wanted to suggest a project focus that could potentially help me, but didn't actually voice it because several of the folks on the team had really great arguments for something different that was also interesting."

A SUPPORTER'S JOURNEY THROUGH DT

Immersion

Supporters truly encapsulate what it means to be human centered. They have a very early focus on those being designed for as people and not just as subjects, and build the social connections necessary to facilitate good interviews and research. Empathy comes naturally to them, and they can gently pull Drivers and Analysts more toward empathy by acknowledging and questioning biases and hyperfocusing on the human side. Supporters face their own challenges, however, with digging deeper into the problem space, which creates more ambiguity and less of a clear path forward. Such ambiguity creates space for more conflict, more biases, and more to do in a short amount of time, all issues they would rather avoid. Supporters are concerned with how their own personal biases, as well as their teammates', could be a detriment to getting to good solutions. They worry that if the team goes wrong during research—not interviewing the right people or failing to understand the real issues their stakeholders are experiencing—they won't be able to get to effective solutions.

What Supporters Say During Immersion

> "I constantly felt that my team and I needed to keep aside our personal and team biases and constantly have our customers and their problem in mind to effectively navigate through the process."

> "We have a bright team full of interesting perspectives that will be vital in solving our team's problem."

FACILITATOR TIPS

While everyone's attention is on the task, Supporters scrutinize the inner workings of the team. To help them shift their focus from team to those being designed for, facilitators can:

Accelerate team bonding: Teams that have a high degree of psychological safety offer Supporters an opportunity to take risks and be vulnerable in front of others. Supporters will not feel comfortable without this, so plan a team activity to kick-start team bonding.

Use team members' strengths to assign roles and responsibilities: Supporters will seek to ensure that team members are given the right roles and responsibilities for their skills and talents. This is very helpful when the right roles are assigned, but can derail them if there is a mismatch on the team. Feedback tools that allow individuals to share their results with teammates, like the DiSC or Myers-Briggs, can be very helpful here.

Establish team norms: Creating team norms is really about creating mutual accountability. Supporters will seek to discover how the team will hold each other accountable and what the team will do if there is no progress. Simple activities like Start, Stop, Continue (what should the team start doing, stop doing, and continue doing?) go a long way toward breaking down norms into specific behaviors and prioritizing the most important norms.

Coachable Moment

DEAR ANA,

As my team settled on the scope of our challenge, I had so much anxiety. It's very difficult for me to challenge group dynamics that might not be working for me. Facilitating a group discussion to include everyone's ideas or move in a new direction is so hard. As we carry out interviews, I wonder—are we doing everything we can to maximize our chance of creating meaningful change for this person? And it is difficult to be comfortable with conflicting information! This is all a bit overwhelming.

— SAM

DEAR SAM,

*I agree. Design can be overwhelming. I've always been intrigued by the writings of the architect Frank Gehry. I'm a big Gehry admirer. He once said, "If I knew how a project was going to turn out, I wouldn't do it." How can we honor the power of not knowing like Gehry did? Exploring the ambiguity within every project gives us a chance to find out what the **real** problem is and what a great solution might look like. Also, let yourself off the hook: in our current environment, where we have scarce resources, our objective is not to achieve perfection but instead to move toward goodness. That is hard for all of us because we always hope for that fabulous silver-bullet solution. This doesn't mean that we accept early compromises—but the reality of living in a world of finite resources is that we might not achieve all possibilities perfectly.*

— ANA

Sensemaking

When Sensemaking is done as an independent activity, Supporters often find themselves capable of accepting ambiguity: the freedom from the pressure of "finding the right answer" is liberating and exciting. They still worry about doing it wrong or missing the mark particularly in interpreting the many stories the data could be telling, so they move forward cautiously, anticipating the ways in which their team could respond when they all reunite for team Sensemaking and Alignment. Such worry about the next phase can draw Supporters away from focusing on deep insights and experiencing their own "Aha!" moments. However, if they allow themselves to sit with the data and not rush through, they are fascinated by the learning and deeper empathy they develop.

What Supporters Say During Sensemaking

"One thing that struck me is the importance to give yourself time to digest and go back with a fresh eye."

"Insights aren't as easy as I thought they would be."

"I'm concerned I'm going to focus on the wrong data and get insights way off from the rest of my team."

Coachable Moment

DEAR ANA,

I've been so surprised and excited to learn that there isn't one single correct answer in design thinking! It makes me feel like the answers we need, the solutions that will make the most impact, are out there and just have yet to be realized. With that said, I'm staring at this big pile

---

FACILITATOR TIPS

Supporters are interested in finding insights that help depict the user experience, but they struggle to give themselves permission to come to conclusions that they can share confidently with the team. To help, facilitators can:

Solicit insights in advance: The fear of rejection or ridicule worries Supporters even when they are individually analyzing the data. Free them from the potential pressure by having team members submit their insights anonymously and have them compiled visually before team conversations begin. This will allow Supporters to worry less about their teams and focus more on their reactions to the data.

Give ample time: Supporters are not quick to act; they need time to take it all in and sit with it. Instituting a fast timeline for determining insights will add greater pressure and distraction to Supporters as they try to make sense of the data. Providing multiple days before team Alignment conversations is a critical step to make Supporters feel settled and confident with their learning.

of data points, and I can't help but worry—am I doing this right? Will this actually work? Is this what the interview subject really meant, or am I misremembering? It is interesting to see what data confirms all we thought coming into the process, but it's a little overwhelming to see all that it doesn't.
— SAM

DEAR SAM,
*I know that the volume of data seems overwhelming. It's natural to concentrate on the quantity of data that we have collected because that seems like a good measurement of performance—more data = better performance. But I am **more focused** on the quality of data that we are receiving and the learning that we are achieving. You are modeling inquisitiveness for the team by asking questions and genuinely listening to the responses. Listening with curiosity is more important than talking right now, and we have a lot of talkers on the team. But you must also find the space and confidence to listen to yourself. Trust your gut with the insights that pop out to you. There is no "wrong" way to take in this data, so remove all that pressure, take a breath, and let the data speak to you.*
— ANA

Alignment

Supporters achieve the mindset shift fairly naturally in Alignment. They appreciate how much can be learned through diverse perspectives and their immense empathy for the users keeps their needs front and center. Supporters play a major role in reminding the rest of the team about keeping the focus on the users' needs, and they also pay close attention to the team dynamics during discussion. They are the ones to suggest processes and norms as ways to mitigate any strain or power imbalance. They are the team cheerleader. However, they lose this confidence when other team members do not abide by the norms and instead ignite forceful debate. The Supporter's role (up until now) has been to create a safe space and environment for collaboration. But if and when conflicts arise, Supporters tend to withdraw. The safe space that Supporters cultivated for the team suddenly seems unsafe. It comes as a shock that aligning is much more difficult than empathizing.

What Supporters Say During Alignment

"It's important to help each other and promote each other during insight conversations."

"I didn't consider how polite and happy or smiley I can be. . . . That is something that is not necessarily true for other people."

"I struggle to work with the team without being shy or getting offended."

FACILITATOR TIPS

Alignment can be a very vulnerable and volatile experience for Supporters. To help them find confidence and security in the process, facilitators can:

Enforce turn taking and shut down debates: Supporters need to be encouraged to share their point of view, especially when it differs from other members of the team.

Build in energizers and plenty of breaks: This keeps Supporters' mood light when conversations get emotionally charged.

Agree to a predetermined structure before alignment conversations begin: This ensures there is no misunderstanding about how to proceed. Preempting conflict about how to handle the data and how to develop insights will go a long way toward mitigating doubt in the process when conflict arises.

Coachable Moment

DEAR ANA,
I feel really good about the insights I developed. Getting to know the users and their needs really put into perspective what was most important to them, which should be what is most important to us. I'm excited to hear what different insights my teammates gleaned. I'm just nervous about what conflicts may arise. We need a way to share ideas safely and promote each other, and a respectful way to challenge one another without getting into an all-out debate. Without those things, I doubt it will be effective.
— SAM

DEAR SAM,
I have always been a believer in the notion that even though we complain about the lack of resources, in the end, the thing that is most finite is our own time and attention. The most strategic choice we make as a team is where we put the precious time that we've got. Many of our team members are highly action oriented, so it seems wasteful and time consuming to them to immerse everyone in our qualitative data collection. But there is so much to learn and so many perspectives to listen to before we take action. I know you see the value of this investment. If we make the investment up front, we will save time later by avoiding implementing ideas that turn out to have serious problems with them. In the end, design thinking is the right way to address our challenge because there is so much uncertainty around why our donors have disengaged. Aligning the team now around what the attributes of an ideal future might look like for our donors will help generate the enthusiasm, energy, and optimism that we need before we move into testing. This dialogue may not be easy, but your leadership will

benefit the team in redirecting the conversation away from debate and toward the possibility of serving our donors in a reimagined way.

— ANA

Emergence

A Supporter's confidence in Emergence seems to mirror the mood and energy of the team. If the team is high performing and led with energy and enthusiasm, a Supporter's creative confidence is high. However, if the team is struggling, overly cautious, or bogged down in debate, then their own personal confidence is weakened. This is a red flag for the entire team because strong-willed, stubborn teammates (read: Drivers) who are tired and waning in energy in ideation activities can negatively impact the energy and resilience of the Supporters on their team. Supporters may also be easily swayed by energetic, superconfident Influencers who overwhelm them with ideas, unintentionally stifling Supporters' voices. Because Supporters are nonconfrontational and are hesitant to give feedback to other team members, they are also not likely to initiate strategies or activities to address overbearing voices, but they bounce back quickly when they utilize fresh thinking from outsiders.

What Confident Supporters Say During Emergence

"Although I always wanted to be creative, I thought it wasn't 'my thing,' but I am impressed with myself."

"I was taken aback by the number of ideas that we generated—the ideas were so diverse."

What Less-Confident Supporters Say During Emergence

"We struggled with some of the individual ideas—it was easy to shoot them down and say 'someone's already doing that.'"

"I struggled with the ideation process more than I would have expected."

"I found it difficult to organize our ideas into a coherent design that could generate a prototype."

FACILITATOR TIPS

Supporters can either thrive or shrink during Emergence, and it has less to do with them and more to do with the dynamics of the team. To help, facilitators can:

Create the right environment for Emergence: Supporters have the potential to be creative, but need more than just structure to get them there. Creating a positive environment with attention to detail about the choice of room (spacious), lighting (soft), colors (relaxing), and noise (ambient) promotes a positive mood and creativity for all, especially Supporters.

Neutralize hierarchy: Hierarchy is a big inhibitor to creating psychological safety in a group, especially for Supporters. It makes it hard for them to tell the truth, a critical component to reach Emergence. A safe space is critical for Supporters to let down their guard.

Praise them for their contribution: While it is unproductive to show support for individual ideas as they arise, Supporters value encouragement just for playing the game. Find a way to objectively value the participation of the entire team, and Supporters will rise to the occasion.

Coachable Moment

DEAR ANA,

Follow the rules. That's all we had to do, just follow the rules of brainstorming agreed upon by the team. And yet, after just two rounds of trigger questions, my team was injecting judgment into the process. A few times, team members responded to ideas in debate (even though we clearly were not supposed to do so). Sometimes responses were subtle, like an "ahh" following a "good" idea or the eye rolls or snickers at a clearly subpar idea. Maybe no one else noticed, but I did, and it totally clouded my ability to think freely. Is there such a thing as a judgment-free zone?
— SAM

DEAR SAM,

Despite setting up the rules for a judgment-free zone in our brainstorming session, obviously some people on our team couldn't help themselves. I know it's a bummer, but I think it is safe to say that most of us are not used to playing by strict rules, so this new way of collaborating will take some getting used to. I am not justifying their behavior, but I think it is another reminder of why establishing rules will help us get better outcomes and will get us closer to the mark. If you want a laugh, remind me to play you a clip from the TV show Parks and Recreation *when Leslie Knope (played by the hilarious Amy Poehler) leads her team through the worst brainstorming session ever. It's awful. Thank goodness we were not that bad. I will remind the team and I know we will do better next time.*
— ANA

Imagining

Supporters breathe a sigh of relief when the team reaches Imagining. The team has converged (and worked through all the conflict that comes with it), and Supporters love the concreteness of prototyping for its good social interaction and its inclusive process. They appreciate taking a step back to ensure consensus on what works in reality and the accuracy of assumptions, which allows all team members to contribute their unique skills and perspectives. In this arena of critique and iteration, Supporters are hyper-aware of the dynamics of the team, to the point where they struggle to avoid critique rather than trying to learn. Fearful of critique, they have trouble looking beyond imperfections in the design of their initial sketches and prototypes and may lose the creative confidence they developed in Emergence, causing them to mute their ideas and later regret and criticize themselves for their inaction. If they do voice their opinions, Supporters take criticism personally, rather than as baseline learning material. They often feel they must "sell" their ideas to be considered valid, and their visualizations tend to hover at surface level, sacrificing key learning opportunities in order to play it safe. This can be mitigated by mutual respect and a consistent focus back on the user's needs (because serving the user's needs motivates the Supporter almost as much as team dynamics do).

What Supporters Say During Imagining

"In the prototype working session, I found myself constantly explaining things or feeling embarrassed that we didn't consider certain details, instead of being more open-minded to feedback."

"I learned I have a hard time not 'selling.'"

"I see the people around me coming up with such cool ideas, and often feel that mine aren't great. This process has allowed me to practice generating new ideas and showed me that I, too, can be creative!"

Coachable Moment

DEAR ANA,

Our team has certainly grown since we started this journey, and I thought it would get easier. I thought that the hardest part would be agreeing about which ideas to use. However, imagining these ideas so that they feel real brings a whole new level of risk and judgment. It seems easier for others on the team, but to me, nothing is less comfortable than exposing myself to criticism as we try to build our ideas to function in the real world. I don't like giving critiques, and I definitely would rather not get them either.

— SAM

FACILITATOR TIPS

When venturing into the more subjective experience of Imagining, Supporters often retreat into their default ways of avoiding critique and keeping the peace, which makes it all but impossible to test and learn. To help, facilitators can:

Set the stage for feedback: Supporters struggle to engage in arenas of conflict and critique, two concepts Imagining brings in abundance. Remind them that the purpose of early prototyping is to learn so they can iterate, test, and learn some more, and set norms and structures in place so that there are clear procedures for objectively giving and accepting feedback. Initiating sentence starters for warm feedback ("I found it interesting that you . . .") or cool feedback ("Have you thought about . . . ?") can ensure that critique is constructive and useful.

Remove the pressure of perfection: Of all team members, Supporters have the greatest fear of being wrong and may fixate on finding and finessing the "perfect" option. Remind them that successful prototyping relies more on the ability to generate lots of options and less on a talent to generate perfect concepts on the spot.

Reiterate and celebrate detachment: Supporters are least comfortable when they feel like rugs have been swept out from under their feet. To them, visualizing an idea makes it real and meaningful, which may make changes difficult to accept. Remind them that the iterative process brings with it unexpected changes to ideas that should be expected and embraced.

DEAR SAM,

I found this great research that shows that helping our donors do something called "pre-experience" a new future can actually be a proxy for experiencing the real thing. And it can significantly improve their ability to give us more accurate feedback. This just reinforces for me that the most important thing we need to remember here is that our donors are the real experts—not us. We should expect that we may well get most of the ideas wrong, but showing rather than telling our ideas will get us closer. We could postpone making our concepts concrete until we work out the details ourselves, but I think that would actually slow us down. It is easy to stay in the safety space of debate and dialogue, but pushing through this discomfort will help us avoid costly mistakes later. We can make some good hunches, but ultimately, getting our ideas in front of our donors and getting their feedback is the only thing that matters. We can only do that by making our ideas concrete and real.

— ANA

Learning in Action (LIA)

Unlike Imagining, where individual members had to make themselves vulnerable when sharing their personal perspectives, LIA is all about the team. Supporters love that they can rally behind team solutions, which every member has had a hand in forming. The pressure leaves the individual; succeed or fail, they do so as a team, and because of this, they can easily detach themselves from the idea and its outcomes. The ability for Supporters to test to learn and not worry about being wrong depends, again, on the dynamic of their team. If Supporters find themselves surrounded with a positive team cohesion with a strong focus on learning, they will approach experimentation with little fear of being wrong. However, if their team is toxic, cynical, and dog-eat-dog, they will greatly fear the "failure" and may sway experimental designs to confirm the desired result.

What Supporters Say During LIA

"It's a lot easier to stomach a failed solution when the blame isn't entirely on you."

"I'm a bit sad our team time has to end."

"I'm so proud of the solutions our team put forward to test. Whatever happens, our efforts will impact the lives of our users, one way or another."

Mitigate the mystery: Create a space for team members to safely share their feelings during an experiment's success or failure so that all feelings can be validated and addressed with team support.

Host an After Action Review (AAR): As the process comes to a close (or begins a new journey) Supporters feel a bit deflated that their time with this team they have spent supporting and managing is coming to an end. Appoint the Supporter to conduct an AAR documenting the key takeaways and recommendations for the process. The ability to celebrate and commemorate the journey of the team will bring closure to a Supporter, and the practice of reflection will help all members see just how far they have come.

Coachable Moment

DEAR ANA,
It took this long, but I finally feel free. We still need to test validity in the real world, but I don't feel as worried or vulnerable about whether our idea succeeds or fails. The solutions we have created are mosaics of all of our opinions, discussions, critiques, and compromises. Perhaps I feel less risk because they are not mine alone—we share

the burden of their effectiveness. I do, however, worry about our experiments failing, mostly because I don't know how my team will take it. What happens next, and how do we pick up the pieces and move forward?
— SAM

DEAR SAM,
I think many of us on the team grew up thinking that being smart equates to being right, but that is just not true when we work in the innovation space. We are stepping into a world that looks more like venture capital. And we need to think like an investor. The highest-performing VCs in Silicon Valley still expect that 8 out of 10 of their projects will fail. And these are people who are at the top of their game and do it for a living. Why should it be different in our world? What we are used to instead is having 10 tasks and succeeding at all of them. So part of my job as a leader is to help everyone adjust their expectations. We don't talk about failure enough. I need to help the team differentiate intelligent failure from dumb mistakes. I want us to recognize that we can't analyze away uncertainty. We have to live with it! I am trying to help the team step away from a fear of failure and instead think about experimenting our way to success. If we fail, then we will simply pivot to our other options, just like a VC would approach the problem. It's all about the learning.
— ANA

WRAP-UP

It may seem that DT would be much too harrowing for our friendly, peaceful, predictable Supporters. But we suspect that, without them and their ever-present focus on other team members, DT would not work as well. While everyone else is free to think about project success, supportive data, and those they are designing for, Supporters take responsibility for making the team run as smoothly as possible. They organize scheduling and send group communication. They make sure everyone has a strong understanding of the user. They recognize when a team member is struggling and do all they can to restore balance and inclusion. They keep the team on track, sometimes at the expense of their own time, confidence, and opinions. While they will never actively take the "leader" role, their silent stewardship ensures that the team works as optimally as possible to deliver the best results for the user.

PART FIVE
THE DESTINATION

THE DESTINATION

In this book, we have explored the many ways DT enriches the experience of innovators, helping them improve their abilities to:

- Understand latent biases that hinder innovation
- Collaborate more productively and more intentionally with others
- Empathize with the pain points of those for whom they are designing
- Make sense of large amounts of qualitative data
- Mitigate risks while also becoming more comfortable with risk
- Imagine a future so vividly it inspires others
- Recognize their own journey with DT and the ways it differs from that of others

In Part 4, we looked at the role innovators' personal preferences play in how each phase is experienced. Our four personas—Driver, Influencer, Analyst, and Supporter—each face different challenges as the process unfolds. Acknowledging and supporting their unique journeys spurs more successful collaboration across diverse groups of people. By understanding the different personas in your group, you can better enable individual engagement and team dynamics in real time, tailoring your own actions based on the differing needs of the different personas. Knowing team members' limitations and constraints also helps guide selection of "just right" challenges. Novices can get deeply frustrated—hindering their ability to learn DT methodology—if forced to deal with massive challenges in their first projects.

Having done all this, we finally reach the destination this book is all about—You! How do you put all of the information we have shared on experiencing design into practice? Getting you off to a good start is Chapter 14, which focuses on how to assess and accelerate your own personal progress in the journey of DT. Whether you are looking for ways to plot your own course or helping another colleague with their growth, you will benefit from the Personal Development Plan (PDP) in Chapter 14. If you want to influence the broader journey to DT competence in your organization, you will benefit from the organizational focus of Chapter 15. Each chapter contains a diagnostic tool that will help you to identify developmental needs. Each also offers a case illustrating the development process in action, and a set of suggestions for next steps.

Before we dive into your personal development planning with the PDP, we want to acknowledge that at this point, you might feel daunted by the amount of work it takes to become a design thinker. Take a deep breath. The subtitle of this book is *The Innovator's Journey*. All journeys have to start somewhere. Your ultimate destination may look distant—but it's not as far away as you think. So enjoy the ride. Albert Einstein may have said it best: "Life is like a bicycle. To keep your balance, you must keep moving."

So, ever onward . . .

CHAPTER 14

PERSONAL DEVELOPMENT PLANNING

A PERSONAL DEVELOPMENT PLAN (PDP) helps you excel by focusing your attention on thinking proactively and strategically about the what, where, why, when, and how of personal growth. A good PDP highlights your strengths and weaknesses, shows where you need to improve, and includes plans for how to do so, complete with timelines. A DT PDP (we couldn't resist!) maps where your abilities currently are, describes where you want them to be (and why it matters to you), creates measurable goals, and specifies activities to get there.

PDP OVERVIEW

We have already shared a lot of suggestions to help you grow as an innovator at each individual phase of the DT journey. The process starts with *what* you measure—the MVCs for each phase. Recall that in Chapter 2, we reported on research showing that the sweet spot for achieving DT's transformative effects involved crossing over the threshold from beginner skills to design literacy at an intermediate level. The MVCs specify a set of behaviors to look for as evidence that you've gone beyond *doing* DT to *experiencing* each of our six phases in ways that foster *becoming*. We shared, for each phase, a critical set of questions to ask yourself (or your group). When you can answer yes to most of them (honestly!), we believe you are where you need to be to reap the full benefits of DT.

In a process that is fuzzy, abstract, and highly personal, MVCs provide measurable targets that allow you to reflect on where your mindsets and behaviors are and set goals for these that specify *how* you want to grow.

MVCs THROUGHOUT THE PHASES

IMMERSION

I am aware of my own biases and blinders.
I listen to understand rather than to test.
I ask good questions.
I search for areas of opportunity rather than solutions.
I develop an emotional engagement and empathetic bond with those for whom I design.
I probe deeply for unarticulated needs and beliefs.
I am fully present in the moment to the lived experience of my colleagues and those for whom I am designing.

SENSEMAKING

I distinguish between an observation and an interpretation.
I remain patient with iteration and search.
I summarize key interview takeaways cogently and clearly.
I dig deeper beyond the obvious and clearly stated needs of a user.
I gain more clarity on what is the most relevant problem to solve.
I develop informed inferences that are actionable.
I allow myself to question the norms, rules and status quo.
I articulate the "why" behind my own perspective to teammates.
I control my need for closure.
I treat differing views as an opportunity to understand and learn, not debate.
I listen openly to those who disagree with my interpretations.
I (productively) challenge the perspective of others.

ALIGNMENT

I give careful thought to how we structure our conversations.

I am attentive to the rules of dialogue, like turn taking.

I focus on the issues that really matter, as expressed in the design criteria.

I listen heedfully and respectfully to my team, ensuring that everyone feels heard.

I am able to make our different perspectives visible to each other.

I am willing to let go of my perspective to be open to that of others.

I am capable of achieving a shared definition of the problem that we want to solve.

I align with others on a prioritized understanding of the qualities of the ideal solution.

I contribute to the learning of others and learning together.

EMERGENCE

I pursue multiple possibilities.

I actively engage in co-creation, looking for opportunities to build on the ideas of others.

I avoid allegiance to particular solutions during the process.

I explore nontraditional and unexpected ideas.

I work positively, constructively and collaboratively with my team to form new possibilities.

I focus on "What if anything were possible?" in idea generation.

I stay in the possibility despite time pressures and discomfort.

I control the urge to compromise prematurely.

I value and appreciate the diverse perspectives represented within our team.

IMAGINING

I am able to capture, in my mind's eye, a vivid image of the experience a concept will create for users.

I translate what I see to others in ways that make a concept come to life for them.

I build artifacts that bring concepts to life and allow users to "pre-experience."

I translate ideas in a clear and compelling way from text to image.

I develop immersive prototypes that facilitate feedback conversations.

I am able to surface and prioritize assumptions to be tested.

I am able to capture these assumptions in a prototype.

I find the trade-off between emptiness and vividness, using the right level and kind of detail.

I invite co-creation, actively entering conversations with users and partners.

LEARNING IN ACTION

I recognize when my knowing is interfering with my learning.

I explore disconfirming data with curiosity, rather than rejecting it.

I actively seek feedback on my new ideas from critical users and partners.

I am able to detach my ego from my creation.

I practice a hypothesis-driven approach.

I am focused on testing critical assumptions.

I listen nondefensively to critique.

I accept imperfect data and move on.

I design rigorous experiments.

I identify and gather the data needed to test.

I use findings to iterate hypotheses.

I am clear on what kinds of experiments to do at each stage.

I think creatively about how to triangulate data.

In the following steps, we recommend ways to integrate MVCs into your own plan for professional growth.

STEP 1: **Collect**

The first step is to gather data to help you reflect on your own situation. You likely have an assortment of personal data already collected that can help inform your personal DT journey. This data could include personality assessments, performance reviews from your bosses, or peer reviews from your colleagues. All are valuable, and have a place within the larger scope of your PDP. We also highly recommend completing the DiSC assessment. As we discussed in Part 4, the personas we describe are built around DiSC preferences. Taking the DiSC and learning more about your own personal preferences, and those of your teammates, will help you home in on the ways you are motivating—or impeding—both your personal and your team's DT journey.

Most important to your prework, we have developed a personal diagnostic—the MVC 360—based specifically around the MVCs. The MVC 360 tool provides you with the opportunity to assess where you rank your competence prior to the start of your DT journey, as well as a postphase evaluation to map your progress towards mastery. We also include a 360-degree evaluation that invites your teammates, coaches, and leadership to weigh in with their own assessment of your MVC performance. The Likert scale format makes it easy to set improvement goals for how successfully you build these behaviors into your daily practices.

As a starting point, begin by assessing your performance against all of the MVCs, across all six phases. Then, as you move into each phase, you will select a smaller set of specific MVCs for that phase that you want to focus on. At the conclusion of that phase, you'll get some feedback on how you've done. Then as you move onto the next phase, you'll select a few more MVCs from the new phase to focus on. When that phase ends, you will get some feedback on those. And so on. . . . You get the picture!

So—imagine yourself going into the first phase of Immersion . . .

STEP 2: **Reflect**

Among the mass of wisdom bestowed upon us by Maya Angelou lies this sage advice: *You can't really know where you are going until you know where you have been.* This is critical for our next step of reflection. Throughout the chapters, we provided specific FROM-TO mindset shifts as well as the MVCs. Your job is to decide which are most relevant to you at each phase of your journey. Your FROM-TO journey needs to be informed by all the feedback you have received and by your own personal reflection on what you'd like to achieve for that phase. For instance, in Immersion:

- If you want to be a better listener, how does that show up at work in terms of how you engage?

What does your boss say about you as a listener? What do your peers say about you as a listener? What would being a better listener look like?

- If you want to be more curious, how does that show up at work? What did you learn from your DiSC assessment (or a related tool) about your level of curiosity? What would being more curious look like for you?

Based on the personal diagnostic from the MVC 360 that you did in Step 1 you will likely see that you (like most of us) are already practicing some MVC behaviors. For others, you have room to grow. Take a minute and reflect; while all MVCs are important, some will resonate more than others. Which align most with your values at this phase? Which do you have the most interest in improving? Which seem most (and least) challenging to improve? We suggest that you focus on one to three MVCs per phase as you progress.

STEP 3: **Set Goals**

Recognizing areas of growth is a critical first step, but now we need accountability as well. One way to accomplish this is in a FROM-TO statement of your own, for the particular MVCs you have selected to work on during that phase. A FROM-TO statement includes (1) an identification of the area that you want to work on (like listening or curiosity), (2) a statement of your current behavior (from your personal diagnostic), and (3) your desired behavior. With your coach, mentor, or team leader, we recommend completing these steps to turn the growth opportunities you see into action goals for your chosen MVCs.

Craft a sentence or two depicting your current level of competency. This is your FROM statement. For instance, if working on active listening is your goal during the Immersion phase, your FROM statement might read something like this:

"I'm a person who often gets distracted, who sometimes feels embarrassed, and who doesn't want to pry, so I often look at my phone instead of asking people questions. I get feedback from people that says that I'm kind of standoffish, which really irritates me because I feel like I try to be nice, so I don't know what that's all about."

Then craft a sentence or two describing what "good" looks like to you. It is important that this is not copied out of a guide that says what a perfect listener is—it must be authentic to you. This is your TO statement, which, for active listening, may look like this:

"I'm a person who invites others to share and who people trust with their confidences. When I'm meeting new people, I get to know them quickly and I build rapport. Others say that I'm a person who helps bring a room together and makes it easy to share insights and new information."

STEP 4: **Plan and Act**

The hardest step is to figure out how to get from where you (think you) are to where you want to be during each phase. Spoiler alert: your growth will not happen overnight. Think of where you want to be as the final destination on the map. Whether you call it task analysis or backwards planning, the premise is the same: what small changes or behaviors must happen first, then next, then after that, and so forth to reach your goal?

In this step, we encourage innovators to consider each of their FROM statements, their TO statements, and the gray spaces in between. What needs to take place first, then next, then after that? Challenge yourself to build three actionable steps with as much specificity as possible. Plot the points needed to grow your competency. Make sure your steps are clear, measurable, and time bound so you know exactly whether or not you have reached them.

Within our given FROM-TO statements around active listening, the innovator may commit to the following three steps:

1. I will put my phone away and keep it away throughout an entire conversation.
2. I will pay more attention to my body language when others are speaking, like turning to face the speaker, making eye contact, nodding, smiling if appropriate, and uncrossing my arms.
3. Instead of jumping in to offer my own thoughts, I will probe first for a deeper explanation of how my teammates are thinking by asking "Why?" or prompting "Tell me more." My goal will be to ask one or two follow-up questions before adding my own thoughts.

70-20-10 PLAN

Experts in personal development often advocate developing a 70-20-10 plan. This suggests that 70% of your learning and growth should come through your experience and practice in your day-to-day work, 20% should come through socialization and the support you get from others (whether that's a mentor, a coach, or your boss) and 10% should come from formal learning.

Activities that are in the 10% are concrete learning activities or formal, structured learning opportunities. These could be things like reading this book or taking a class. Activities that fall into the 20% are activities that help you take some ownership of your relationship capital. These are activities from a relationship perspective that can help you with your desired goals, such as identifying one or two people in your organization who are really good at the behavior you are trying to improve whom you could contact for an informational interview. Anything that can help share the learning from someone's experience and encourages you to use your network to move you in the direction that you are trying to go. Activities that fall into the 70% are activities that can create accountability for your day-to-day work. These are deliberate and intentional efforts to do something new like apply a new structure to something or experiment with a new set of behaviors. It's important to remember that you can't just go to a class to change your behavior. In order to change and grow, you have to focus on the 70%.

To help you achieve these goals, we also encourage you to identify two people who could help you further develop your skills as well as one book or article to supplement your development in your chosen area.

You will rinse and repeat this for each phase as you enter it.

STEP 5: **Reflect (Again)**

Congratulations! Making it this far in your PDP is admirable—putting in the hard work to shift behaviors and mindsets is difficult, honest work. Now, it is important to stop and reflect on your progress (with as much objectivity as you can muster). At the conclusion of each phase, assess your own progress but also invite others to weigh in with their perspectives. Completing the self-postassessment and having teammates complete the 360 evaluation provides a good gut check on your progress and the way it manifests outwardly toward others. Your coach, mentor, or team leader should compile all of the feedback, making sure to keep it anonymous so that everyone feels safe to be honest. It is also critical that the team commits to this process to empower and develop one another and form a stronger, more creative whole.

As the pace of your DT project work accelerates, you will be tempted to let the PDP work be the first casualty when you and your team feel pressed for time. Fight that urge! Taking some time to reflect on your individual performance improvement goals, and those of your teammates, and gathering feedback against your progress, will pay big dividends in the longer term, for you, your team, and the success of both the current and future projects. Remember the power of learning to learn, of double-loop thinking. This is your chance to rise above the rat race that goes with being trapped in single-loop, System 1 habitual *doing* as a way of life. You want to be a design thinker in your life, not just within the narrow confines of today's project—so "Physician, heal thyself!" Insist on building attention to your *becoming* into your doing. Make it part of your daily practice.

STEP 6: **Repeat, Repeat, Repeat**

Just like Rome wasn't built in a day, full competence isn't achieved in one phase. Just like mastering the activities of DT, innovators must repeatedly reflect and actively revisit their current status within the MVCs—not sometimes, but *every* time the innovator engages in DT. It is this commitment to not only doing, but *experiencing* DT that will unlock the true power of the process. One option is to continue to revisit your MVC goals and simply up your game. Make the goals more challenging. Add more repetitions. Combine two actions so that they have to happen simultaneously instead of separately. Or challenge yourself to choose an MVC that is already in your wheelhouse and push yourself to improve, or help others improve. There is always more to work toward in DT—that's what makes it perfect for PDPs. We have included the full MVC 360 evaluation tool in appendix 1.

AMAN AND THE MVC 360

What does the MVC 360 look like in practice? Let's look at how Aman, our Analyst from Part 4, works with the tool as he approaches the Immersion phase.

Aman is starting the DT process with a multidisciplinary project team at work. He is apprehensive because he is typically not a "people" person and feels overwhelmed with the level of involvement DT requires. Additionally, he has no experience with qualitative research, enjoying his work with his perfectly synchronized spreadsheets. However, Ana, his supervisor, has encouraged him to participate in the experience as part of a PDP, and Aman feels like it seems a safe space to explore new knowledge, skills, and abilities.

Prior to embarking on their DT journey, Aman and his teammates filled out a self-assessment on all of the MVCs across the six experience phases of the DT process. Let's look at the process as he steps into his first phase. Entering Immersion, Aman examines his self-assessment on the **MVC 360: Immersion** (figure A).

It worries Aman that none of these MVCs feel comfortable to him. However, when he meets with Ana, his supervisor, prior to the start of interviews, he chooses two MVCs to focus on and reflects on where he feels he is currently operating and where he would like to be (figure B).

A

Immersion

I am aware of my own biases and blinders.

1	2	3	4	5
not at all	not often	sometimes	frequently	all the time

(3 is circled)

I listen to understand rather than to test.

1	2	3	4	5

(1 is circled)

I search for areas of opportunities, not solutions.

1	2	3	4	5

(2 is circled)

I develop an emotional engagement and empathetic bond with those for whom I design.

1	2	3	4	5

(1 is circled)

I probe deeply for unarticulated needs and beliefs.

1	2	3	4	5

(2 is circled)

I am fully present in the moment to the lived experience of my colleagues and those for whom I design.

1	2	3	4	5

(2 is circled)

I ask good questions.

1	2	3	4	5

(2 is circled)

Preassessment Total   (13)

B

MVC #1:

I probe deeply for unarticulated needs and beliefs.

From:
CURRENT STATE

I come into a problem with solutions stirring in my mind. Therefore, I approach conversations and interviews driven to clarify and confirm which direction I should go. I may be filtering what I hear.

To:
DESIRED STATE

I quiet the solutions stirring in my mind and instead aim to fully understand, even (and especially) if what I hear differs from all of my initial assumptions. I walk away wiser and more confident in my listening skills.

MVC #2:

I develop an emotional engagement and empathetic bond with those for whom I design.

From:
CURRENT STATE

I am intimidated to speak to people I don't know, so I am reluctant to ask personal questions and hear intimate details about strangers' lives. I fear they will see right through my front, recognize my discomfort, and assume I am disinterested. Really, however, I just have trouble connecting.

To:
DESIRED STATE

I am warm, open, and vulnerable in my conversations with others. I show them the same openness I need them to show me, and I walk away feeling deeply what they feel—the highs and the lows.

The next day, Aman and Ana walk through how Aman might make such transformations. What could he do? What could he say? What could he think (or not think)? Together, they craft actionable steps to get Aman closer to proficiency on his chosen MVCs (figure C).

C

MVC #1:

I probe deeply for unarticulated needs and beliefs.

Three actionable, measurable steps I can take to make this transition are:

1   *Ask open-ended questions that allow the person to share a full experience with limited direction.*

2   *Approach each interview with curiosity—ask follow-up questions that engage emotional responses.*

3   *Take a breath before responding and ask, "Is this question to learn more, or is it guiding the person to something I want them to say?"*

Two people I can have a conversation with to improve my listening skills:

1   *Mary Pat, Director of Qualitative Research*

2   *Ken Singer, Customer Call Center Manager*

One book I can read to improve my listening skills:

1   *Power Listening: Mastering the Most Critical Business Skill of All, Bernard T. Ferrari*

MVC #2:

I develop an emotional engagement and empathetic bond with those for whom I design.

Three actionable, measurable steps I can take to make this transition are:

1   *I will not pretend I understand or relate to the person at all. I will approach the interview with a blank slate and an open mind.*

2   *I will actively listen and use probing questions that relate to particular emotions and experiences.*

3   *I will run point on at least four interviews our team completes, and I will follow up personally to each interview subject with a note of gratitude.*

Two people I can have a conversation with to improve my listening skills:

1   *Chandra Smith, Director of Diversity and Inclusion*

2   *Jim Laksimm, Night Manager*

One book I can read to improve my listening skills:

1   *Permission to Feel: Unlocking the Power of Emotions to Help Our Kids, Ourselves, and Our Society Thrive, Marc Brackett*

D

Aman continues through the ethnographic interviews, focusing on the actionable steps he crafted. He is impressed that by focusing on these somewhat small aspects of the task, the confidence and enjoyment he feels seem to grow, and the acceptance from his teammates is warm and encouraging. The greatest evidence of growth, however, is in the level of connectedness he experiences with those he interviews. By listening to understand and allowing connection on a human-to-human level, Aman realizes that these people are more than data points. They have strengths, motivations, hardships and pain points. As the interview process wraps up, he has developed a bond with those he speaks with, and feels driven to make it easier for them to thrive.

As he fills out the postassessment (figure D), and gets 360 feedback from his teammates, he is shocked to see that while the MVCs he chose to focus on have improved, other MVCs have also benefited from his practice as well. He leaves the data-gathering phase with a new understanding of the experience and is excited to continue the DT journey as he prepares to identify insights.

Immersion

I am aware of my own biases and blinders.

1	2	3	4	5
not at all	not often	sometimes	frequently	all the time

I listen to understand rather than to test.

1	2	3	4	5

I search for areas of opportunities, not solutions.

1	2	3	4	5

I develop an emotional engagement and empathetic bond with those for whom I design.

1	2	3	4	5

I probe deeply for unarticulated needs and beliefs.

1	2	3	4	5

I am fully present in the moment to the lived experience of my colleagues and those for whom I design.

1	2	3	4	5

I ask good questions.

1	2	3	4	5

Postassessment Total   26

Throughout this chapter, our aim has been to help you put the contents of this book into action in ways that improve your practice and deepen your DT experience at each phase, so that you and your team can maximize the impact of DT. We hope we've succeeded!

Time to shift gears to explore how these principles and processes can help transform your organization as well.

CHAPTER 15

ORGANIZATIONAL DEVELOPMENT PLANNING

IN CHAPTER 14, we talked about assessing your personal DT competencies and creating a PDP. But what about the development of your organization, as well as the other groups you work with? How do you assess whether they are taking full advantage of DT's social technology to produce transformational outcomes we have talked about in this book? In this chapter, we take a more collective look at the activities being performed and the outcomes achieved. As in Chapter 14, we will offer you a diagnostic tool (contained in full in appendix 2) that you can use with your team, the larger group of stakeholders you are working with, your business unit or department, or even your organization as a whole to examine where you are, as a basis for exploring together where you want to be. As with the PDP, we will suggest a set of steps for collecting, reflecting, goal setting and development planning—but this time at an organizational level.

Before diving into the *how*, let's spend a minute summing up *why* organizational leaders need to focus on building DT competencies in the first place. We've highlighted a set of positive benefits at different levels.

At the level of the *individual innovator*, DT can build engagement, creative confidence, a sense of ownership, self-efficacy, and psychological safety. It can foster positive emotions and spur more risk-taking.

These individual outcomes all benefit the *organization* as well. In *Harvard Business Review*, Professors Clark and Saxberg review the causes of lack of motivation on the part of employees. They stress four prominent ones: (1) employees may not connect with the task and simply not care; (2) they may lack self-efficacy and confidence in their own abilities; (3) they may lack an understanding of why the solution being implemented makes sense; or (4) they may lack positive emotions and be trapped by negative thoughts.[104] DT directly addresses each one of these motivational traps. Furthermore, it increases both the quality of solutions and their likelihoods of implementation.

DT benefits other kinds of collectives as well, whether these be internal teams, groups of external stakeholders or communities. It creates the opportunity to build and deepen trust, to broaden networks, to foster the creation of more systemic higher-order solutions, and to pool and extend resources.

There are two other critical areas of opportunity we want to highlight here as well. Though neither has received much attention to date as a place where DT can really make a difference, we believe that these are sweet spots for DT—and that they deserve recognition. Both are critical to organizational health and adaptation. The first of these is in the area of equity and inclusion. The second concerns strategic planning.

EQUITY AND INCLUSION

It is not hard to see why DT is a great approach for building more equitable and inclusive organizations. Its underlying values—respecting the uniqueness of each individual, giving voice to a broader cross-section of people, reducing the negative effects of hierarchy, encouraging small experiments that give more people the opportunity to act—all support creating more collaborative and inclusive organizations. But DT contributes more than just values—it builds competencies. *Immersion* develops perspective-taking abilities that help us escape the blinders of our egocentric biases to appreciate difference in a more meaningful way. *Sensemaking* teaches us how to recognize both emotional and cognitive data and translate these into deeper insights that improve the solutions we create for those we design for. *Alignment* offers mechanisms for building action-oriented communities through activities like creating shared design criteria that specify critical attributes of any future design and embody joint priorities. *Emergence* equips diverse stakeholders with tools for facilitating conversations which produce higher-order solutions by inviting individuals to bring their authentic selves into the dialogue. *Imagining* brings tools to help us make our visions tangible and shareable with others. *LIA* sets up a structure for co-creation with those we design for and explicitly gives decision-making power to that community rather than to authorities or hierarchies.

DT also encourages another critical component of

equity and inclusion: humility. In their *Equity-Centered Community Design Field Guide*, Creative Reaction Lab[105] defines humility as recognizing the influence of biases and perspectives when trying to understand another's emotions, thoughts, experiences and actions. While humility sparks from within individuals, organizations can provide an environment that supports it, replacing an expert-focused "knowing" culture with a "learning" culture that rewards openness, experimentation and effort. Valuing humility also tasks organizations to address power imbalances, privilege and systemic inequities people may not have previously recognized or acknowledged. At its core, DT provides a safe space to have the kind of potentially scary conversations that help us get comfortable with *not* knowing. If everyone is asking "What don't I know?" at every phase, the humility that invites and values inclusion will flow naturally.

We are equally intrigued by DT's potential to contribute to the equity and inclusion conversation at a pragmatic level, as well, by encouraging polarized groups to explicitly step away from ideological battles to focus instead on improving concrete experiences. Take, as just one example, police traffic stops. Is there anyone—on either side of that conversation—who does *not* think that this experience is in need of dramatic improvement? What if we tried putting aside, just temporarily and as a first step, the moral and ideological discussions inherent in the battle and used DT tools and methods to concentrate on fixing an experience that is badly broken for all stakeholders

involved? We believe that this approach has the potential to help polarized stakeholder groups move into positive action, and out of unproductive debates, even in the absence of agreement on ideology.

STRATEGIC PLANNING

The second area we want to note as a special opportunity is tied to strategic planning. When the goal is innovation, strategic planning's track record at engaging employees and motivating them to action is terrible. An *Economist* study found that only about 60% of new strategies' promised returns were actually delivered,[106] with other studies placing the frequency of successful implementation of new strategies at less than 10%.[107] One global study noted that while more than 80% of the firms studied *had* mission statements, 60% of their managers did not believe that those statements had *anything* to do with the reality of their daily work.[108]

When strategy is decided and stated by a few, the rest of us will never fully understand or be motivated when we are simply *told* about it. DT allows us all to have a hand in creating strategy—and that makes it come alive. DT moves our thinking beyond the world of cognition and logic (strategy as *thought*), to thinking of strategy as *experienced*. Strategy as *thought* is grounded in a belief in rationality and objectivity, and focuses on gaining employees' intellectual understanding and acceptance of a new strategy. The idea of experiencing strategy (like experiencing design), makes strategy personal, emotional and embodied, as well as cognitive. Strategies are, by nature, abstract. They begin to take on form and concreteness only when translated into new behaviors. Yet, such translation is often not enough for them to be experienced as real by members of the organization not involved in their creation. DT can help.

Our story of the botanical garden, in Chapter 6, with its widely inclusive planning process, offers a case in point. Do you recall a leader there who argued that their plan allowed people to see the garden vividly as the amazing place it could *become*, not as the decaying and long neglected institution it actually was? The vividness he notes did not happen because employees and donors *read* the plan—it was because employees had a hand in creating it. And their passion made it real to donors. This kind of presencing of the future in the present is what translates abstract ideas into something meaningful to the individuals who must implement them. By making the abstract concrete in a believable way, strategic intention is linked to the details of daily practice. This approach incorporates Michael Benedikt's four qualities for making something feel real: attention-getting presence, personal significance, materiality, and an emptiness that invites participation and engagement. Democratizing strategy creation and giving the permission, process and tools to put opportunity finding in the hands of employees throughout the organization is where DT practices can make a difference. They make the work of strategic innovation accessible to all employees, by offering simple rules and a teachable and scalable tool kit. Design practices can foster and guide a widely participative strategic conversation, one that empowers employees to identify otherwise invisible opportunities.

By now, we hope that we have convinced you that building a DT competency is essential to your organization's ability to innovate and adapt to change. Now we turn to how you get there. As with personal development, it involves assessing where you are, where you want to be, and specific plans and timelines for reducing the gap between them.

DEVELOPING YOUR ORGANIZATION'S DT CAPABILITIES

Why is assessing DT outcomes so hard?

One of the universal refrains in the DT world is the absence of quantitative evidence of its effectiveness. Sure—those of us who experience it *know* it works—but rarely is that good enough to gain the kind of corporate support needed for organization-wide competency building. We need to be as creative in our assessment efforts as we are in the creation of new products and services for those we serve.

How do we get a grip on the current reality of the kinds of outcome that DT is producing? Assessing that reality may be the biggest hurdle in the entire process. It begins with an understanding of today's performance. Otherwise, how can we know that we are actually improving as we move forward?

This requires having measurable targets. In our experience with DT, this is more challenging at the organizational level than it is for individuals. For individuals, we have the MVCs to work with—specific behaviors that we can observe. Of course, we could assess organizational progress by just accumulating the total of all individuals' MVCs. But building an organizational competency for innovation is about more than bringing together a set of competent individuals—it involves surrounding them with an infrastructure that includes supportive culture and facilitating processes. We need to push towards gathering data on identifiable *collective outcomes*, not just individual behaviors, recognizing that these collective outcomes show up as new collective behaviors.

This kind of evidence is challenging to establish for *any* new methodology that we introduce into the complex world of an organization, where there are many moving parts and interactions both within it and between it and its outside environment. DT use is just one aspect of this complicated picture. Because of this, direct cause and effect between its introduction and corporate outcomes can rarely be determined with the accuracy we would like. Even beyond these complications (which scientists would call "intervening variables"), significant time often elapses between introducing new behaviors and achieving final outcomes like revenue growth or profitability. These traditional measures of performance are usually too far down the road to be of much assistance to leaders trying to manage the development of new organizational competencies. In addition, we face the problem that we talked about in Chapter 8: though we are tempted to work with the measures we've *got* (like new product revenues and profits), these are likely not the measures we *need*. The measures we need will help us trace not only *what* but *how* DT impacts outcomes, in ways that help us actively manage its development.

To understand DT's impacts deeply enough to intelligently manage development efforts, we need to return to behaviors—but this time focus on the behavioral outcomes that DT produces that are the intermediate mechanisms that lead to the ultimate outcomes we want. For example, instead of just assessing whether innovators are listening openly and with empathy, we need to assess whether that listening is actually producing more user-centered products. How do we do that? Our solution has been to ask those involved.

In Chapter 2, we talked about the research we have been conducting on DT outcomes, and now invite you to use the diagnostic survey we developed to do that work (contained in full in Appendix 2). It allows you to see your organization's strength and weaknesses in both the practices being implemented and outcomes produced. The survey can be taken by any group within your organization that makes sense to you. As with the personal development planning process, we suggest that you consider engaging a broad cross-section of your organization to be part of the assessment process—different functions, levels, and geographies. This will allow you to compare and contrast, identifying your high performers who can serve as role models and mentors, as well as your low performers whose outcomes are in need of improvement.

The survey consists of two scales—one on practices, the other on outcomes. In creating the items for each scale, we started with the data accumulated from years of research on the outcomes produced by specific projects utilizing well-developed DT methodologies—our own as well as that of others.[109]

From this body of work, we identified a comprehensive set of practices and outcomes. Most importantly, we didn't create our outcomes scale by imagining what DT outcomes *might* look like; instead we studied the outcomes that were actually being produced in real-life projects by the innovators we studied.

In order to quantify impact in a rigorous way (a favorite academic descriptor of solid research), it is important to first understand what activities are

PART 1: DESIGN PRACTICES WE ASKED ABOUT

The following items relate to various design thinking practices that you may have used. **Please rate the extent to which you, in your own design thinking practice, have . . .** (*circle your response*):

	NEVER		SOMETIMES		ALMOST ALWAYS
. . . Followed a structured process	1	2	3	4	5
. . . Formed a diverse team	1	2	3	4	5
. . . Emphasized active listening among team members in order to find shared meaning	1	2	3	4	5
. . . Done user research using ethnographic tools (e.g., interviewing and observation, journey mapping, job-to-be-done, etc.)	1	2	3	4	5
. . . Focused your problem definition on the user's perspective rather than the organization's	1	2	3	4	5
. . . Created a set of design criteria that described an ideal solution, based on user research	1	2	3	4	5
. . . Generated a diverse set of ideas based on your user research	1	2	3	4	5
. . . Created prototypes of your ideas (e.g., storyboards, videos, mock-ups of offerings)	1	2	3	4	5
. . . Moved multiple ideas into prototyping and testing	1	2	3	4	5
. . . Got feedback from users and other stakeholders on the prototype	1	2	3	4	5
. . . Executed real-world experiments to test your ideas	1	2	3	4	5

being performed under the DT umbrella. So in Part 1 of this survey tool we developed, respondents are asked to evaluate how often they used each of the 11 different DT practices on a scale of 1 (never), 2 (rarely), 3 (sometimes), 4 (frequently), or 5 (almost always).

Part 2 of the diagnostic tool addresses the outcomes, highlighting for consideration a wide array of different outcomes that we saw DT produce, and asks respondents to note to what extent, in their own experience of DT, they have personally observed each of the potential outcomes listed, on the same scale of 1 (never) to 5 (almost always). These DT outcomes include impacts at multiple levels: individual, team, organizational and even systemic.

These are intermediate outcomes, taking the form of collective behaviors that are the path to producing ultimate and quantifiable outcomes like sales and profits.

PART 2: OUTCOMES WE ASKED ABOUT

The following items seek to capture a variety of possible outcomes produced by the use of design thinking practices. **Please rate how often, in your own experience, the use of design thinking resulted in the following** (circle your response):

		NEVER		SOMETIMES		ALMOST ALWAYS
1	Created deeper understanding of stakeholder needs	1	2	3	4	5
2	Helped teams see the problems in new ways, resulting in solving more promising problems	1	2	3	4	5
3	Helped team members find alignment across their different perspectives	1	2	3	4	5
4	Enhanced your ability to pivot when initial solution didn't work	1	2	3	4	5
5	Increased engagement of employees involved in the design thinking process	1	2	3	4	5
6	Leveraged diversity on team to find more creative solutions	1	2	3	4	5
7	Built new relationships locally that continued after the initial project was completed	1	2	3	4	5
8	Expanded access to new resources for individuals and teams	1	2	3	4	5

Full survey with all items listed can be found in the appendix.

It turns out that they also produce the competencies on the innovation wish list we talked about in Chapter 1. There, we suggested four simple and straightforward outcomes that we wanted our innovation efforts to result in:

1. Better choices—ones that that create better value in the moment.
2. Reduced risk and cost of innovation efforts.
3. Increased likelihood that new ideas actually get implemented.
4. Making both individuals and organizations more adaptable to change and uncertainty.

All of the outcomes on our survey can be linked back to these goals on our wish list.

Because collaboration is so crucial to producing these wish list outcomes, our survey tool also contains a set of items specifically targeted at measuring enhanced collaboration at both team and network levels.

Working with what you find

After conducting your survey using our diagnostic tool, you can reflect on your results in multiple ways:

- You can look at your practices at an organization-wide level and compare what your portfolio of activities looks like today with where you would like to be.

OUTCOMES* BY WISH LIST

WISH LIST 1: **Better Choices**

1	Created deeper understanding of stakeholder needs	☐
2	Helped teams see the problem in new ways, resulting in solving more promising problems	☐
5	Increased engagement of employees involved in the design thinking process	☐
17	Allowed new and better solutions, not visible at the beginning of the process, to emerge during it	☐
18	Fostered the inclusion of user input	☐
20	Helped people involved to examine their own biases and preconceptions	☐
27	Improved the creativity of new solutions	☐
	TOTAL BETTER CHOICES AVERAGE	☐

Numbers correlate to assessment line item.

WISH LIST 2: **Reduced Risk**

4   Enhanced your ability to pivot when initial solution didn't work ☐

12   Helped to surface critical assumptions being made about new ideas so that they could be tested ☐

13   Helped teams to gather more accurate feedback on ideas from users and other stakeholders ☐

19   Reduced the risk of pursuing ideas that will likely fail ☐

30   Made it easier to discard solutions that didn't work as planned ☐

TOTAL REDUCED RISK AVERAGE ☐

WISH LIST 3:
Increased Likelihood of Implementation

28   Improved the likelihood of the implementation of new solutions ☐

36   Kept people motivated to work on a project to achieve impact ☐

40   Increased a sense of ownership and acceptance of a solution ☐

21   Helped champions for new ideas who were enthusiastic about their implementation emerge during the design thinking process ☐

24   Allowed for involvement of key stakeholders who were not on the core team ☐

TOTAL IMPLEMENTATION AVERAGE ☐

WISH LIST 4:
Individual and Organizational Adaptability

INDIVIDUAL

22   Increased people's willingness to take action ☐

23   Created a sense of safety to try new things ☐

26   Gave employees more confidence in their own creative abilities ☐

31   Helped people interested in trying new things to connect and support each other ☐

32   Encouraged people's open-mindedness to try new things ☐

SUBTOTAL ____

ORGANIZATION

33   Encouraged shifts in organizational culture to make it more customer-focused ☐

34   Encouraged changes in organizational culture that made risk-taking more acceptable ☐

37   Broadened organization's definition of what innovation is ☐

41   Increased appreciation for use of data to help drive decisions ☐

35   Equipped team members with new capabilities that can be applied to other projects ☐

38   Created a common language/framework among team members ☐

SUBTOTAL ____

TOTAL ADAPTABILITY AVERAGE ☐

WISH LIST 4: **Assessing Collaboration**

TEAM

3   Helped team members find alignment across their different perspectives ☐

14   Built trust among team members ☐

29   Made working together more enjoyable ☐

25   Helped teams to persist despite challenges along the way ☐

16   Improved the ability to talk to each other in ways that produced better outcomes ☐

6   Leveraged diversity on team to find more creative solutions ☐

SUBTOTAL _____

NETWORK

7   Built new relationships locally that continued after the initial project was completed ☐

8   Expanded access to new resources for individuals and teams ☐

9   Helped pool resources for greater impact ☐

39   Increased willingness to collaborate with others (cross-functionally and cross-departmentally) ☐

10   Helped to build alignment across diverse stakeholders ☐

11   Enhanced other stakeholders' willingness to collaborate on new solutions ☐

15   Built trust between problem-solving teams and other stakeholders ☐

SUBTOTAL _____

TOTAL COLLABORATION AVERAGE ☐

- You can repeat this same process for outcomes. What is your organization doing the most of (using averages from Part 1)? What are you best at (using averages from Part 2)? What skills or opportunities are you missing (the lowest averages)?

- You can also look across different teams or departments and compare their performance. Who are your lead performers, in terms of either usage of tools or the outcomes they create? Who is struggling? Can you establish a system where they can learn from each other to help each other improve?

- Comparing the outcomes that the managers who sponsored projects observed, relative to what those directly involved observed, provides an interesting outside perspective and strengthens confidence in innovators' self-reports.

- A final approach is to compare your results to the averages of those of other organizations in our study whose results we can share (anonymously and aggregated, of course).[110] We keep an updated listing of our results on our website, *experiencingdesign.org*, sorted by type of organization—business, government, and nonprofit.

Chances are, when you review your results using any of the above approaches, you will find many areas that represent opportunities to accelerate your organization's ability to tap into the kinds of transformational outcomes we have talked about in this book.

The next step, then, is to lay out a plan for how you will move forward and accelerate your progress. As with the PDP, we suggest that you highlight just a few areas to target for development. First, figure out what is in the way of moving forward (do some ethnography on the experience of your own employees as they navigate the DT process). Then lay out a detailed plan for how to get where you want to go, depending upon what you learn. Here are some examples:

Problem: People are confused about what DT is and how it can be applied to their work.
Solution: Think about establishing a common language and process methodology.

Problem: Novices are being expected to apply tools they don't fully grasp.
Solution: Deeper training in particular tools or processes and mentoring to support their use.

Problem: The availability of important resources like time (often the biggest impediment) or access to customers is lacking.
Solution: More visible leadership support, including an explicit advance agreement with supervisors about the percentage of time to be devoted to DT projects. Or infrastructure support to make the new behaviors less time consuming and more efficient—like bringing volunteer customers in once a week to make ethnography and co-creation easier.

Problem: Old mindsets around fear of failure lingering that impede your implementation of new skills.
Solution: A new campaign to highlight internal stories of successful experimentation in which both those that support people's ingoing hypotheses and those that disprove them are celebrated. Or we love the idea of one organization that issues a monthly award for the most intelligent instance of "calling the baby ugly."

Problem: An internal myopia that ignores opportunities to work with outside partners who bring important new perspectives and resources.
Solution: A plan for more systematic involvement with critical stakeholders outside of the organization that sets up the kind of "collisions with uncommon partners" that Saul Kaplan talked about in Chapter 5. When you seek partners, invest time in practices designed to build relationships and trust.

Each organization is unique. Only by understanding the particulars of the current reality of your organization's performance and identifying the specific gaps that stand in the way of moving to your desired future can you craft an effective developmental path to organization-wide competency development. Like so much of the worlds we encounter as we experience design, there is no silver bullet, no one size fits all.

USE CASE: **FLOWERPOWER AND THE ORGANIZATIONAL OUTCOMES TOOL**

As Head of Design Strategy at FlowerPower (FP), a leading wholesaler of fresh flowers, Lucy had worked hard over the past five years to infuse DT in all areas of the organization. Working closely with colleagues in FP Human Resources, together they had offered training, mentoring, and personal development plans for interested employees throughout the firm. At present, they had a core group of over 150 "Design Catalysts" deployed across all departments, from Finance to Communications. As she prepared her organizational development plan for the coming year, Lucy wondered what new steps her group should take to deepen DT competency at FP and help the Catalysts succeed. She also realized that in order to maximize buy-in and senior leadership support to expand DT's reach, she needed to demonstrate its impact on organizational performance and the subsequent return on investment that DT was actually producing. As she began to compile data for the next annual report, Lucy decided this would be a good time to step back and assess progress to date.

She decided to administer the DT Organizational Assessment survey organization-wide to those involved in the effort, as well as to those they reported to. She reached out to her Catalysts with a request that they complete the survey—answering as honestly as possible to what extent they had personally: (1) used the key elements listed in Part 1 in their work and (2) observed any of the design outcomes listed in Part 2. She also requested that they furnish the name and email of managers, not directly involved in the efforts, who sponsored the DT work they had done, who would also have a view of the outcomes. Promising strict confidentiality, and with a minimum of five surveys completed per department,

the effort had achieved about a 70% response rate, so she felt good about the data she had collected as she rolled up her sleeves to begin her assessment.

Results and Reflections

First, Lucy focused on practice use. Looking at the usage of particular design practices across the organization, at an aggregate level, she was pleased to see that most of them were being very actively used, suggesting to her that the training focusing on DT as an end-to-end process was taking hold.

She did note, however, that some testing practices at DT's back end were not used as frequently as front-end practices. Lucy also observed that those managers not directly involved with DT projects reported lower practice usage than the Catalysts themselves, making her wonder if she had some educational outreach work to do helping the Catalysts to better engage their sponsors at critical points during the DT process.

Next, she compared design practice averages across departments. When broken down this way, the inconsistencies widened in range.

She noted that some areas were real stars—they seemed to have gone beyond thinking of DT as a series of projects, and had begun to embed these practices into their day-to-day work lives. But there was more variety in usage than she expected. Marketing, for instance, seemed to favor DT's front-end ethnographic tools, using these considerably more frequently that the testing tools like prototyping and real-world experimentation. Operations, on the other hand, almost alone among the departments, was using experimentation heavily.

TESTING PRACTICE AVERAGES ACROSS DEPARTMENTS

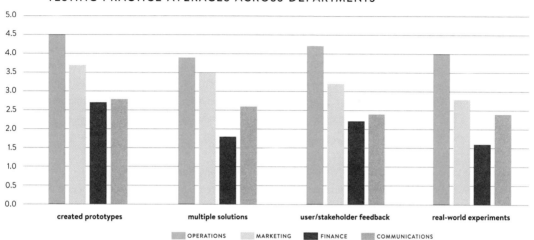

OPERATIONS   MARKETING   FINANCE   COMMUNICATIONS

COMPARISON OF FLOWERPOWER PRACTICE AVERAGES WITH WEBSITE AVERAGE

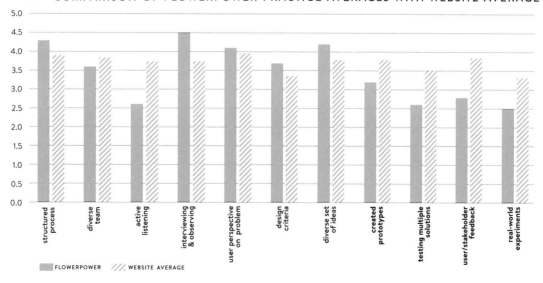

FLOWERPOWER   WEBSITE AVERAGE

Finally, she compared the Catalysts' frequency of usage for selected tools with the latest averages she found on the website *experiencingdesign.org*. These were based on data from over 1,000 people actively using DT. She was pleased to see that, for most of the activities, they were at or above these averages.

In some cases, like the use of ethnographic interviewing and observation, and the creation of a diverse set of ideas, they truly shone. As she had expected, the data confirmed her fears that experimentation was being underutilized at FP.

Next, Lucy turned to look at the data on outcomes. She was pleased that, on most of their innovation priorities, they were seeing solid results. She was especially pleased that responses showed that important psychological benefits were being experienced at the individual level and that people were reporting feeling more security, creative confidence and openness to risk taking. The one exception, she noted, was in the area of collaboration.

Digging deeper, she saw that while collaboration among teams was thriving, on the network side, it lagged. Catalysts were not seeing much in the way of expanded access to new resources or the pooling of resources for greater impact. Lucy believed that, in a resource-strapped environment, it was important for DT to deliver on these outcomes. This lag was apparent in comparison to other organizations as well.

Development Planning

As a next step in her planning process, Lucy identified the key areas that she felt organizational efforts should focus on: (1) improved use of testing practices and (2) achieving better

COMPARISON OF FLOWERPOWER OUTCOME AVERAGES WITH OTHER ORGANIZATIONS

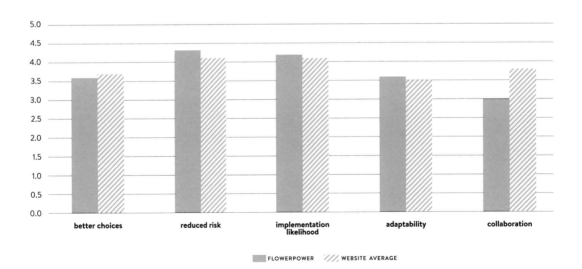

outcomes around network collaboration. She pulled together a group of Catalysts from all across FP for a special session to identify the underlying drivers of the deficiency in these areas and brainstorm possible solutions.

As they examined testing, some expected pain points surfaced as people reported being uncomfortable with the specifics of designing experiments. But other reasons surprised her. Marketing reported hesitation with gathering feedback from customers in real-world experiments because the team did not want to send a mixed message about what products and services were available. What if customers liked a new service that FP testing concluded should be discontinued? Finance worried that testing new practices might come across as disorganized to their internal customers, reducing the department's credibility. In brainstorming solutions, multiple ideas were generated:

- Offering a new workshop focused specifically on the design and execution of experiments.
- Creating some department-to-department partner groups to support each other. For instance, Operations can share their strategies for testing with other departments.
- Identifying both internal and external clients with whom the department in question had good rapport and who would understand and value partnering in experiments.

On the network side, Catalysts from numerous departments described how curtailed travel budgets had made it difficult to go on the road to meet with important constituencies. Lack of time also seemed an issue—others reported that it was only after a dispute of some kind arose that attention was paid to serious conversation with stakeholder groups. This made it difficult to build trust. To address these issues, potential solutions were brainstormed. These included:

- Inviting stakeholders to come to FP to get to know them and their needs and perspectives, rather than FP traveling to them.
- Developing a proactive strategy that identified key partners and supported working with them in advance of troubles arising.
- Setting aside some additional travel funds that allowed relationship building with particularly strategic members of their networks at conferences and industry trade shows.

Lucy settled down to pull together both a report to senior leadership on the ROI of FP's investment in DT to date and a plan for further organizational development. She felt that she now had the depth of understanding that she needed to paint a reasonably accurate picture of current reality, offer clear and concrete options for moving forward, and lay out a strategy for achieving their developmental goals. She felt good about the Catalyst team they had assembled and her colleagues' commitment to working together to take FP to a whole new level of DT usage and benefits.

SOME PARTING THOUGHTS

Despite having stressed that each individual innovator and his or her organization needs to be looked at as unique, our experiences working with many organizations have led us to develop some universal advice. The headline for improving the kinds of outcomes your DT process produces are already obvious from our conversation thus far: *senior leaders need to put in place a supportive infrastructure that deepens their employees' experience of all phases of their DT journeys—and helps them feel safe to explore these new ways of thinking and behaving with humility, curiosity and creativity.*

Let's get specific. We will start with the easy stuff.

SPECIFY A STRUCTURED PROCESS METHODOLOGY. At the risk of repeating ourselves one last time, we will say it again: designers may not need a lot of structure to do DT, but the rest of us do. Rather than dampen creativity, all of our evidence says that the *right* kind of tools and process inspire it. Pick one approach that resonates with your organization and use it to create a common language and set of processes and guidelines for how you will practice DT together.

OFFER THE OPPORTUNITY TO LEARN IT WELL. We're not enthusiastic about hackatons because, although they generate enthusiasm and basic DT knowledge, they also produce widespread misconception that short workshops are all an organization

needs to unleash creative potential. *Experiencing* each phase of DT, as learners work through a real, live project of their own choice, not just *doing* a scattering of activities, is what it takes to shift the mindsets of innovators and equip them with the MVCs they need. This need not be expensive or time consuming. You don't need to fly everybody off to California for boot camp (though we'd gladly join you!). We have been surprised and thrilled to observe how effective inexpensive and easily scalable online instruction can be, coupled with some local coaching and leadership support delivered just in time as learners work through real projects. Seven years of teaching this way, along with more than 300,000 enrollments in our introductory offerings, gives us confidence about that.

PROVIDE EXPERIENCED COACHES. Good coaches really help. Yes, our research has documented some pretty impressive successes of teams of nondesigners learning on their own, online and without any formal mentoring,[111] but that is not ideal. Coaches who have been around the block themselves a few times can help to calm the nerves of jittery teams and unstick stuck ones. They are invaluable.

SUPPORT STARTING SMALL AND LEARNING. One of our favorite aspects of DT is the ability to start small. Take advantage of that. It need not take a big budget or a massive top-down initiative. Start with volunteers who are *already* dying to innovate. Support them with some training, coaching, time and room to experiment. Then publicize their successes—people will get in line to get some of what they've got.

Now for some more challenging suggestions:

PROVIDE BLOCKS OF UNDISTURBED TIME.
Innovators with blocks of undisturbed time can very quickly focus on the work required. In our research, lack of time is the top reason behind a failure to do DT well. It doesn't take giant chunks of time, but you can't expect people to learn new ways of thinking and behaving all on their own time.

KEEP A POSITIVE ENVIRONMENT.
We have already talked a lot about recent psychological research that demonstrates that positive emotion increases the number and breadth of ideas and the brain's ability to triangulate information. Pay attention to the general atmosphere that innovators operate in. Music, snacks and spaces that allow for interaction and sharing all really help.

BEWARE THE UNINTENDED CONSEQUENCE OF RIGID CUSTOMER FOCUS.
This one is really interesting to us. Overly zealous implementation of a mandate to deliver 100% satisfaction to customers at all times can actually impede the kind of experimentation innovators need to do to continue to improve the customer experience. Make it okay to show customers stuff that isn't perfect. Be willing to give them something to try that you may later need to take away. These behaviors, essential to experimentation, feel just plain wrong after drinking the Kool-Aid of "the customer always comes first." As one of our interviewees noted:

> *Many company cultures resist this openness to experiment. Many fear the risk associated with a failed idea being tested directly with customers. So they push for speed, deciding to forgo careful design and the need for sequential testing of hypotheses to tease out the drivers of what works and what doesn't.*

In this mindset, you can't even ask customers what they *think* without creating a sense of obligation to actually give it to them. Offering a trial product that you may never deliver—or if you do, later take back—seems unthinkable. This limits data gathering to "say" data, which is far inferior to "do" data, for testing purposes. Getting to "do" data necessitates inviting actions that you sometimes will deliberately not follow through on. This means finding a set of partners who are themselves interested in experimentation and learning.

TRY TO LOWER THE STAKES.
The constant coupling of DT with "wicked problems" alarms us. Yes—it is good for those big, messy, hard-to-solve problems—but novices certainly shouldn't start there. The more we can lower their anxiety as they learn DT, the more they will fully experience it and shift. Small is beautiful.

And now here are some thoughts on the really hard-to-do stuff:

INCREASE SENIOR LEADERSHIP ATTENTION. Executive attention and interaction is a big deal when teams are wading through uncertainty and feeling untethered. Increasing executive access reinforces positive behaviors and provides assurance that innovators' work is valued and is sanctioned by the executive team. Even short executive check-ins can help rebuild creative confidence in team members who suddenly feel skeptical that their efforts will lead to success, or have lost energy fighting a bureaucracy that doesn't support them.

The specifics of leadership support will look different at different phases:

STARTING OUT: As teams are composed, think carefully about requisite variety—the repertoire of perspectives and experience needed in an innovation effort to match the solution space. Don't forget the importance of local voices.

LEADERSHIP SUPPORT AT EACH PHASE

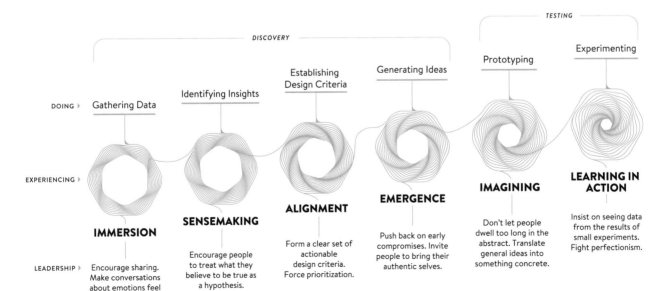

DISCOVERY

TESTING

DOING ▶ Gathering Data   Identifying Insights   Establishing Design Criteria   Generating Ideas   Prototyping   Experimenting

EXPERIENCING ▶

IMMERSION   **SENSEMAKING**   **ALIGNMENT**   **EMERGENCE**   **IMAGINING**   **LEARNING IN ACTION**

LEADERSHIP ▶ Encourage sharing. Make conversations about emotions feel normal and valuable.

Encourage people to treat what they believe to be true as a hypothesis.

Form a clear set of actionable design criteria. Force prioritization.

Push back on early compromises. Invite people to bring their authentic selves.

Don't let people dwell too long in the abstract. Translate general ideas into something concrete.

Insist on seeing data from the results of small experiments. Fight perfectionism.

IMMERSION: Encourage not only the use of DT's ethnographic research tools to broaden individual members' perspectives beyond their own worldviews, but the sharing of what they learn with a broader group of stakeholders through stories, posters—whatever it takes. Begin to make conversations about emotions feel as normal—and valuable—as talking about financials.

SENSEMAKING: Encourage people to treat what they believe to be true as a hypothesis. Make that a norm you enforce. That especially applies to the definition of the problem. Invite a larger collective to spend time exploring the problem before they explore solutions.

ALIGNMENT: Insist that groups drill down to agreement on what really matters in the form of a clear and succinct set of actionable *design criteria* about the kind of user experience that an ideal design would create. Force prioritization. When you have too many priorities, you actually have none.

EMERGENCE: Obsessively focus on creating and protecting the conditions that foster the emergence of higher-order solutions. Push back on early compromises. Invite people to bring their authentic selves, their withheld, into a conversation for possibilities.

IMAGINING: Don't let people dwell too long in the abstract. Insist that they translate general ideas into something concrete and tangible enough so that we all know what they are talking about.

LEARNING IN ACTION: Insist on seeing data from the results of small experiments. Then use it to assess ideas against previously agreed-upon design criteria, and then force decisions as to what moves forward, and how it needs to be iterated. Fight perfectionism and make it easy to find and talk with customers. Make it okay to show rough stuff to them.

HOW WE TESTED THIS BOOK'S THEME

Determined to take our own advice, we enlisted feedback from several partners we have worked closely with over the years, who seemed to personify the reader we were hoping to add value to with this book. They reviewed an early draft and were generous with their thoughts—both positive and negative. They helped us see what they loved best and found real value in, where our arguments and examples confused them—and where they needed us to go deeper to really help. They loved the Velveteen Rabbit opening and told us to keep it. They weren't sure what to do with our "social technology" emphasis and suggested that we dial it down. They wanted specifics about the behaviors we were talking about. Their input was invaluable and we are so grateful for the time they invested in helping us see what we were missing. Thank you! You know who you are.

And finally some thoughts on the really, REALLY hard stuff:

CREATE A CULTURE OF CONTINUOUS LEARNING AND ADAPTATION. We now get to the challenging topic of changing organizational culture. DT prospers in a particular culture—customer-centric, open to new ways of doing things, tolerant of intelligent mistakes and focused on long-term success. Many organizations talk about these things, but actually only reward what looks like efficiency in the short term, always being right, focusing on the bottom line only and getting to decisions quickly rather than thoughtfully. As one seasoned innovator observed:

> *The learning needs to be rewarded even in times that an idea fails. While the learning will hopefully contribute to better decision-making, it should be separated from merely demonstrating an outcome. While many organizations now talk this talk, I'd argue hierarchy, a sense of pressure from shareholders and current performance-review criteria incentivizes the opposite behavior. Organizations that focus too tightly on getting quick success, even if they incorporate innovative methods, are less likely to sustain this success.*

WATCH FOR THE NEGATIVE IMPACT OF HIER-ARCHY. Whose voice matters in deciding? The indisputable rule of thumb for who decides is nearly always the person in charge. Ideas are run up and down the ladder. The notion that those you are designing for, supported by the innovation team itself, should be empowered to call the shots is a radical (almost subversive) change. Another innovator commented:

> *What keeps innovation from happening in any sort of bureaucracy is you have chain of command and you have new ideas only from the top. Because it's people at the top who have the political capital to actually take some risks and do some of that experimentation. Whereas folks at the bottom, who ironically have the most entrée and understanding, and who see the different opportunities that are available, don't have the political capital.*

Having to constantly ask permission not only puts the locus of decision in the wrong place, it can slow innovation itself to a crawl.

ROOT OUT ORGANIZATIONAL STRUCTURES THAT MAKE COOPERATION DIFFICULT. One of the issues in large, complicated organizations is the sheer number of stakeholders involved in any particular problem. Their competing needs pit them against each other in a winner-take-all battle. Silos and fiefdoms make collaboration difficult. When something becomes difficult, people stop doing it. There's nothing complicated about that.

FIND BESPOKE MEASURES THAT MEASURE THE RIGHT THING. How many times have we heard "what

DESIGN 3.0 AT LOGITECH

Logitech has been working to embed design thinking in the Logitech culture for a number of years. Focused on the application to the experiences they develop and deliver to their consumers, Logitech development teams have grown in experience and competence. Their approach has earned them recognition as a leading design company, and, most importantly, connected them with their consumers in a more meaningful and emotionally engaging way. However, leadership there realizes that this is only the start of the journey. Stephen Harvey, Logitech's Global Head of Design Transformation, reflected on their next stage of development:

To become a true design company our design thinking journey must infuse into everything we do, whether it's a new service, how we run board meetings or how we hire new talent. It must influence our creation of systems of experiences, which speak intentionally and holistically to our consumers. This requires us to work across, regions, functions and business groups through a common language and innovative culture united around the DNA of design thinking. Ultimately our next chapter, Design 3.0, is about people. How to inspire, energize and scale the transformation across our organization in a meaningful way so that people can apply design thinking in their day-to-day jobs, as leaders, as game changers, as colleagues, as parents, as friends, as people who want to make the world a better place. We embrace the journey, the learning and the challenge. It's how we will grow and transform.

gets measured, gets managed"? We ask for new behaviors and then we measure the same old stuff. Use your creativity to create new *measures*, as well as new ideas—ones that pay attention to the right stuff, not ones that are easy to pull off the shelf.

OUR BOTTOM LINE: Leaders need to *own the conversation* and let go of controlling its output. Leaders who successfully tap into the potential of DT see themselves as *conveners* and *guardians* of a culture and a dialogue, rather than architects of solutions. The kind of possibility thinking that lies at the heart of DT's success is fragile. It takes only a few skeptical and strident voices to destroy the positive, collaborative spirit so essential to productive conversations. Building a supportive scaffolding that safeguards the innovation conversation itself is the most important contribution leaders can make.

And how do we know when we've reached our final destination? We probably never will. But the best evidence to look for is when DT becomes so embedded in the way we (and our organizations) think and act, and live our lives day to day, that we no longer need to call it anything special—it's just the way we operate.

All of the above may seem a tall order for both innovators and their leaders. But if transformation was easy, everybody would be doing it!

We wrote this book with a goal of deepening your innovation journey—wherever that takes you. We'd love to continue to tag along with you as you move forward. Share your new adventures at our website, *experiencingdesign.org*. We are cheering you on and wish you the best of luck!

APPENDIX 1: PERSONAL DEVELOPMENT PLAN

The MVC 360 feedback tool kit is designed to help you obtain the greatest personal growth from the design thinking experience. Design thinking not only leads to better outcomes and solutions; it also has the capability to transform you—the innovator. Research shows that achieving minimum viable competencies—behaviors and actions required to maximize the benefits of design thinking—marks the level of expertise needed to go beyond *doing* design thinking to *experiencing* the ways in which it shapes the way you approach challenges and solutions.

This process includes:

- **A self-reported assessment**, which documents your starting point at the beginning as well as end of your design thinking journey and draws attention to mindsets and behaviors you want to improve as you complete each phase.

- **A 360 evaluation** that provides the opportunity to receive (and give) feedback from peers and managers after each phase is complete. This allows you to gauge your own perception of your progress with the feedback from those working with you.

The goal of this tool kit is to provide a personal development roadmap for you to get the most out of your design thinking experience while also helping your team build trust and collaboration.

Why 360?
By surveying up, down and across the team (360 degrees), we can glean information normally unobtainable from conventional assessment instruments. The activity is anonymous so that it can facilitate honest, objective and user-friendly feedback that, research shows, improves performance, interpersonal communication and working relationships. While feedback always requires a level of vulnerability, it can help you gain a level of self-awareness about the strengths you bring and the ways in which you can continue to grow.

PERSONAL ASSESSMENT SURVEY

Immersion
Name of person evaluated: ☐ SELF-EVALUATION

I am aware of my own biases and blinders.

1	2	3	4	5
not at all	not often	sometimes	frequently	all the time

I listen to understand rather than to test.

1	2	3	4	5
not at all	not often	sometimes	frequently	all the time

I search for areas of opportunities, not solutions.

1	2	3	4	5
not at all	not often	sometimes	frequently	all the time

I develop an emotional engagement and empathetic bond with those for whom I design.

1	2	3	4	5
not at all	not often	sometimes	frequently	all the time

I probe deeply for unarticulated needs and beliefs.

1	2	3	4	5
not at all	not often	sometimes	frequently	all the time

I am fully present in the moment to the lived experience of my colleagues and those for whom I design.

1	2	3	4	5
not at all	not often	sometimes	frequently	all the time

I ask good questions.

1	2	3	4	5
not at all	not often	sometimes	frequently	all the time

Immersion Assessment Total _____

Sensemaking
Name of person evaluated: ☐ SELF-EVALUATION

I distinguish between an observation and an interpretation.

1	2	3	4	5
not at all	not often	sometimes	frequently	all the time

I remain patient with iteration and search.

1	2	3	4	5
not at all	not often	sometimes	frequently	all the time

I summarize key interview takeaways cogently and clearly.

1	2	3	4	5
not at all	not often	sometimes	frequently	all the time

I dig deeper beyond the obvious and clearly stated needs of a user.

1	2	3	4	5
not at all	not often	sometimes	frequently	all the time

I gain more clarity on what is the most relevant problem to solve.

1	2	3	4	5
not at all	not often	sometimes	frequently	all the time

I develop informed inferences that are actionable.

1	2	3	4	5
not at all	not often	sometimes	frequently	all the time

I allow myself to question the norms, rules and status quo.

1	2	3	4	5
not at all	not often	sometimes	frequently	all the time

I articulate the "why" behind my own perspective to teammates.

1	2	3	4	5
not at all	not often	sometimes	frequently	all the time

I control my need for closure.

1	2	3	4	5
not at all	not often	sometimes	frequently	all the time

I treat differing views as an opportunity to understand and learn, not debate.

1	2	3	4	5
not at all	not often	sometimes	frequently	all the time

I listen openly to those who disagree with my interpretations.

1	2	3	4	5
not at all	not often	sometimes	frequently	all the time

I (productively) challenge the perspective of others.

1	2	3	4	5
not at all	not often	sometimes	frequently	all the time

Sensemaking Assessment Total _____

Alignment

Name of person evaluated: _____   ☐ SELF-EVALUATION

I give careful thought to how we structure our conversations.

1	2	3	4	5
not at all	not often	sometimes	frequently	all the time

I am attentive to the rules of dialogue, such as turn taking.

1	2	3	4	5
not at all	not often	sometimes	frequently	all the time

I am able to make our different perspectives visible to others.

1	2	3	4	5
not at all	not often	sometimes	frequently	all the time

I am willing to let go of my own perspective to be open to that of others.

1	2	3	4	5
not at all	not often	sometimes	frequently	all the time

I am capable of achieving a shared definition of the problem the team wants to solve.

1	2	3	4	5
not at all	not often	sometimes	frequently	all the time

I am able to align on a prioritized understanding of the qualities of the ideal solution.

1	2	3	4	5
not at all	not often	sometimes	frequently	all the time

I focus on the issues that really matter, as expressed in the design criteria.

1	2	3	4	5
not at all	not often	sometimes	frequently	all the time

I listen heedfully and respectfully to others, ensuring that everyone feels heard.

1	2	3	4	5
not at all	not often	sometimes	frequently	all the time

I contribute to the learning of others and learning together.

1	2	3	4	5
not at all	not often	sometimes	frequently	all the time

Alignment Assessment Total   _____

Emergence

Name of person evaluated: ☐ SELF-EVALUATION

I pursue multiple possibilities.

1	2	3	4	5
not at all	not often	sometimes	frequently	all the time

I actively engage in co-creation, looking for opportunities to build on the ideas of others.

1	2	3	4	5
not at all	not often	sometimes	frequently	all the time

I avoid allegiance to particular solutions during the process.

1	2	3	4	5
not at all	not often	sometimes	frequently	all the time

I explore nontraditional and unexpected ideas.

1	2	3	4	5
not at all	not often	sometimes	frequently	all the time

I work positively, constructively and collaboratively with my team to form new possibilities.

1	2	3	4	5
not at all	not often	sometimes	frequently	all the time

I focus on "What if anything were possible?" in idea generation.

1	2	3	4	5
not at all	not often	sometimes	frequently	all the time

I stay in the possibility despite time pressures and discomfort.

1	2	3	4	5
not at all	not often	sometimes	frequently	all the time

I control the urge to compromise prematurely.

1	2	3	4	5
not at all	not often	sometimes	frequently	all the time

I value and appreciate the diverse perspectives represented within our team.

1	2	3	4	5
not at all	not often	sometimes	frequently	all the time

Emergence Assessment Total   _____

Imagining

Name of person evaluated: _____   ☐ SELF-EVALUATION

I am able to capture, in my mind's eye, a vivid image of the experience a concept will create for users.

1	2	3	4	5
not at all	not often	sometimes	frequently	all the time

I translate what I see to others in ways that make a concept come to life for them.

1	2	3	4	5
not at all	not often	sometimes	frequently	all the time

I build artifacts that bring concepts to life and allow users to "pre-experience".

1	2	3	4	5
not at all	not often	sometimes	frequently	all the time

I translate ideas in a clear and compelling way from text to image.

1	2	3	4	5
not at all	not often	sometimes	frequently	all the time

I develop immersive prototypes that facilitate feedback conversations.

1	2	3	4	5
not at all	not often	sometimes	frequently	all the time

I am able to surface and prioritize assumptions to be tested.

1	2	3	4	5
not at all	not often	sometimes	frequently	all the time

I am able to capture these assumptions in a prototype.

1	2	3	4	5
not at all	not often	sometimes	frequently	all the time

I find the trade-off between emptiness and vividness, using the right level and kind of detail.

1	2	3	4	5
not at all	not often	sometimes	frequently	all the time

I invite co-creation, actively entering conversations with users and partners.

1	2	3	4	5
not at all	not often	sometimes	frequently	all the time

Imagining Assessment Total _____

Learning in Action

Name of person evaluated: _____   ☐ SELF-EVALUATION

I recognize when my knowing is interfering with my learning.

1	2	3	4	5
not at all	not often	sometimes	frequently	all the time

I explore disconfirming data with curiosity, rather than rejecting it.

1	2	3	4	5
not at all	not often	sometimes	frequently	all the time

I actively seek feedback on my new ideas from critical users and partners.

1	2	3	4	5
not at all	not often	sometimes	frequently	all the time

I am able to detach my ego from my creation.

1	2	3	4	5
not at all	not often	sometimes	frequently	all the time

I practice a hypothesis-driven approach.

1	2	3	4	5
not at all	not often	sometimes	frequently	all the time

I am focused on testing critical assumptions.

1	2	3	4	5
not at all	not often	sometimes	frequently	all the time

I listen nondefensively to critique.

1	2	3	4	5
not at all	not often	sometimes	frequently	all the time

I accept imperfect data and move on.

1	2	3	4	5
not at all	not often	sometimes	frequently	all the time

I design rigorous experiments.

1	2	3	4	5
not at all	not often	sometimes	frequently	all the time

I identify and gather the data needed to test.

1	2	3	4	5
not at all	not often	sometimes	frequently	all the time

I use findings to iterate hypotheses.

1	2	3	4	5
not at all	not often	sometimes	frequently	all the time

I am clear on what kinds of experiments to do at each stage.

1	2	3	4	5
not at all	not often	sometimes	frequently	all the time

I think creatively about how to triangulate data.

1	2	3	4	5
not at all	not often	sometimes	frequently	all the time

Learning in Action Assessment Total _____

360 EVALUATION

Innovator: _____ **Phase:** _____

Choose up to 3 MVCs to focus on developing during this phase. Complete a table for each.

MVC #1:

From:
(current state)

To:
(desired state)

Three actionable, measurable steps I can take to make this transition are:

1

2

3

Two people I can have a conversation with to improve my listening skills:

1

2

One book I can read to improve my listening skills:

1

MVC #2:

From:
(current state)

To:
(desired state)

Three actionable, measurable steps I can take to make this transition are:

1

2

3

Two people I can have a conversation with to improve my listening skills:

1

2

One book I can read to improve my listening skills:

1

MVC #3:

From:
(current state)

To:
(desired state)

Three actionable, measurable steps I can take to make this transition are:

1

2

3

Two people I can have a conversation with to improve my listening skills:

1

2

One book I can read to improve my listening skills:

1

Complete with your coach, supervisor, mentor or team leader before moving on to the next phase.

After completing this phase, I feel that my status on the MVCs:			
MVC #1	☐ improved	☐ stayed the same	☐ declined
MVC #2	☐ improved	☐ stayed the same	☐ declined
MVC #3	☐ improved	☐ stayed the same	☐ declined
Use this space to write any justifying behaviors or reflections to support your responses.			

Coach, supervisor, mentor or team leader will review peer 360 feedback on MVCs.

Next Steps: How do you plan to continue to make progress on your chosen MVCs? Are there other MVCs you'd focus on in future projects? What most surprised you about this process and your abilities?

APPENDIX 2:
ORGANIZATIONAL OUTCOMES ASSESSMENT SURVEY

PART 1: DESIGN THINKING PRACTICES

The following items relate to various design thinking practices that you may have used. **Please rate the extent to which you, in your own design thinking practice, have . . .** (*circle your response*):

	NEVER		SOMETIMES		ALMOST ALWAYS
. . . Followed a structured process	1	2	3	4	5
. . . Formed a diverse team	1	2	3	4	5
. . . Emphasized active listening among team members in order to find shared meaning	1	2	3	4	5
. . . Done user research using ethnographic tools (e.g., interviewing and observation, journey mapping, job-to-be-done, etc.)	1	2	3	4	5
. . . Focused your problem definition on the user's perspective rather than the organization's	1	2	3	4	5
. . . Created a set of design criteria that described an ideal solution, based on user research	1	2	3	4	5
. . . Generated a diverse set of ideas based on your user research	1	2	3	4	5
. . . Created prototypes of your ideas (e.g., storyboards, videos, mock-ups of offerings)	1	2	3	4	5
. . . Moved multiple ideas into prototyping and testing	1	2	3	4	5
. . . Got feedback from users and other stakeholders on the prototype	1	2	3	4	5
. . . Executed real-world experiments to test your ideas	1	2	3	4	5

Please list any other additional design practices you used that you consider important:

PART 2: OUTCOMES WE ASKED ABOUT

The following items seek to capture a variety of possible outcomes produced by the use of design thinking practices. **Please rate how often, in your own experience, the use of design thinking resulted in the following** (*circle your response*):

		NEVER		SOMETIMES		ALMOST ALWAYS
1	Created deeper understanding of stakeholder needs	1	2	3	4	5
2	Helped teams see the problem in new ways, resulting in solving more promising problems	1	2	3	4	5
3	Helped team members find alignment across their different perspectives	1	2	3	4	5
4	Enhanced your ability to pivot when initial solution didn't work	1	2	3	4	5
5	Increased engagement of employees involved in the design thinking process	1	2	3	4	5
6	Leveraged diversity on team to find more creative solutions	1	2	3	4	5
7	Built new relationships locally that continued after the initial project was completed	1	2	3	4	5
8	Expanded access to new resources for individuals and teams	1	2	3	4	5
9	Helped pool resources for greater impact	1	2	3	4	5
10	Helped to build alignment across diverse stakeholders	1	2	3	4	5
11	Enhanced other stakeholders' willingness to collaborate on new solutions	1	2	3	4	5
12	Helped to surface critical assumptions being made about new ideas so that they could be tested	1	2	3	4	5
13	Helped teams to gather more accurate feedback on ideas from users and other stakeholders	1	2	3	4	5
14	Built trust among team members	1	2	3	4	5
15	Built trust between problem-solving teams and other stakeholders	1	2	3	4	5

#	Statement	1	2	3	4	5
16	Improved the ability to talk to each other in ways that produced better outcomes	1	2	3	4	5
17	Allowed new and better solutions, not visible at the beginning of the process, to emerge during it	1	2	3	4	5
18	Fostered the inclusion of user input	1	2	3	4	5
19	Reduced the risk of pursuing ideas that will likely fail	1	2	3	4	5
20	Helped people involved to examine their own biases and preconceptions	1	2	3	4	5
21	Helped champions for new ideas who were enthusiastic about their implementation emerge during the design thinking process	1	2	3	4	5
22	Increased people's willingness to take action	1	2	3	4	5
23	Created a sense of safety to try new things	1	2	3	4	5
24	Allowed for involvement of key stakeholders who were not on the core team	1	2	3	4	5
25	Helped teams to persist despite challenges along the way	1	2	3	4	5
26	Gave employees more confidence in their own creative abilities	1	2	3	4	5
27	Improved the creativity of new solutions	1	2	3	4	5
28	Improved the likelihood of the implementation of new solutions	1	2	3	4	5
29	Made working together more enjoyable	1	2	3	4	5
30	Made it easier to discard solutions that didn't work as planned	1	2	3	4	5
31	Helped people interested in trying new things to connect and support each other	1	2	3	4	5
32	Encouraged people's open-mindedness to try new things	1	2	3	4	5
33	Encouraged shifts in organizational culture to make it more customer-focused	1	2	3	4	5

34	Encouraged changes in organizational culture that made risk-taking more acceptable	1	2	3	4	5
35	Equipped team members with new capabilities that can be applied to other projects	1	2	3	4	5
36	Kept people motivated to work on a project to achieve impact	1	2	3	4	5
37	Broadened organization's definition of what innovation is	1	2	3	4	5
38	Created a common language/framework among team members	1	2	3	4	5
39	Increased willingness to collaborate with others (cross-functionally and cross-departmentally)	1	2	3	4	5
40	Increased a sense of ownership and acceptance of a solution	1	2	3	4	5
41	Increased appreciation for use of data to help drive decisions	1	2	3	4	5

Please list any other positive outcomes you observed from the use of design practices not discussed here:

Please list any negative outcomes you observed from the use of design thinking:

PART 3: ADDITIONAL QUESTIONS

1   **What type of organization do you work for?** (check one)

☐ Business   ☐ Nonprofit   ☐ Government

2   **What position do you hold in your organization?**

3   **How would you assess your own experience with design thinking?** (check one)

☐ 1—No experience at all   ☐ 2—Some limited experience   ☐ 3—A moderate level of experience

☐ 4—Extensive experience

4   **What kinds of aims did the design thinking projects you were involved in have?** (check all that apply)

☐ Improve the delivery of customer-facing product or service   ☐ Redesign or create new internal processes

☐ Develop new strategies, policies, or business models   ☐ Meeting facilitation

☐ Other (please specify):

NOTES

CHAPTER 1

1 Margery Williams Bianco and William Nicholson, *The Velveteen Rabbit: Or, How Toys Become Real* (New York: Avon Books, 1975).

2 Fred Kofman and Peter Senge, "Communities of Commitment: The Heart of Learning Organizations," *Organizational Dynamics* 22, no. 2 (1993): 5–23.

3 João Ferreira, "Writing Is Seeing—Towards a Designerly Way of Writing," *The Design Journal* 23, no. 5 (2020): 697–714, 708.

4 Kevin Slavin, "Design as Participation," *Journal of Design and Science* (2016), https://doi.org/10.21428/a39a747c.

5 Mary Uhl-Bien and Michael Arena, "Complexity Leadership: Enabling People and Organizations for Adaptability," *Organizational Dynamics* 46, no. 1 (2017): 9–20.

CHAPTER 2

6 Ranulph Glanville, "How Design and Cybernetics Reflect Each Other," Relating Systems Thinking and Design 2014 Working Paper, https://systemic-design.net/wp-content /uploads/2014/08/Ranulph_Glanville.pdf.

7 For those interested in learning more about DT and cognitive bias, see Jeanne Liedtka, "Linking Design Thinking with Innovation Outcomes Through Cognitive Bias Reduction," *Journal of Product Innovation Management* 32, no. 6 (2015): 925–938.

8 Kimberly D. Elsbach and Ileana Stigliani, "Design Thinking and Organizational Culture: A Review and Framework for Future Research," *Journal of Management* 44, no. 6 (2018): 2274–2306.

9 The idea of simple rules relates to the need to give employees in high-velocity environments a set of simple rules. For more information, see Kathleen Eisenhardt and Donald Sull, "Simple Rules for a Complex World," *Harvard Business Review* (2012), https://hbr.org/2012/09/simple -rules-for-a-complex-world.

10 Forrester, "The Total Economic Impact™ of IBM's Design Thinking Practice: How IBM Drives Client Value and Measurable Outcomes with Its Design Thinking Framework" (2018), https://www.ibm.com/design/ thinking/static/Enterprise-Design-Thinking-Report -8ab1e9e1622899654844a5fe1d760ed5.pdf; Benedict Sheppard, Hugo Sarrazin, Garen Kouyoumijan, and Fabricio Dore, "The Business Value of Design," *McKinsey Quarterly* 4 (2018): 58–72.

11   We have made this point before. See Jeanne Liedtka, Andrew King, and Kevin Bennett, *Solving Problems with Design Thinking: Ten Stories of What Works* (New York: Columbia Business School Publishing, 2013).

12   Trust building was the exception here—and these are self-reports.

13   Jeanne Liedtka and Kristina Jaskyte Bahr, "Assessing Design Thinking's Impact: Report on the Development of a New Instrument," Darden School Working Paper, DSWP 19–13, November 2019.

CHAPTER 3

14   For these (and most of the activities we mention), see Jeanne Liedtka, Tim Ogilvie, and Rachel Brozenske, *The Designing for Growth Field Book: A Step-By-Step Project Guide*, 2nd edition (New York: Columbia Business School Publishing, 2019).
- Ethnographic observation: pp. 50–53
- Job to be done: pp. 54–55
- Journey maps: pp. 58–59
- Mirroring or shadowing users, see Direct Observation on pp. 48–49
- Capturing key takeaways, see 360 Empathy on pp. 62–63

15   Mark Goulston, *Just Listen: Discover the Secret to Getting Through to Absolutely Anyone* (New York: Amacom, 2015).

16   Pier Francesco Ferrari and Giacomo Rizzolatti, "Mirror Neuron Research: The Past and the Future," *Philosophical Transactions B: Biological Sciences* 369, no. 1644 (2014): 1–4.

17   Paul J. Silvia, "Interest—The Curious Emotion," *Current Directions in Psychological Science* 17, no. 1 (2008): 57–60.

18   Leaf Van Boven, David Dunning, and George Loewenstein, "Egocentric Empathy Gaps Between Owners and Buyers: Misperceptions of the Endowment Effect," *Journal of Personality and Social Psychology* 79, no. 1 (2000): 66–76.

19   Raymond S. Nickerson, "Confirmation Bias: A Ubiquitous Phenomenon in Many Guises," *Review of General Psychology* 2 (1998): 175–220.

20   Of course, Sir Arthur Conan Doyle, creator of Sherlock Holmes, actually wrote this.

21   For full story, see Jeanne Liedtka, Randy Salzman, and Daisy Azer, *Design Thinking for the Greater Good: Innovation in the Social Sector*, Chapter 4 (Kingwood Institute) (New York: Columbia Business Press, 2017).

22   Rainer Maria Rilke, Franz Kappus, and K. W. Maurer, *Letters to a Young Poet* (London: Euston Press, 1943).

CHAPTER 4

23   John Kounios and Mark Beeman, "The Aha! Moment: The Cognitive Neuroscience of Insight," *Current Directions in Psychological Science* 18, no. 4 (2009): 210–216.

24   Andy Dong and Erin MacDonald, "From Observations to Insights: The Hilly Road to Value Creation," paper presented at the Design Thinking Research Symposium of the Copenhagen Business School, Copenhagen, Denmark, November 2016.

25   Again, we refer you to the *Designing for Growth Field Book* for these activities:
- Summarizing interview takeaways, see Creating Posters on pp. 64–65
- Crafting personas, see Personas on pp. 60–61
- Empathy Maps, see 360 Empathy on pp. 62–63

26   The Five Whys is a root cause analysis tool. By asking "Why" five times in a row, you can get to the root of a person's beliefs, assumptions and motivations. It is used to understand underlying behaviors or attitudes that may not be easily articulated. See Olivier Serrat, "The Five Whys Technique," *Knowledge Solutions* (2017): 307–310.

27   Nicholas Dew, "Abduction: A Pre-Condition for the Intelligent Design of Strategy," *Journal of Business Strategy* 28, no. 4 (2007): 38–45.

28   Daniel Kahneman, *Thinking, Fast and Slow* (New York: Farrar, Straus and Giroux, 2011).

29 Chris Argyris, "Double Loop Learning in Organizations," *Harvard Business Review* 55, no. 5 (1977): 115–125.

30 Jon Kolko, "Abductive Thinking and Sensemaking: The Drivers of Design Synthesis," *Design Issues* 26, no. 1 (2010): 15–28.

31 Lenny T. Mendoca and Hayagreeva Rao, "Lessons from Innovation's Front Lines: An Interview with IDEO's CEO," *McKinsey Quarterly*, no. 2 (2008), https://www.mckinsey.com/quarterly/the-magazine/2019-issue-2-mckinsey-quarterly.

32 Alan Gregerman, *The Necessity of Strangers: The Intriguing Truth About Insight, Innovation, and Success* (San Francisco: John Wiley & Sons, 2013).

CHAPTER 5

33 Again, we refer you to the *Designing for Growth Field Book* for these activities:
   • Creating design criteria: pp. 24–25
   • Point of View Insight Statements, see Storytelling Narratives on pp. 84–85

34 Boris Ewenstein and Jennifer Whyte, "Beyond Words: Aesthetic Knowledge and Knowing in Organizations," *Organization Studies* 28, no. 5 (2007): 689–708.

35 Betsy Campbell, *Practice Theory in Action* (New York: Routledge, 2019).

36 The product development team literature, in particular, offers ample research evidence that difference often drives team disagreement and dysfunction. For example, see Shona Brown and Kathleen M. Eisenhardt, "Product Development: Past Research, Present Findings, and Future Directions," *Academy of Management Review* 20, no. 2 (1995): 343–378; Kay Lovelace, Debra L. Shapiro, and Laurie R. Weingart, "Maximizing Cross-Functional New Product Teams' Innovativeness and Constraint Adherence: A Conflict Communications Perspective," *Academy of Management Journal* 44, no. 4 (2001): 779–793.

37 The idea of simple rules relates to the need to give employees in high velocity environments a set of simple rules. For more information, see Eisenhardt and Sull, "Simple Rules."

38 Mary Uhl-Bien and Michael Arena, "Complexity Leadership: Enabling People and Organizations for Adaptability," *Organizational Dynamics* 46, no. 1 (2017): 9–20.

39 Richard J. Boland and Ramkrishnan V. Tenkasi, "Perspective Making and Perspective Taking in Communities of Knowing," *Organization Science* 6, no. 4 (1995): 350–372.

40 William Isaacs, *Dialogue and the Art of Thinking Together* (New York: Random House, 1999).

41 Hal Saunders, *A Public Peace Process: Sustained Dialogue to Transform Racial and Ethnic Conflicts* (New York: Palgrave, 1999).

42 Fred Kofman and Peter Senge, "Communities of Commitment."

43 Charles J. Walker, "Experiencing Flow: Is Doing It Together Better Than Doing It Alone?" *The Journal of Positive Psychology* 5, no. 1 (2010): 3–11, https://doi.org/10.1080/17439760903271116.

44 Marisa Salanova, Alma M. Rodríguez-Sánchez, Wilmar B. Schaufeli, and Eva Cifre, "Flowing Together: A Longitudinal Study of Collective Efficacy and Collective Flow Among Workgroups," *The Journal of Psychology* 148, no. 4 (2014): 435–455.

45 Henri Lipmanowicz and Keith McCandless, *The Surprising Power of Liberating Structures* (Liberating Structures Press, 2013).

46 Bettye Pruitt and Philip Thomas, *Democratic Dialogue: A Handbook for Practitioners* (New York: United Nations Development Program, 2007).

47   Complexity theorist Stuart Kauffman explained the idea of the adjacent possible in his seminal work, *At Home in the Universe: The Search for the Laws of Self-Organization and Complexity* (London: Oxford University Press, 1999). The idea has been extended into a variety of fields, including, for instance, analysis of big data. See https://www.wired.com/insights/2014/12/the-adjacent-possible-of-big-data/.

48   Saul Kaplan, *The Business Model Innovation Factory* (Hoboken, NJ: John Wiley & Sons, 2012).

CHAPTER 6

49   Again, we refer you to the *Designing for Growth Field Book* for these activities:
- Brainstorming: pp. 68–71
- "Chili Tables," see Anchors on pp. 72–73
- Napkin pitches: pp. 30–31
- Mashing up/combining ideas, see Forced Connections on pp. 76–77
- Buy, Build, Bring, see 5Bs Supply Chain on pp. 74–75
- Trigger Questions: pp. 68–71

50   Scenario creation offers a way to have a group conversation about what a range of possible futures should/could look like. Multiple possible futures, or scenarios, are created that pivot around the outcomes of key unknowns.

51   David Colander and Roland Kupers, *Complexity and the Art of Public Policy: Solving Society's Problems from the Bottom Up* (Princeton, NJ: Princeton University Press, 2014).

52   George Henry Lewes, *Problems of Life and Mind*, vol. 2 (Boston: James R. Osgood and Company, 1875), 369.

53   M. Mitchell Waldrop, *Complexity: The Emerging Science at the Edge of Order and Chaos* (New York: Simon and Schuster, 1993).

54   Steven Johnson, *Where Good Ideas Come From* (New York: Penguin Random House, 2010).

55   W. Ross Ashby, "Requisite Variety and Its Implications for the Control of Complex Systems," *Cybernetica* 1, no. 2 (1958), http://pcp.vub.ac.be/Books/AshbyReqVar.

56   Michael Lissack, "Understanding Is a Design Problem: Cognizing from a Designerly Thinking Perspective. Part I," *She Ji: The Journal of Design, Economics, and Innovation* 5, no. 3 (2019): 238.

57   Barbara L. Fredrickson, "The Broaden-and-Build Theory of Positive Emotions," *Philosophical Transactions of the Royal Society of London B, Biological Sciences* 359, no. 1449 (2004): 1367–1378, https://doi.org/10.1098/rstb.2004.1512.

58   Peggy Holman, *Engaging Emergence* (San Francisco: Berrett-Koehler Publishers, 2010).

59   W. Brian Arthur, "Coming from Your Inner Self," interview by Joe Jaworski, Gary Jusela, and C. Otto Scharmer, April 16, 1999, https://www.presencing.org/aboutus/theory-uq/leadership-interview/W_Brian_Arthur.

60   C. Otto Scharmer, *Theory U: Learning from the Future as It Emerges* (San Francisco: Berrett-Koehler Publishers, 2009).

61   Reuven Gorsht, "SAP BrandVoice: When Is 'Good Enough' No Longer Good Enough?" Forbes, January 2, 2014, https://www.forbes.com/sites/sap/2014/01/02/when-is-good-enough-no-longer-good-enough/#662ccb847108.

62   Max Boisot, *Information Space: A Framework for Learning in Organizations, Institutions and Culture* (New York: Routledge, 2013).

63   Michael Benedikt, *For an Architecture of Reality* (New York: Lumen Books, 1987).

64   Alison Reynolds and David Lewis, "Teams Solve Problems Faster When They're More Cognitively Diverse," Harvard Business Review Online, March 30, 2017, https://hbr.org/2017/03/teams-solve-problems-faster-when-theyre-more-cognitively-diverse; Alison Reynolds and David Lewis, "The Two Traits of the Best Problem-Solving Teams," Harvard Business Review Online, April 2, 2018, https://hbr.org/2018/04/the-two-traits-of-the-best-problem-solving-teams.

65 For more on these examples and others presented in this chapter, see Jeanne Liedtka, Randy Salzman, and Daisy Azer, *Design Thinking for the Greater Good*.

CHAPTER 7

66 Michael Benedikt, *For an Architecture of Reality*.
67 Again, we refer you to the *Designing for Growth Field Book* for these activities:
   • Storytelling, see Storytelling Narratives on pp. 84–85
   • Sketching, see Visualization Basics on pp. 80–81
   • Metaphors, see Analogies on pp. 66–67
   • Videos, see Co-Creation Tools on pp. 88–89
   • Storyboards: pp. 86–87
68 William James, *Principles of Psychology* (Chicago: University of Chicago Press, 1952).
69 Murray S. Davis, "That's Interesting! Towards a Phenomenology of Sociology and a Sociology of Phenomenology," *Philosophy of Social Science* 1, no. 4 (1971): 308–344.
70 Beatrice de Gelder, Marco Tamietto, Alan J. Pegna, and Jan Van den Stock, "Visual Imagery Influences Brain Responses to Visual Stimulation in Bilateral Cortical Blindness," *Cortex* 72 (2015): 15–26.
71 Dan Roam, *The Back of the Napkin: Solving Problems and Selling Ideas with Pictures* (London: Portfolio, 2009).
72 Christopher Taibbi, "Brain Basics, Part One: The Power of Visualization," *Psychology Today* (blog), November 4, 2012, https://www.psychologytoday.com/us/blog/gifted-ed-guru/201211/brain-basics-part-one-the-power-visualization.
73 Denise Grady, "The Vision Thing: Mainly in the Brain," *Discover Magazine* 14, no. 6 (1993): 57.
74 Allan Paivio, "Dual Coding Theory: Retrospect and Current Status," *Canadian Journal of Psychology* 45 (1991): 255–287.
75 Mary Susan Weldon and Henry L. Roediger III, "Altering Retrieval Demands Reverses the Picture Superiority Effect," *Memory & Cognition* 15 (1987): 269–280.
76 W. J. T. Mitchell, "Showing Seeing: A Critique of Visual Culture," *Visual Culture* 1, no. 2 (2002): 165–181.
77 John Paul Stephens and Brodie J. Boland, "The Aesthetic Knowledge Problem of Problem-Solving with Design Thinking," *Journal of Management Inquiry* 24, no. 3 (2015): 219–232.
78 George Lakoff and Mark Leonard Johnson, *Metaphors We Live By* (Chicago: University of Chicago Press, 1980).
79 Melissa Burkley, "Why Metaphors Are Important," *Psychology Today* (blog), November 28, 2017, https://www.psychologytoday.com/us/blog/the-social-thinker/201711/why-metaphors-are-important.
80 Alex Marin, Martin Reimann, and Raquel Castaño, "Metaphor and Creativity: Direct, Moderating, and Mediating Effects," *Journal of Consumer Psychology* 24, no. 2 (2014): 290–297.
81 Michael Slepian, Max Weisbuch, Abraham M. Rutchick, Leonard S. Newman, and Nalini Ambady, "Shedding Light on Insight: Priming Bright Ideas," *Journal of Experimental Social Psychology* 46 (2010): 696–700.
82 João Ferreira, "Writing Is Seeing."
83 Michael Lissack, "Understanding Is a Design Problem: Cognizing from a Designerly Thinking Perspective: Part II," *The Journal of Design, Economics, and Innovation* 5, no. 4 (2019): 327–342.
84 Marian Diamond, Arnold B. Scheibel, Greer M. Murphy Jr., and Thomas Harvey, "On the Brain of a Scientist: Albert Einstein," *Experimental Neurology* 88 (1985): 198–204.
85 João Ferreira, "Writing Is Seeing."
86 Richard Thruelsen, *The Grumman Story* (New York: Praeger, 1976).
87 Praveen Sidyal, "Sketching for Design," *Medium* (blog), November 20, 2019, https://medium.com/@designthinker_97912/sketching-for-design-5370f5b077e4.
88 Coosje Van Bruggen and Frank O. Gehry, *Guggenheim Museum Bilbao* (New York: Guggenheim Museum Publications, 1998).

89   João Ferreira, "Writing Is Seeing," 710.

CHAPTER 8

90   Kathryn Schulz, *Being Wrong: Adventures in the Margin of Error* (New York: HarperCollins, 2010), 319.

91   Carol S. Dweck, *Mindset: The New Psychology of Success* (New York: Random House, 2008).

92   E. Tory Higgins, "Promotion and Prevention: Regulatory Focus as a Motivational Principle," in *Advances in Experimental Social Psychology* Volume 30, edited by Mark Zanna, 1–46 (San Diego: Academic Press, 1998).

93   Kathryn Schulz, *Being Wrong*.

94   Otto Rank, *The Trauma of Birth* (Oxfordshire: Routledge, Trench & Trubner, 1929).

95   For research on unlearning, Ali E. Akgün, John C. Byrne, Gary S. Lynn, and Halit Keskin, "Organizational Unlearning as Changes in Beliefs and Routines in Organizations," *Journal of Organizational Change Management* 20, no. 6 (2007): 794–812.

96   David Kolb, *The Kolb Learning Style Inventory* (Boston: Hay Resources Direct, 2007).

97   Kimberly D. Elsbach and Ileana Stigliani, "Design Thinking and Organizational Culture."

98   For more information on after-action reviews, see Lloyd Baird, Philip Holland, and Sandra Deacon, "Learning from Action: Imbedding More Learning into the Performance Fast Enough to Make a Difference," *Organizational Dynamics* 27, no. 4 (1999): 19–32; Shmuel Ellis and Inbar Davidi, "After-Event Reviews: Drawing Lessons from Successful and Failed Experience," *Journal of Applied Psychology* 90, no. 5 (2005): 857–871.

99   John W. Creswell and Dana L. Miller, "Determining Validity in Qualitative Inquiry" *Theory Into Practice* 39, no. 3 (2000): 124–131.

100 Fred Kofman and Peter Senge, "Communities of Commitment."

101 Richard Beckhard (originally published in *Sloan Management Review*, 1975), citing David Gleicher; quoted in Steven H. Cady, Robert "Jake" Jacobs, Ron Koller, and John Spalding, "The Change Formula: Myth, Legend, or Lore?" *OD Practitioner* 46, no. 3 (2014): 32–39.

102 Andrew Grove, *Only the Paranoid Survive: How to Exploit the Crisis Points That Challenge Every Company* (New York: Random House, 1996).

CHAPTER 9

103 Otto Scharmer, *Theory U*.

CHAPTER 15

104 Richard E. Clark and Bror Saxberg, "4 Reasons Good Employees Lose Their Motivation," *Harvard Business Review* (March 13, 2009), https://hbr.org/2019/03/4-reasons-good-employees-lose-their-motivation.

105 Creative Reaction Lab, *Equity-Centered Community Design Field Guide* (2018), https://static1.squarespace.com/static/5e3b20447d777f2b32c1bc1c/t/5e667103feb2830f1b1b68d4/1583771908636/ECCD+FIELD+GUIDE+-+DOWNLOAD.pdf.

106 Michael Mankins and Richard Steele, "Turning Great Strategy Into Great Performance," *Harvard Business Review* (July/August 2005): 65–72

107 Robert Kaplan and David Norton, *The Strategy-Focused Organization* (Cambridge, MA: Harvard Business School Press, 2000).

108 J. Nevan Wright, "Mission and Reality and Why Not?" *Journal of Change Management* 3, no. 1 (2002): 30–45.

109 This is the research we introduced in Chapter 2. For additional examples, see Lisa Carlgren, Ingo Rauth, and Maria Elmquist, "Framing Design Thinking: The Concept in Idea and Enactment," *Creativity and Innovation Management* 25, no. 1 (2016): 38–57; Kimberly Elsbach and Ileana Stigliani, "Design Thinking and Organizational Culture"; Jeanne Liedtka, "Putting Technology in Its Place: Design Thinking's Social Technology at Work," *California Management Review* 62, no. 2 (2020): 53–83; Pietro Micheli, Sarah J. S. Wilner, Sabeen Hussain Bhatti, Matteo Mura, and Michael B. Beverland, "Doing Design Thinking: Conceptual Review, Synthesis, and Research Agenda," *Journal of Product Innovation Management* 36, no. 2 (2019): 124–148.

110 For details on this, check out our website, experiencingdesign.org.

111 For more details, see Jeanne Liedtka, Randy Salzman, and Daisy Azer, *Design Thinking for the Greater Good*, Chapter 5 (Monash) and Chapters 13 and 14 (Gateway).

ACKNOWLEDGMENTS

This book is the result of 20+ years of support for our research from the UVA Darden School and its Batten Institute. The encouragement of a series of leaders there—Deans Harris, Bruner and Beardsley—has been fundamental to our ability to do this work. Tim Ogilvie and his team at Peer Insight helped us to understand experimentation at a completely new level, and Rachel Brozenske taught us to be wary of the Cosmo quiz approach to development planning. To them, and to all of the good friends around the world that we have met during our DT adventures—from far away and close to home—thank you! And special thanks to our wonderful designer, Leigh Ayers, who made our words beautiful.

FROM JEANNE:

As I look back over 60+ years of decision-making on my part, three particularly good ones stand out to me (I will not go into the bad ones). The first was the decision to spend my career at Darden. Thank you, Ed Freeman! The wisdom and collegiality of my colleagues there, and all that they have taught me over the years, have brought me to where (and who) I am today, and made this book possible. Many of my favorite people—Susan Chaplinsky, Lynn Isabella, and Karen Musselman to name just a few—have made coming to work something to look forward to for many years. The decades there have flown by—I guess because I was having so much fun. The second choice was becoming a mother. My children and their spouses and children are the very light of my life—and taught me what empathy really means. Though it often seemed hard to try and "have it all," they made the effort to do that rewarding beyond measure (and I sometimes feel I have gotten really close). The third choice was my husband, Salz, the truth teller. His seemingly limitless ability to both work and love with a level of passion and commitment that I have never seen in anyone else, and that is remarkably undeterred by the slings of reality, is inspirational. A final great decision I want to note was hitching my wagon to my two wonderful co-authors. This book exists only because of their insights, persistence, ingenuity and wisdom. They kept me going when the going got tough. Not to mention, they are among the nicest people in the world—and a total joy to work with. And a final thank you to the people who have been there for me my entire life—my beloved Loudka siblings, and my cherished old porch friends in Onset, and in life.

FROM KAREN:

Writing a book with Jeanne Liedtka is like training with an Olympic athlete at the top of her game. Jeanne is always pushing the boundaries of possibility with bigger, bolder and more brilliant ideas. It was the adventure of a lifetime to write this book with her and I am eternally grateful for her generosity and optimism while breaking new ground and understanding. I am also deeply grateful for our ride-or-die partner, Jessica, who was always ready for every adventure coupled with an incredible ability to keep us organized, focused and laughing. Thank you to Stephanie Rowe and my DT: DC and Summer of Design family, who inspire me every day. You are the dreamers, change agents and innovators aspiring to make our beautiful home of Washington, DC, a kinder, more inclusive and equitable city. I am grateful for the many colleagues who joined me in leading Summer of Design the last six years, including Rob Colenso, Amy Conrick, Carol Hamilton, Ken Holmes, Angela Long, Lael Lyons, Peter Kale, Trish Martinelli, Jay Miles, Seul Rhee, Arty Rivera, Niko Sommaripa, Rachel Thompson and Sergio Venegas and for the many sponsors of our design challenges, including Toby Chaudhuri and the Public Broadcasting System (PBS); Denita Takemoto, Pierre Vigilance and the Milken Institute School of Public Health at George Washington University; Adam Siegel and the Retail Innovation Leaders Association; Hope Costanzo, Aram Terminassian and Capital One Bank; and Chris Bagley, Jamie Bowerman, John Gray Parker, Santiago Pikula, Kat Siedlecki and Booz Allen Hamilton. Thank you to my teaching colleagues Erica Estrada-Liou and Dean Chang at UMD; Mira Azarm and Adam Richardson at MICA; Alon Rozen, Saman Sarbazvatan, and Younes Sekkouri at École des Ponts, and the entire team at Darden Executive Education, for stretching my thinking and providing a platform to share our work. A big thank you to Rob Colenso, Sabrina Blowers and Jaymes Cloninger for their valuable feedback. Finally, thank you to my beautiful family for their love and support, especially my darling daughter, Caroline, who is the light of my life. My passion for design was inspired by the pioneering work of Caroline's great-grandfather, Leroy Grumman, who taught me that it is better to have a rough answer to the right question than a detailed answer to the wrong question. I hope his words inspire you as much as they inspire me.

FROM JESSICA:

I'd like to primarily thank my co-authors for the opportunity to learn from their rich and engaging experiences with DT. First, to Jeanne, who graciously welcomed me into the Darden family and introduced me to the truly transformational power of DT. In true educator fashion, Jeanne's ability to mentor, coach, stretch and inspire set me on a new path of purpose and possibility, embodied in the pages of this book. Pinch me, as I still can't believe that I get to call her my colleague and friend. Then, to Karen, who balances her tremendous repertoire and impressive skill set with a humility and empathy that only a true superhero would have. Writing a book is a winding journey, and as the absolute Supporter of our group, Karen brought a positivity and thoughtful levity to this process that kept me moving forward. I'm a better leader, design thinker and person because of these two amazing women. I'd also like to thank my family, especially my husband, Dylan, whose confidence in me is unwavering, and my son, Oliver, whose imagination helps re-kindle my own sense of creativity and wonder. Lastly, I'd like to dedicate this book to my father, Michael Warren, the master storyteller.

INDEX